In the Eye of the Storm

In the Eye of the Storm

Middle Eastern Christians in the Twenty-First Century

Edited by
MITRI RAHEB

PICKWICK *Publications* · Eugene, Oregon

IN THE EYE OF THE STORM
Middle Eastern Christians in the Twenty-First Century

Pickwick Publications
An Imprint of Wipf and Stock Publishers
199 W. 8th Ave., Suite 3
Eugene, OR 97401

www.wipfandstock.com

PAPERBACK ISBN: 978-1-6667-4893-2
HARDCOVER ISBN: 978-1-6667-4894-9
EBOOK ISBN: 978-1-6667-4895-6

Cataloguing-in-Publication data:

Names: Raheb, Mitri, editor.

Title: In the eye of the storm : middle eastern Christians in the twenty-first century / edited by Mitri Raheb.

Description: Eugene, OR : Pickwick Publications, 2023 | Includes bibliographical references.

Identifiers: ISBN 978-1-6667-4893-2 (paperback) | ISBN 978-1-6667-4894-9 (hardcover) | ISBN 978-1-6667-4895-6 (ebook)

Subjects: LCSH: Middle East. | Christians—Middle East—History. | Christianity and other religions—Middle East.

Classification: BR1070 .I56 2023 (paperback) | BR1070 .I56 (ebook)

06/21/23

To Shirin Abu Akleh,
a Palestinian Christian journalist who dedicated her life to being a witness in the eye of the storm. Shirin was murdered by an Israeli sniper on May 11, 2022.

Contents

Contributors

KHALED ANABTAWI is a PhD student in the Department of Sociology and Anthropology at the Geneva Graduate Institute (IHEID). His PhD project addresses the reshaping of sectarianism and communitarianism in a settler-colonial context (the case of the Palestinian citizens of Israel). His research interests are focused on identity studies, sociology of space, and everyday life.

PAOLO MAGGIOLINI is a research fellow and adjunct professor at the Catholic University of Milan (Italy). His publications include *Minorities and State-Building in the Middle East: The Case of Jordan* (with Idir Ouahes).

AMIR MARSHI is a master's student at the University of Chicago and a researcher and writer for the Jerusalem Story website.

MIRAY PHILIPS is a PhD candidate in sociology at the University of Minnesota and a visiting researcher at Georgetown University's Berkley Center for Religion, Peace, and World Affairs.

MITRI RAHEB is the founder and president of Dar al-Kalima University in Bethlehem, Palestine. The most widely published Palestinian theologian to date, Raheb is the author of more than forty books, including *Faith in the Face of Empire* and *The Politics of Persecution*.

BERNARD SABELLA is a retired associate professor of sociology at Bethlehem University. His publications include *A Life Worth Living: The Story of a Palestinian Catholic*.

ANTOINE SALAMEH is a lecturer at Saint Joseph University and Makassed University of Beirut. His latest research interests have resulted in a book regarding religious dialogue in Lebanon, in addition to several academic published papers on the following subjects: religious pluralism, comparative religious studies, and Islamo-Christian relationships with specific emphasis on the Maronite-Druze interrelationship and the religious aspects of the Maronite and Druze.

ROULA TALHOUK is a professor in practical theology and in anthropology of religions, director of the Institute of Muslim-Christian Studies at Saint Joseph University of Beirut, and coordinator of the master's degree in the religious sciences faculty. Her publications include a book and several papers on the perceptions between religious communities in Lebanon, especially the Shia and the Maronites.

Preface

THIS BOOK IS THE outcome of a research project initiated by Dar al-Kalima University (DAK) in Bethlehem, Palestine, in 2009. The religion and state project has a long-term goal of achieving more peaceful and inclusive societies in the region to ensure gender equality, human dignity, justice, and freedom, with the United Nations' Sustainable Development Goal #16 as its framework. The project was implemented in cooperation with the Christian Academic Forum for Citizenship in the Arab World (CAFCAW). The target groups of the research are Christian communities in Egypt, Lebanon, Jordan, and Israel/Palestine. The scope of the research includes the following:

a. The sociopolitical and economic context of the countries

b. Demography, facts and figures: religious and denominational composition

c. Religion/church and state relations

d. Freedom of religion, societal discrimination—invisibilities, stereotypes, and possible harassment or attacks faced by Christians

e. The sociocultural impact of Christian communities

f. Major institutions and movements within the churches

g. Major challenges

h. Future prospects

i. References and resources

Based on the assumption that the twenty-first century has given rise to some of the toughest challenges ever, the focus of the research was confined to developments during the past two decades. The collapse of the so-called peace process; the devastating wars in Iraq and Syria; the destabilization of the region, including Egypt, due to the Arab Spring; and the economic collapse of Lebanon have posed unprecedented challenges and put Christians in the eye of the storm.

The research was conducted mainly by indigenous researchers in the respective countries. It was important to include both established researchers, like Prof. Bernard Sabella, Prof. Roula Talhouk, and Dr. Antoine Salameh, and young and emerging scholars in the region, like Meray Phillips, Amir Marshi, and Khaled Anabtawi. Jordan was the exception in having an Italian researcher, Dr. Paolo Maggiolini, to write the country chapter. The research included desk reviews, interviews, and focus groups during 2021, and the manuscript was finalized in 2022.

I would like to take this opportunity to thank all the researchers involved. Special thanks go to Wipf and Stock publishers for their support in publishing this book. I would like to thank both Hiba Nasser Atrash, my assistant, and Theresa Pfenig for their administrative support.

Introduction

Mitri Raheb

TWO DECADES IN REVIEW

In March 2000, Pope John Paul II visited Bethlehem in occupied Palestine and held a Mass at Manger Square. The visit was part and parcel of the millennium celebrations commemorating two thousand years of Christianity. It was, after all, in Palestine that Christianity began. It was here that Jesus was born, lived, worked, and proclaimed the reign of God. It was in Jerusalem that the first church was established. For twenty centuries, Christianity in Palestine survived successive empires from the Roman to the Byzantine, Arab, Crusader, Ottoman, British, and Israelis. As tens of thousands of Palestinian Christians and pilgrims gathered in front of the Church of the Nativity, the pope's message to a dwindling Christian community was none other than "Do not lose heart!"

The city of Bethlehem was chosen by the pope not only because it is the birthplace of Christ, but also because it has the largest Christian concentration in the West Bank; about half of all West Bank Christians reside there. However, the pope did not address only the Palestinian Christian community but the Palestinian people as a whole. It was clear to the pope that Christians do not exist in a vacuum but are an integral part of the sociopolitical and economic context, and of the larger community. Addressing a group of dignitaries at the Palestinian presidential residence later that day, the pope explicitly referred to the greater context in which Palestinian Christians live: "No one can ignore how much the Palestinian people have had to suffer in recent decades. Your torment is before the eyes of the world.

1

And it has gone on too long."[1] That same day, he visited the largest refugee camp in Bethlehem, Deheisheh, where residents reminded the pope of their Nakba, the catastrophe that took place in 1948, over half a century ago, that led to the displacement of over seven hundred thousand Palestinians, including over fifty thousand Palestinian Christians.

Bethlehem was planning for the millennium celebrations. The city had many projects ready for implementation, and over 200 million US dollars were invested in infrastructure and cultural projects. The city was decorated to receive heads of states, diplomats, and celebrities. Cultural activities were planned for the entire year and there was hope in the air. The pope prayed in the grotto for lasting peace in the region.

The peace negotiations were being conducted by the Clinton administration with the Palestinian leadership under Arafat and with Ehud Barak of Israel. The Oslo Accords signed at the White House in September 1993 were intended to lead to a negotiated and final peace settlement. To that end, President Clinton called both leaders to a two-week retreat at Camp David in July 2000. The summit concluded without agreement on two disputed issues: the status of Jerusalem and the right of return for Palestinian refugees. Two months later, Ariel Sharon stormed al-Aqsa Mosque compound in Jerusalem in a provocative demonstration of his opposition to any division of the city and to demand that al-Aqsa be under Israeli control. This visit on September 28, 2000, triggered al-Aqsa Intifada, the second Palestinian uprising. Ehud Barak lost the Israeli elections of 2001, and Ariel Sharon was elected as prime minister.

One year later, Sharon invaded all West Bank cities, including Bethlehem. In April 2002, Israeli tanks rolled into Bethlehem and destroyed the infrastructure built for the millennium celebrations.[2] Israeli tanks shelled Christian neighborhoods, and Apache helicopters bombed Palestinian security buildings. A new wave of Christian emigration was triggered as the hopes raised by the millennium celebrations and the "peace process" were dashed and shattered. In the two decades since then, it has become clear that the Israeli occupation of Palestine has no clear end. Most Israelis accept the religious-based settler-colonial ideology that has produced an apartheid regime.[3] Sharon unilaterally withdrew his troops and settlers

1. Stanley, "Pope in Holy Land."

2. Raheb, *Bethlehem Besieged*, 3–49.

3. For an overview of the use and development of the settler-colonial paradigm to Israel, I recommend Sabbagh-Khoury, "Tracing Settler Colonialism."

Three human rights organizations recently defined Israel as an apartheid state: Amnesty International, B'Tselem, and Human Rights Watch (Amnesty International, "Israel's Apartheid against Palestinians"; B'Tselem, "Apartheid"; Shakir, "Israeli Apartheid").

from Gaza while controlling all access points via air, sea, and land, making the small 140 square miles of the Gaza Strip the largest open-air prison in the world. Under such circumstances, the number of Christians in the Gaza Strip has declined rapidly to less than one thousand, and it is foreseeable that Christianity in Gaza will cease to exist.

Nazareth, the city of the annunciation, was also preparing for the millennium celebrations, named Nazareth 2000, like the Bethlehem 2000 project in its twin city of Bethlehem. Like Bethlehem, Nazareth had been a city with a mixed Christian-Muslim population living together for centuries with good neighborly relations.[4] Both cities had a Christian mayor despite Christians no longer being the majority. Like Bethlehem, Nazareth is a Palestinian enclave, a city strangled by the surrounding Jewish colonies that prevent the city from expanding. Sectarian identity politics are entrenched in the identity of the state of Israel, which defines itself as a Jewish state for the Jewish people, and where 93 percent of the land is reserved exclusively for Jewish use. In the context of confined space, a small piece of land in the town center known as Shihab ad-Din became a tool for sectarian identity politics by the Islamic party in Israel against the leftist municipality led by secular Christians and Muslims. The rise of Islamic parties in Palestine (Hamas) and in Israel (two Islamic movements) are a symptom of growing sectarianism in society and an important factor in the deepening sectarian identity politics. The rise of religious Zionist and Islamist movements are part and parcel of a wider phenomenon of the political being sacralized.[5]

Islamist parties of all shapes have mushroomed worldwide. One specific Saudi-led militant transnational Islamist movement named al-Qaeda made headlines on September 11, 2001, when four commercial airliners were hijacked, two of them crashing into the World Trade Center, a third into the Pentagon building, and the fourth in a field in Pennsylvania. With almost 3,000 fatalities and over 25,000 injured, September 11 became the deadliest terror attack and one with global magnitude. The attack took place on American soil and coincided with a Republican administration under George W. Bush, with Dick Cheney as vice-president, Donald Rumsfeld as secretary of defense, and many neoconservative advisors such as Paul Wolfowitz, Elliot Abrams, and Richard Perle, along with considerable influence from the Israel lobby.[6] In fact, neoconservatives and al-Qaeda had many things in common in that they both believed in a metaphysical war between

4. A study on Christian-Muslim relation in Nazareth was conducted in 1992 (Emmett, *Beyond the Basilica*).

5. For an interreligious and cross-national study on this phenomenon, see Rouhana and Shalhoub-Kevorkian, *When Politics Are Sacralized*.

6. Mearsheimer and Walt, *Israel Lobby*, 229–62.

good and evil. Both believed themselves to be on the side of the righteous called to defeat evil in the world and to use whatever military force necessary. Both focused on Israel, the Middle East, and Islam: the Christians of the region were irrelevant. Yet, it was these Christians in the region who experienced the collateral damage of such policies.

Secretary of Defense Donald Rumsfeld, under the influence of neo-conservatives and the Israel lobby, fabricated evidence of weapons of mass destruction in Iraq and a link between Saddam Hussein and al-Qaeda. Based on these allegations, and under the banner of bringing democracy and freedom to the Iraqi people, the United States launched war on Iraq on March 20, 2003. The situation of the 1.4 million Iraqi Christians under Saddam was poor. The Iran-Iraq war from 1980 to 1988, followed by the invasion of Kuwait in 1991, the war to liberate Kuwait, and the subsequent sanctions imposed on Iraq,[7] exerted a major toll on the country, particularly on Christians. Many Christians fled Iraq during the Iran-Iraq war to avoid being drafted into that deadly conflict. Christian migration accelerated after the 1991 conflict, mainly to the US but also to Europe, Australia, and New Zealand. Sanctions in the 1990s led 30 percent of the population to emigrate. It is estimated that of the 2 million Iraqis who emigrated between 1980 and 2003, one-eighth (250,000) were Christian.[8] However, the largest wave of Christian emigration from Iraq was triggered by the American invasion of Iraq in 2003. Under the false pretext of a smoking gun, the US invaded Iraq and dismantled the Baath Party of Iraq and the Iraqi military. This brought chaos to the country and paved the way for ISIS to take over. Three years after the invasion, al-Qaida and other religious Sunni groups declared the Islamic State of Iraq, taking control of large areas of the country and proclaiming an Islamic Caliphate. This led to the largest displacement and migration of Christians ever seen from the region. Over 1 million Christians felt defenseless and fled Iraq to neighboring countries such as Jordan, Lebanon, and Syria, while many migrated to North America and Australia. It is very sad to see how an ancient and once-thriving Christian community shrank from 1.5 million in 2003 to less than 200,000 today, many of them internally displaced in Irbil.[9]

Lebanon was also optimistic in 2000. The Israeli withdrawal from Southern Lebanon in May 2000 was a reason for celebration for a country that had been partly occupied for almost two decades. The South Lebanon Army, which had cooperated with the Israeli occupation, was dismantled,

---

7. For the impact of the siege, see Arnove, *Iraq under Siege*.
8. Chatelard, "Migration from Iraq."
9. Personal interview with minority expert Dr. Saad Saaloum, July 22, 2022.

and many of their members and their families fled to the Galilee. The popularity of Hezbollah grew following the Israeli withdrawal from South Lebanon. After the Israeli war on Lebanon in 2006, Hezbollah's strength was celebrated as a force capable of fighting Israel and forcing it to withdraw. This sharpened the popularity of Shia resistance over and against compliant Sunni Gulf states. The toppling of Saddam Hussein and his Sunni-based system in 2003 gave prominence to the Iraqi Shia community, which had previously been marginalized but had increasing transnational ties to Iran. These developments heightened the Sunni-Shia divide and the identity sectarian politics of the region.[10]

The sectarian divide developed into an intra-Muslim phenomenon along Shia-Sunni lines with the two Muslim groups injecting billions of petrodollars to export their Shiite or Wahhabi version of Islam and to support their allies financially and military, including the funding of proxy wars. The ultimate goal of the oil-producing countries was to buy allies and expand their influence in the region. Lebanon became the battleground for Saudi Arabia and Iran. A Shiite-led government under Aoun prompted Saudi Arabia and the Gulf countries to halt their financial support to Lebanon. The corrupt sectarian regime built on political dynasties, plus rocketing national debt, forced the country to declare bankruptcy and caused the devaluation of the Lebanese lira amid the most serious economic problems ever. Many Christians emigrated to France, Europe, and North America. The country once celebrated as the Switzerland of the Middle East has become another example of a failed state.

The so-called Arab Spring that began in December 2010 in Tunisia raised the expectations of populations in the Middle East for a better future and triggered a ripple effect throughout the Arab world. A revolution began in Egypt on January 25, 2011, and a civil uprising in Syria one day later, in two countries that were key locations for the Christian presence in the Middle East. The largest Christian community in the region lives in Egypt. Syria also had a substantial Christian presence, especially in and around Damascus, Aleppo, and Homs. It is important to understand that Christian attitudes towards the Arab Spring ranged from skepticism to strong support. At the beginning of the uprising, traditional church leaders tended to side with those in power politically (Pope Shenoudah with President Mubarak, Syrian Church leaders with Assad) whereas young Christian theologians and more secular Christian activists like George Sabra and Michel Kilo in Syria favored change and supported the uprising. Christian youth, both Orthodox such as the Mespiro Youth Union and Protestant like Qasr ad-Dubara,

---

10. For an in-depth analysis, see Wehrey, *Sectarian Politics in Gulf.*

participated actively at Tahrir Square and demonstrated a visible Christian presence in the public realm. The rise to power of Islamic parties in Egypt with the electoral victory of the Muslim Brotherhood's Freedom and Justice Party on December 3, 2011, provoked fear and concern among both secular Muslims and Christians in the country. This did not deter the Evangelical Presbyterian Church of Egypt from opening a dialogue with the leadership of the Muslim Brotherhood. On February 28, 2012, seventeen leaders of the Evangelical Presbyterian Church met with five leaders from the Muslim Brotherhood at their headquarters and issued a joint statement on issues related to citizenship, freedom of religious practice, and Egyptian unity and identity. The election of Mohammad Morsi as president of Egypt on June 17, 2012, and Morsi's policies of Islamization caused serious disquiet among secular Muslims, Christians, and the military. For this reason, various Coptic religious establishments welcomed the June 30, 2013, counter-revolution as an expression of genuine dissatisfaction by the majority of Egyptians with the ambitious rule of the Muslim Brotherhood, rather than viewing it as a coup d'état, as perceived in the West. Several Christian leaders went on to establish political parties. Nagib Sawiris began the Free Egyptians Party, and Emad Gad and other Christian intellectuals were among the founders of the Egyptian Social Democratic Party. While many Egyptian Christians have a sense of security under President Sisi, many have doubts about whether the situation is sustainable in the long term.

In Syria, the civil war became militarized and witnessed the rise of ISIS and an-Nusra in attempts to control territory. This new reality represented an existential threat to the Christian presence in the areas controlled by these Islamist groups. Many Christian communities were forced to leave their villages for relatively safe zones such as Damascus. A few Christian groups created quasi-Christian militias to take up arms and defend their villages, as was the case with the Sotoro in Syria. For the thriving Armenian community in cities like Aleppo, the war meant not only a loss of businesses and property but another wave of displacement and ultimately a total loss of faith and hope in the region. It is estimated that the percentage of Christians in Syria fell from 10 to 3 percent.

The events of the Arab Spring presented a huge challenge for the people of the Middle East, and particularly for the Christians of the region. Those marching on the streets overestimated their own power and the role of regional and international players, as well as the depth of the problems facing the region. The Arab Spring highlighted the dire need for a new social contract based on equal citizenship and social cohesion. It also demonstrated the value of freedom, especially for young people. Studies show that one-fourth of young people in the region belong to the so-called "creative class" that can develop and market new ideas. It is crucial for a better future that these talents are harnessed and space be expanded for freedom, creativity, and innovation.

A GEOPOLITICAL VIEW

The status of Christians in the Middle East cannot be discussed without looking at the larger geopolitical picture. Over the last two centuries, the Middle East has experienced twenty-six wars, an average of one war every eight years. The region never recovered from the neocolonialism of the first half of the twentieth century, including the implanting of Israel at the heart of the region, nor from the many wars and civil wars that became a marker of the second half of the twentieth century. The region has been unable to really recover from the economic stagnation and de-development of the later period of the century. Nor can we ignore the influence of three regional powers in the last five decades—Israel, Saudi Arabia, and Iran—and their religious affiliations: Jewish, Sunni and Shiite Islam. The twenty-first century has been marked by Israeli military hegemony over the region and its settler-colonial project in historic Palestine. Saudi Arabia and Iran, and to some degree Qatar and UAE, have been heavily involved in the civil wars in Iraq, Syria, and Yemen, and in the destabilization of Lebanon. In almost all these countries, proxy wars involving a complex web of local, regional, and international players with shifting configurations have created huge losses in human capital and natural resources. Turkey, Russia, the US, and Israel were, and are still, heavily involved in Iraq, Syria, and Lebanon.

To understand the larger context in which Middle Eastern Christians live today, a quick look at the *Arab Human Development Report* of 2022 is helpful. The Middle East is home to 5.5 percent of the world's population and yet is home to 25 percent of the world's conflicts, 58 percent of the world's refugees, and 45 percent of the world's displaced people.[11] Iraqi and Syrian refugees have added to the chronic Palestinian refugee problem. Palestinian and Syrian refugees continue to constitute the largest number of refugees globally with over six million each.

By 2050, three out of four people in the Middle East will be living in countries with a high risk of conflict. The number of Middle Eastern countries affected by conflict grew from five in 2002 to eleven in 2016. The Israeli occupation of Palestinian land is the longest occupation in modern history. The infrastructure of several countries has been destroyed: Palestine, Iraq, Syria, Yemen, and Lebanon, and there is no end in sight. Several groups have been displaced multiple times (Armenians, Lebanese, Palestinians),

11. Akhtar et al., *Arab Human Development Report*, 4.

and many have had to start anew several times during their lifetime. Wars do not distinguish between Christians, Muslims, or atheists. Many people in the Middle East have seen their hopes shattered over and over again, and have given up on the region. They have lost their hopes for peace and security for themselves and for their children. Many have resorted to emigration. Thousands of people from the Middle East, including many Christians, have opted to start a new life in North America, Australia, Europe, and South America. Emigration and displacement continue to be an open wound, and healing is delayed. Without peace, this wound will continue to bleed. Without peace, Christians will continue to leave. Without peace, it will be difficult to keep Christianity alive in the lands of its origin.

The Middle East and North Africa region (MENA) is one of the fastest growing regions in the world, next only in Africa. There were over 100 million people living in the MENA region in 1960, a number that has grown today to over 460 million. With lower mortality rates and a steady birth rate (though starting to decline), the region is expected to reach one billion by 2100. The number of Christians in the Middle East cannot keep pace with this demographic explosion. Lower birth rates among Middle Eastern Christians and the migration patterns that have resulted from the brain drain or wars, unrest, and occupation (Iraq, Syria, Lebanon, Palestine) have resulted in a steady decline in their total percentage of the population. Most Middle Eastern countries do not publish separate figures for their Christian population, but it is estimated that there are between 10 to 15 million indigenous Christians living today in the Middle East, making up between 2 to 3 percent of the region's population. The trend is clear: from 20 percent in the Ottoman Empire in the second half of the nineteenth century to 10 percent in the Middle East by the early twentieth century, and down to 2 or 3 percent today. The role of Christians in society is not what it used to be. Their influence in social, economic, and political spheres is diminishing. Nevertheless, they continue to play a vital role in certain sectors like health, education, and not-for-profit, albeit to a lesser degree than before.

The population explosion constitutes a major challenge for the region, as the available resources cannot sustain such numbers and governments are not equipped to face this challenge. Population growth is felt especially in the major regional capitals. The development of infrastructure in urban settings has been unable to keep pace with demographic growth and has resulted in densely populated, polluted, and congested cities surrounded by large slums with inadequate transportation systems, education, or health services. Since the majority of Middle Eastern Christians live in urban areas, they have seen on a daily basis how their quality of life has deteriorated with congested streets; polluted air, sea, and land; plus rising violence and social tensions.

Another feature of the last two decades is the failed state. Who would have thought that two major countries like Iraq and Syria with strict security apparatuses and trained military personnel would lose control over geography so easily and fall like a house of cards within weeks? In Lebanon, sectarianism and corrupt dynasties have led to the total collapse of the Lebanese financial system and the bankruptcy of the state and society. No wonder there is a lack of trust between the government and the people.[12] The region has a very high unemployment rate (12.5 percent in 2021 compared with 6.2 percent globally) and the highest number of unemployed young people worldwide (28.6 percent). The unemployment rate among young women is the highest in the world at 49.1 percent.[13] In 2020 the region lost ten million jobs. At the same time, the Middle East has the highest rate of illiteracy worldwide at 36 percent, compared with 18 percent globally. Equal access to education and health services is lacking, and there is a divide between those with private schooling in city centers versus very poor schooling, especially in rural areas. This became very apparent during the pandemic when 55 percent of schoolchildren in the Middle East had no access to online teaching and could not be educated.[14]

A major challenge facing the region is access to water. The region has only 1.4 percent of global water resources, eighteen of the twenty-two countries have water scarcity, and over one hundred million people have no access to clean water. With rising demand, the water deficit in the region is expected to reach 75.4 billion cubic meters by 2023, compared with 28.3 in 2000. Currently, over two hundred million people are exposed to water stress that puts increased pressure on groundwater resources, which are frequently being extracted beyond the recharge potential of the aquifers.

A further challenge facing the Middle East is militarization. Five of the top ten most militarized countries globally are found in the Middle East. Israel is the most militarized country in the world. Based on military expenditure in relation to GDP, the number of military personnel per capita and the amount of military hardware, the region as a whole is the most heavily militarized on the planet. In 2015, four countries in the Middle East spent over 100 billion US dollars on defense: 56 billion by Saudi Arabia (third only after the US and China), 18 billion by Turkey, 15 billion by Israel, and 14 billion by the UAE. Our region also receives over half of all weapons deliveries to developing countries and over one-fourth of all arms shipments worldwide. Ranked by military spending per capita, six of the seven top countries are found in the Middle East. Natural resources like oil are

12. Akhtar et al., *Arab Human Development Report*, 4.

13. Akhtar et al., *Arab Human Development Report*, 6–7.

14. Akhtar et al., *Arab Human Development Report*, 10.

exploited to pay for these weapons, which are either not used at all or are used against the citizens of the region themselves.

A further challenge is climate change. The Middle East is particularly vulnerable to climate change, as it is one of the world's driest and most water-scarce regions with high dependency on climate-sensitive agriculture. Much of its population and economic activity are located in flood-prone urban coastal zones. Higher temperatures and reduced precipitation will increase the occurrence of droughts. In urban areas in North Africa and the Gulf region, a temperature increase of one to three degrees could expose six to twenty-five million people to coastal flooding. Climate change in large parts of the Middle East and North Africa could put the very survival of the inhabitants in jeopardy. By 2050, during the warmest periods, temperatures will not fall below thirty degrees at night, and could rise to forty-six degrees Celsius during the day. By 2100, midday temperatures on hot days could climb even to fifty degrees Celsius, with heatwaves occurring ten times more often than they do now. Between 1986 and 2005, it was very hot for an average of about 16 days per year; by 2050 it may be hot for 80 days per year, and up to 120 days by 2100. Researchers from MIT are predicting that future temperatures in southwest Asia will exceed the threshold of human adaptability. By 2100 the Middle East will become almost uninhabitable, as heat and humidity will be fundamentally hostile to human life.[15] "Climate change will significantly worsen living conditions in the Middle East and North Africa. Prolonged heatwaves and desert dust storms may render some regions uninhabitable, which will surely contribute to the pressure to migrate."[16] Middle Eastern Christians are already especially vulnerable to emigration, and climate change will take its toll on the Christian community.

Last but not least, there is a huge divide between the oil-exporting countries like Saudi Arabia and the Gulf States on the one hand, and oil-importing countries like Jordan and Lebanon on the other. This divide widened recently due to the war in Ukraine as oil prices rocketed, and the region is the most food-dependent globally. There is also a widening gap between rich and poor in the region. Income inequality is extreme in the Middle East, and there is almost no middle class left in the region, a class that in the past was largely comprised of Christians.

Geopolitically speaking, Christians in the twenty-first century Middle East are not major players and have seldom been the immediate target of regional politics. Yet, like their Muslim compatriots, they are directly affected by the overall geopolitical context. They face the same challenges as the rest

15. Pal and Eltahir, "Future Temperature," 198.
16. SB/PH, "Climate-Exodus Expected."

of the population, but their small numbers in highly unstable and volatile socioeconomic and political situations make them more vulnerable, quicker to emigrate, and more liable to lose hope and heart. These chronic realities and challenges are expected to continue for coming decades and make the future bleak for the region in general, particularly for Christians. Nevertheless, Christians have repeatedly proven themselves to be a resilient community in spite of all the challenges, and capable at times not only of surviving but of thriving.

BIBLIOGRAPHY

Akhtar, Tehmina, et al. *Arab Human Development Report 2022: Expanding Opportunities for an Inclusive and Resilient Recovery in the Post-Covid Era; Executive Summary.* New York: United Nations Development Programme Regional Bureau for Arab States, 2022.

Amnesty International. "Israel's Apartheid against Palestinians: A Cruel System of Domination and a Crime against Humanity." Amnesty International, Feb. 1, 2022. https://www.amnesty.org/en/latest/news/2022/02/israels-apartheid-against-palestinians-a-cruel-system-of-domination-and-a-crime-against-humanity/.

Arnove, Anthony, ed. *Iraq under Siege: The Deadly Impact of Sanctions and War.* Updated ed. Cambridge, MA: South End, 2003.

Besenyő, János, and Roland Gömöri. "Christians in Syria and the Civil War." In *Panorama of Global Security Environment 2014*, edited by Peter Bator and Robert Ondrejcsak, 219–30. Bratislava: Center for European and North Atlantic Affairs (CENAA), 2015. https://www.academia.edu/68874429/Christians_in_Syria_and_the_civil_war.

Betz, Frederick. "Political Theory of Societal Association and Nation-Building: Case of the Failed State of Lebanon." *Open Journal of Social Sciences* 9 (2021) 333–84.

Brown, Brian J. *Apartheid South Africa . . . Apartheid Israel!: Ticking the Boxes of Occupation and Dispossession.* Independently published, 2022.

B'Tselem. "Apartheid." B'Tselem, Jan. 12, 2021. https://www.btselem.org/apartheid.

Carter, Jimmy. *Palestine: Peace Not Apartheid.* Reprint ed. New York: Simon & Schuster, 2007.

Chatelard, Géraldine. "Migration from Iraq between the Gulf and the Iraq Wars (1990–2003): Historical and Sociospacial Dimensions." Centre on Migration, Policy and Society, Working Paper No. 68, University of Oxford, 2009. https://www.academia.edu/182775/Migration_from_Iraq_between_the_Gulf_and_the_Iraq_Wars_1990-2003_Historical_and_Sociospacial_Dimensions.

Diyar Consortium. *From the Nile to the Euphrates: The Call of Faith and Citizenship; A Statement of the Christian Academic Forum for Citizenship in the Arab World.* Bethlehem: Diyar, 2015.

Emmett, Chad F. *Beyond the Basilica: Christians and Muslims in Nazareth.* Chicago: University of Chicago Press, 2012.

Guzansky, Yoel, and Benedetta Berti. "Is the New Middle East Stuck in Its Sectarian Past? The Unspoken Dimension of the 'Arab Spring.'" *Orbis* 57 (2013) 135–51.

Halper, Stefan, and Jonathan Clarke. *America Alone: The Neo-Conservatives and the Global Order.* New York: Cambridge University Press, 2004.

Mearsheimer, John J., and Stephen M. Walt. *The Israel Lobby and U.S. Foreign Policy.* New York: Farrar, Straus and Giroux, 2008.

Nadhmi, Faris K. "Consciousness of Stigma, Psychological Disengagement, and Collective Self-Esteem: The Case of Iraqi Christians." *TAARII Newsletter,* Jan 1, 2012. https://www.academia.edu/82156679/Consciousness_of_Stigma_Psychological_ Disengagement_and_Collective_Self_Esteem_The_Case_of_Iraqi_Christians.

Pal, Jeremy S., and Elfatih A. B. Eltahir. "Future Temperature in Southwest Asia Projected to Exceed a Threshold for Human Adaptability." *Nature Climate Change* 6 (Feb. 2016) 197–200. https://doi.org/10.1038/nclimate2833.

Salloum, Saad. "Barriers to Return for Ethno-Religious Minorities in Iraq: Identity Politics and Political Patronage among Yazidi and Christian Communities from Ninewa Governorate." International Organization for Migration, Jan. 2020. https:// www.researchgate.net/publication/343787692_BARRIERS_TO_RETURN_ FOR_ETHNO-RELIGIOUS_MINORITIES_IN_IRAQ_Identity_Politics_and_ Political_Patronage_Among_Yazidi_and_Christian_Communities_from_ Ninewa_Governorate.

Shakir, Omar. "Israeli Apartheid: 'A Threshold Crossed.'" Human Rights Watch, July 19, 2021. https://www.hrw.org/news/2021/07/19/israeli-apartheid-threshold-crossed.

Raheb, Mitri. *Bethlehem Besieged: Stories of Hope in Times of Trouble.* Minneapolis: Fortress, 2004.

———. *The Politics of Persecution: Middle Eastern Christians in an Age of Empire.* Waco, TX: Baylor University Press, 2021.

———. "The Revolution in the Arab World. Liberation: The Promise and the Illusion; A Palestinian Christian Perspective." *The Reemergence of Liberation Theologies: Models for the Twenty-First Century,* edited by Thia Cooper, New Approaches to Religion and Power, 101–10. New York: Palgrave Macmillan, 2013.

Raheb, Mitri, and Mark A. Lamport, eds. *Surviving Jewel: The Enduring Story of Christianity in the Middle East.* Eugene, OR: Cascade, 2022.

———. *The Rowman & Littlefield Handbook of Christianity in the Middle East.* Lanham, MD: Rowman & Littlefield, 2020.

Ross, Kenneth R., et al., eds. *Christianity in North Africa and West Asia.* Edinburgh: Edinburgh University Press, 2018.

Rouhana, Nadim N., and Nadera Shalhoub-Kevorkian, eds. *When Politics Are Sacralized: Comparative Perspectives on Religious Claims and Nationalism.* Cambridge: Cambridge University Press, 2021.

Sabbagh-Khoury, Areej. "Tracing Settler Colonialism: A Genealogy of a Paradigm in the Sociology of Knowledge Production in Israel." *Politics & Society* 50 (Mar. 1, 2022) 44–83.

SB/PH. "Climate-Exodus Expected in the Middle East and North Africa." Max-Planck-Gesellschaft, July 10, 2020. https://www.mpg.de/10481936/climate-change-middle -east-north-africa.

Stanley, Alessandra. "The Pope in the Holy Land: The Overview; Pope, at a Camp, Deplores Plight of Palestinians." *New York Times,* Mar. 23, 2000. https://www. nytimes.com/2000/03/23/world/pope-holy-land-overview-pope-camp-deplores- plight-palestinians.html.

Wehrey, Frederic. *Sectarian Politics in the Gulf: From the Iraq War to the Arab Uprisings.* Reprint, New York: Columbia University Press, 2016.

Christians in Egypt

Transformations in Representational Authority and Narratives of Belonging

Miray Philips

THE REVOLUTION OF 2011 was a defining moment for Egypt in the past two decades. Egyptians, including Coptic Christians, took to the streets calling for bread, freedom, and social justice. Christians specifically brought to the fore questions of religious freedom and citizenship. Yet an analysis that begins ten years prior to the revolution reveals how the oscillating relationship between presidents and patriarchs has defined Coptic affairs, while sidelining Coptic voices both in Egypt and the diaspora. The decade since the revolution reveals how Copts mobilized to challenge the authority of the Coptic Church, seeking to create independent avenues to reconsider an expansive definition of Coptic identity, heritage, and rights. These changing dynamics are considered in this chapter in an attempt to understand how transformations in representational authority have resulted in various, and sometimes conflicting, narratives of belonging.

Egypt is home to many Christian communities and religious minorities. Coptic Christians are the largest religious minority group in Egypt and the largest Christian group in the Middle East. In the absence of a census, there are no official statistics about the religious breakdown of the Egyptian population, though Coptic Christians are estimated to be 10 percent of the population.[1] Of those, 90 percent adhere to the Orthodox tradition. The Church of Alexandria, one of the earliest episcopal sees of Christianity,

---

1. While 10 percent is the most commonly cited population percentage, some official accounts record Copts as low as 5 percent, while the Coptic Church maintains that they are almost 20 percent of the population.

was founded by St. Mark the Evangelist, who brought Christianity to Egypt in AD 42. While Coptic identity is largely construed as a religious one, many scholars and community members emphasize its ethnic and cultural aspects, especially as the community is increasingly becoming a global one[2] and many of its members are increasingly nonreligious. After all, the Arabic word for Copts, *al-qibti*, is an Arabized version of the Coptic word *aiguption*, which is derived from the Greek word for Egypt, *aigytios*. In this vein, Copts emphasize their indigenous history by, for example, reviving the Coptic language,[3] and some even claim direct descent from the pharaohs.[4] Questioning these "ideal" constructions of Coptic identity, Mina Ibrahim's research brings attention to the lives of negated and invisibilized Copts, those whose actions and beliefs do not fit prescribed ideals about Coptic religious and ethnic identity.[5]

While Orthodox Copts dominate politically and numerically, Egypt is also home to Coptic Catholics and Evangelicals. Catholic missionaries arrived in Egypt in the seventeenth century, and by the nineteenth century the pope established the Coptic Catholic Patriarchate of Alexandria. After Antonios I Naguib retired in 2013 for health reasons, Ibrahim Isaac Sidrak became the Coptic Catholic patriarch, leading a congregation of nearly 200,000. The Coptic Evangelical Church was founded in the mid-nineteenth century by American Presbyterian missionaries who proselytized and converted Coptic Orthodox Egyptians. Andrea Zaki is the current president of the Protestant community in Egypt, which numbers nearly 250,000. While the Catholic Church shares more traditions with the Orthodox Church than with the Evangelical Church, they have both contributed considerably to Christian life in Egypt, especially in the realm of education.[6] Other Christian communities in Egypt include Armenian Christians, Greek Orthodox, and Jehovah's Witnesses, among many others. As for Muslim minorities, while Sunnis make up the majority sect, there are a small number of Quranists, Ahmadis, Sufis, and Shi'as. There also remains a Jewish population, although rapidly dwindling. Existing but officially unrecognized communities include the Baha'is and the nonreligious.

In the following text, I begin by charting the relationship between the leadership of the Coptic Church and successive Egyptian regimes over the past two decades. I then turn to the relationship between the Coptic

---

2. Akladios, "Heteroglossia," 631–32.

3. Miyokawa, "Revival of Coptic Language," 151.

4. Van der Vliet, "Copts."

5. See M. Ibrahim, "Minority at the Bar"; M. Ibrahim, "Drinking."

6. Monier, *Whose Heritage Counts*, 30–31.

Church and laity, emphasizing Copts' roles in internal reform, political mobilization, and cultural representation. Having introduced the three key actors—the church, the government, and Coptic laity—I then address how these three actors battle to define Coptic belonging in Egypt through the conflicting rhetoric of national unity, insecurity, martyrdom, and citizenship rights. As Copts are increasingly a global community, I conclude by exploring opportunities and challenges in the diaspora.

CHURCH-STATE RELATIONS: AN OSCILLATING ENTENTE

After a long stretch of autocratic rule in Egypt, the turn of the century has been animated with rapid political transformations. In the past twenty years alone, Egypt has been governed by five different leaders: Hosni Mubarak (1981–2011); the field marshal of the Supreme Council of the Armed Forces Mohamed Tantawi (2011–2012); Mohamed Morsi (2012–2013); interim Adly Mansour (2013–2014); and Abdel Fatah al-Sisi (2014–present). At a time of immense uncertainty, Pope Shenouda III, the patriarch of the Coptic Church of Alexandria, passed away in 2012 after a forty-year papacy. Pope Tawadros II was selected as his successor. These transformations resulted in an oscillating entente between the church and the state, having major implications for the social, cultural, and political standing of Copts in Egypt.

In the 1950s, the Coptic Orthodox Church under the leadership of Pope Cyril VI forged an entente with the Egyptian government during the presidency of Gamal Abdel Nasser, promising political allegiance in exchange for protection and concessions. Nasser's government, with the support of the Coptic Church, adopted policies that compromised the role of Coptic laity, especially within the realm of politics, forging a pathway for the Coptic Church to become the primary political and social representative of Copts.[7] When Anwar al-Sadat assumed power, he buttressed Islamist organizations, adopted Islamization policies, and failed to intervene adequately during sectarian strife, marking a temporary break in the entente between the Coptic Church and the state. After extensive disputes over domestic and foreign affairs, the final blow came when President Sadat sent Pope Shenouda III into exile to a monastery.

After Hosni Mubarak relieved Pope Shenouda III from exile, their relationship marked a return of the entente, although marred by tensions. Pope Shenouda III and President Mubarak found a common enemy in the growing threat of Islamism. Fearing the possibility that the Muslim Brotherhood might

---

7. Tadros, "Vicissitudes in the Entente," 270–72; Hasan, *Christians vs Muslims*, 103–5.

dominate politically, Pope Shenouda III institutionalized public support for President Mubarak, who cracked down on Islamists. During the presidential elections of 2005, for example, Pope Shenouda III demanded that all bishops vote Mubarak into office for a fifth term. Even when President Mubarak proposed constitutional amendments in 2007 that were met with opposition for potentially limiting political freedoms, Pope Shenouda III encouraged parishioners to vote in favor of the referendum. Yet the Mubarak regime engaged in mere lip service, barely holding their end of the entente. Addressing the longstanding problem of church construction, for example, the president filed a decree that transferred the decision-making power from the president to the governor, thereby easing the process. Otherwise, Copts continued to occupy a marginalized status in society, and sectarian violence was rampant. Growing tensions between the Coptic Church and state security services came to a head during the Wafaa Constantine saga, raising questions about the president's role in the entente, the state's interference in conversion cases, and the role of the state security apparatus in managing sectarian affairs.[8]

In 2011, popular protests erupted, calling for Mubarak to step down. While the relationship between Pope Shenouda III and President Mubarak was largely strained during these final years, Pope Shenouda III and leaders of both the Coptic Catholic and Coptic Evangelical Churches initially dissuaded their congregants from joining protests. Defying their leadership, many Christians, including Copts, took to the streets calling for bread, freedom, and social justice, alongside their Muslim conationals. After witnessing the utopic initial days of the revolution and engaging in intense conversations with youth, however, Andrea Zaki, the head of the Coptic Evangelical Church, changed his mind about the Evangelical Church's position and issued a statement in support of the revolution. The Kasr El Dobara Evangelical Church, specifically, played an important role during the revolution.[9] Located nearby Tahrir Square, the church provided a

---

8. Wafaa Constantine had reportedly suffered domestic abuse at the hands of her disabled husband, who was a priest in Beheira Governorate. In 2004, as a way to escape her situation, she approached a police station and claimed that she wanted to convert to Islam. At first, the state security apparatus held her in a secret location, resulting in mass protests among Copts who wanted to know her whereabouts, fearing that she had been abducted and forcefully converted. After Pope Shenouda III retreated to the monastery in protest, President Mubarak intervened, and the state security apparatus agreed to let Constantine meet with a few bishops. Constantine later claimed that she wanted to return to Christianity and agreed to live in a monastery. Her return to the church resulted in mass protests among Muslims asking that she be handed over to al-Azhar. For the questions raised, see Tadros, *Copts at the Crossroads*, 76–81.

9. On how Protestant theology shaped participation in the revolution, see Dowell, "Landscapes of Belonging."

meeting point for people of various religious backgrounds to gather and pray. When violence erupted during the Mohamed Mahmoud protests, the church turned into a hospital for the wounded. Ever since, evangelical theologians have played a key role in conceiving of a Christian theology that addresses the religious and political subjectivities of Egyptian Christians in a marginalized context.[10]

After Mubarak resigned, the Supreme Council of the Armed Forces (SCAF) stepped in to oversee a democratic transition. This critical period was riddled with insecurity, tensions, continued state-sanctioned violence, and sectarian strife. Although the SCAF claimed that it would protect the revolution, it repeatedly instigated violence against protestors and failed to prevent sectarian violence against Copts. Tensions between SCAF and citizens peaked when security forces killed twenty-eight protestors, mostly Copts, in what became known as the Maspero massacre. Throughout this transitory period under SCAF, the Coptic Church largely maintained a low political profile, as it had lost some legitimacy for opposing the revolution. During a very critical time, Pope Shenouda III passed away right before the presidential election, leaving Copts in a state of insecurity and uncertainty about their future. Pope Tawadros II assumed his position only five months after Mohamed Morsi, the Muslim Brotherhood candidate, was elected as president, marking a new era of church-state relations.

Leading up to the elections, the Muslim Brotherhood assured Copts of their rights. Upon assuming power, Mohamed Morsi declared himself the "president of all Egyptians" and met with representatives of the Coptic Orthodox, Catholic, and evangelical churches to discuss national unity, cooperation, and rights.[11] Despite these attempts, the relationship between the brotherhood and the church was strained. While the brotherhood accused the church of encouraging Copts to vote against Islamist policies, the church accused the brotherhood of instrumentalizing religion and stoking sectarianism. Once Morsi assumed power, many of his policy decisions confirmed Copts' fears of being marginalized. The draft of the new constitution designated Islamic Sharia as the source of legislation, elevated the role of al-Azhar to observe the application of Islamic law, omitted protections for marginalized communities, and relegated all personal status affairs under the purview of the Coptic Church.[12] Despite popular protest by Christians, liberals, and secular citizens, Morsi issued a presidential decree allowing him to fast-track

---

10. Hernandez, "At Borders of Identity."

11. Sense of Belonging, القاء مشترك; Kortam, "Morsi Meets Religious Leaders"; *Asia News*, "Mohammed Morsi."

12. See Kirkpatrick, "Egyptian Islamists Approve"; Sedra, "Copts under Morsi."

approval of the constitution. Morsi's only Christian advisor, Samir Morcos, resigned in protest, claiming that he was not consulted on the decree. This structural marginalization emboldened everyday discrimination. When Egyptians protested against Morsi's regime only a year after his appointment, the Coptic Church encouraged its congregants to participate in the protests and consequently supported the military takeover in 2013.

The relationship between Abdel-Fatah al-Sisi and Pope Tawadros II marks a return of the entente. Sisi has deliberately constructed himself as a savior of Copts from Islamism, assuming a policy of "gift-giving" as a way to showcase government support for the Coptic Church. These gestures include building the largest Christian cathedral in the Middle East; appointing a first-ever Christian to the highest court, the Supreme Constitutional Court; and attending to a long-standing source of sectarian tensions by introducing a streamlined church building law. In 2015, he became the first president to officially attend Coptic Mass on Christmas Eve. During his brief speech, the crowd erupted in cheers, to which he jovially responded, "We love you too!" and he affirmed national unity: "We're going to build our country together, and the place is going to hold us all, and we're going to love one another."[13]

The relationships between patriarch and presidents highlights the extent to which the Coptic Church has become the primary political, spiritual, and social representative of Copts, positioned as a mediator between Coptic citizens and the state. However, Mariz Tadros importantly argues that an analysis of church-state relations needs to go beyond the idea that politics on either side are homogenous when, in fact, there are often multiple actors and interests at play.[14] Increasingly, Coptic laity, both in Egypt and the diaspora, have challenged the authority of the Coptic Church, playing a notable role in Coptic affairs and defining Coptic belonging.

LAITY CHALLENGES TO THE AUTHORITY OF THE COPTIC CHURCH

The totalizing representational authority of the Coptic Orthodox Church has increasingly become a source of tension between the church and Coptic laity. Georges Fahmi argues that the church's monopolization of political affairs has ultimately marginalized Copts because church-state alliances have rarely resolved Coptic grievances historically; Copts are discouraged from participating in politics, further entrenching their isolation in civic

13. Christian Youth Channel, "Word of the President."

14. Tadros, *Copts at the Crossroads*, 61.

life; and the church's authority enforces an idea that Copts are a homogenous mass with singular political interests.[15] When the church called on diasporic Copts to support Sisi's visit to the United States in 2016, a group of Coptic activists put forth these critiques in an open letter, asking the church leadership not to assume a political role.[16] Indeed, several lay groups have contested the totalizing authority of the church by calling for internal reform and accountability, organizing alternative avenues for political mobilization and representation, and creating independent platforms for cultural representation.

Calls for internal reform and accountability have largely revolved around matters related to sexual abuse and divorce. Novel among these issues is a MeToo movement based on allegations of sexual abuse by clergy. In July 2020, Sally Zakhari came out publicly about her experience of childhood sexual assault at the hands of a priest, Fr. Reweiss Khalil Aziz, who was visiting Florida from Egypt in the late 1990s. When she informed church authorities of the abuse, they told her that they were already aware of several other incidents. The church, however, did not take swift action and instead relocated him to other parishes. Although he was defrocked in 2014, he continued to serve. After the internal investigation was leaked in 2019, which was followed by public outcry in 2020, Pope Tawadros II eventually issued an official decree defrocking and laicizing Reweiss. While the statute of limitations had expired in Sally's case, there is currently a pending case by Samah Awadalla against Fr. Antonios Baky in California.

Sally's story catapulted a movement within the church, shedding light on the systematic problem of sexual violence and cover-up. Although varying in their responses, representatives of the Coptic Church denied covering up any incidents and tried to control the reputation of the church. While the Coptic Orthodox Archdiocese of North America and the Diocese of New York and New England instituted protocols on how to handle sexual and physical abuse, Pope Tawadros II condemned the publicization of allegations and banned Sally Zakhari from speaking at any churches.[17] Additionally, the spokesperson for the Coptic Orthodox Church claimed that priests are given up to twenty chances at repentance before they are stripped of their position.[18] These conflicting responses raised the ire of many who felt that abusers are protected by the church more than their victims.

15. Fahmi, "Coptic Church and Politics."
16. *Mada Masr*, "Coptic Activists Criticize."
17. CopticSurvivor, "Pope Tawadros's Response."
18. Salama, "Coptic Orthodox Spokesperson."

Calls to ease religious restrictions on divorce have also garnered a lot of attention by Coptic groups, highlighting challenges emanating from personal status laws that relegate family affairs to the authority of the Coptic Church.[19] In the 1970s, Pope Shenouda III restricted divorce to cases of adultery and limited second marriages. In 2008, the Supreme Administrative Court granted a Copt divorce, consequently undermining the authority of the Coptic Church. Some Copts also mobilized through groups such as Copts 38 and Victims of the Christian Personal Status Law, calling for the reinstatement of the 1938 personal status bylaws that permitted divorce on nine grounds, including adultery, imprisonment, abandonment, chronic illness, and incompatibility. Responding to calls for internal reform, Pope Tawadros II instituted more lenient divorce regulations. Disputes over divorce are rooted in challenges pertaining to personal status laws. Indeed, religious autonomy over judicial affairs has turned gender and sexuality into primary sites of contention and, often, sectarian strife.[20]

Facing outwards, Copts have mobilized around political affairs, seeking to create independent avenues for political representation beyond the purview of the Coptic Church. In the wake of sectarian attacks in the 1970s and 80s, diasporic Copts founded several advocacy organizations to raise awareness among US, Canadian, and European policymakers about religious discrimination in Egypt. Though fragmented in their narratives and strategies, many of these organizations have largely remained independent from both the Coptic Church and the Egyptian government, allowing them to hold both accountable for failing to protect Copts from violence and discrimination.[21] As a result of their work, diasporic Copts became the targets of smear campaigns led by the government, with the support of the Coptic Church, who accused diaspora activists of being national traitors for inviting Western intervention in sovereign affairs. Beyond organized political movements, diaspora Copts have responded to sectarian incidents in Egypt by protesting, praying, and singing as a form of dissent.[22] Diasporic Copts have also participated in domestic politics in their new homes by running for office, illustrated by the example of the Coptic American PAC based in New Jersey, and by intervening in public debates and policies about contentious issues such as sex education.[23]

---

19. See Elsässer, "Coptic Divorce Struggle."
20. Mahmood, *Religious Difference*, 111–48.
21. Akladios and Philips, "Contested Politics."
22. Ramzy, "Singing Strategic Multiculturalism."
23. Zacharia, "Tackling Sex Education."

While Coptic protests in Egypt were common, though periodic prior to 2011, the period immediately after the revolution saw a rise in Coptic activism. Copts mobilized to gain control over their political representation and advance political claims. Advocacy organizations such as the Maspero Youth Union (MYU) sought to mobilize Copts beyond the control of the Coptic Orthodox Church. Their calls for citizenship rights did not erase their religious identity, but rather asserted it. In protests, for example, members of MYU employed religious symbolism and pharaonic imagery to claim that Christians, as citizens, are central to Egypt.[24] Along with participating in movements focused narrowly on Coptic affairs, Copts also participated in national movements. Take, for example, the Kefaya movement of 2004 whose cofounder was George Ishak, a Coptic Catholic. Additionally, in the aftermath of the revolution, many Copts joined and led political parties and coalitions. During the first parliamentary elections, for example, the Kotla coalition included the Free Egyptian Party, which was founded by Coptic businessman Naguib Sawiris, and the Social Democratic Party, which had the largest number of Copts in any party.

The obliteration of civil society under President Sisi quashed many of these attempts at Coptic political mobilization. Wrongful incarceration, emigration, and repression have hindered knowledge production and advocacy on Coptic affairs. These concerns became urgent after Ramy Kamel, a Coptic activist and one of the founders of the Maspero Youth Union, was arrested prior to his departure to Geneva to participate in the United Nation's Minority Forum in 2019. A few months later, Patrick Zaki, a Coptic researcher with the Egyptian Initiative for Personal Rights, was arrested in the airport while visiting his family in Egypt from Bologna, where he was an MA student. Zaki was charged with spreading false news for an article he penned on the marginalization of Copts in Egypt. The targeting of Coptic activists as part of a repression campaign has raised questions about whether President Sisi is truly a champion of religious freedom.

Lay Copts have also created sociocultural organizations with the goal of preserving the cultural heritage of Copts, offering a more expansive and inclusive understanding of Coptic identity, history, and memory.[25] These organizations include Egypt Migrations (formerly known as the Coptic Canadian History Project), which was founded by Michael Akladios in 2016. Frustrated by the lack of systemic attempts to preserve family archives that are accessible to the public, Akladios built the first ever repository to document, preserve, and make accessible the experiences of Egypt's migrant

24. Lukasik, "Conquest of Paradise."
25. See Monier, *Whose Heritage Counts*, 29–40.

populations.[26] Through events, conferences, blog posts, and archives, the organization quickly became a platform for diasporic Egyptians to engage in all aspects of their identity, including that which has otherwise been excluded from hegemonic narratives. Egypt Migrations, along with other diasporic organizations and initiatives such as Coptic Queer Stories, Progressive Copts, and the Elmahaba Center, have provided a platform for Copts to talk about contentious issues relating to gender, sexuality, race, and belonging. For example, after the Coptic Church organized a convention on homosexuality in 2019, a group of mental health experts, academics, community activists, and members in the diaspora published an open letter condemning the church's framing of queerness as a mental illness and an addiction.[27]

Attention to lay initiatives by Copts challenges the notion that Copts are a homogenous mass governed by the Coptic Church. Calls for internal reform, political mobilization, and cultural representation reflect the heterogeneity of Coptic communities.

BATTLING TO DEFINE COPTIC BELONGING: UNITY, INSECURITY, MARTYRDOM, AND RIGHTS

Copts in Egypt are a marginalized group, facing discrimination and violence on an interpersonal, societal, and structural level. Their experiences entail quotidian microaggressions, institutional discrimination, structural and legalized inequality, state-sanctioned violence, and targeted terrorist attacks. Defining the plight of Copts in Egypt is not a straightforward endeavor, however. Several actors, including the Coptic Church, the Egyptian government, and Coptic groups and rights organizations, battle to define the problem of sectarianism and religious freedom, revealing the multitude of actors, interests, and politics that shape narratives of Coptic belonging in Egypt. Circulating discourses of national unity, citizenship, insecurity, and martyrdom—advanced by these different actors—offer conflicting representations of the nature of violence, the perpetrators, those responsible, and pathways for solutions. Each discourse ultimately offers a different lens through which Copts relate to their church, the government, and their co-citizens.

26. The repository can be found at the Clara Thomas Archives and Special Collections at York University in Canada.

27. Progressive Copts, "Open Statement."

National Unity and the Erasure of Religious Difference

The Mubarak regime downplayed the reality of sectarianism in the name of national unity, overemphasizing harmony between Muslims and Christians while erasing any traces of religious difference. This rhetoric framed Muslims and Christians as united against the threat of an external other, whether Islamism or a foreign power. This rhetoric of unity finds its origins in the 1919 revolution against British occupation, when Copts and Muslims united as Egyptians against colonialism, employing the symbolism of cross and crescent.

One key element of national unity discourses is Coptic patriotism. Perhaps this is best illustrated by Pope Shenouda III's famous saying that "Egypt is not a homeland that we live in, but a homeland that lives within us."[28] Constructions of Copts as patriotic serve the purpose of dispelling any suspicions that they might be traitors to the nation, allying with foreign coreligionists rather than Muslim conationals. This is especially sensitive for the Coptic Evangelical Church, as its origins are rooted in foreign influence. As Sebastian Elsässer rightly observes, however, the discourse of Coptic patriotism, while intended to build cohesion between Muslims and Christians as equal citizens, instead further entrenches a stereotype that Christian communities in the region are traitors and foreign agents.[29]

Discussions of Coptic patriotism are deeply intertwined in debates about whether Copts qualify as a minority community or not. On the one hand, the Coptic Church, along with some Copts, rejects the status of a minority, asserting, instead, that they are central to the Egyptian national fabric and citizenry. Importantly, when Copts reject a minority identity in the name of national unity, this discourse does not altogether erase their religious identity.[30] Rather, they emphasize the unique contributions of both religious and secular Copts to Egyptian history, culture, and politics.[31] On the other hand, Copts, including many in the diaspora, suggest that a minority identity recognizes Coptic marginalization in Egypt and allows them to call for equality within an international framework of rights and freedoms. The minority discourse was rejected by the Mubarak regime, which wanted to avoid international intervention, as well as the Coptic Church, which wanted to assert its loyalty to the nation.

28. Elsässer, *Coptic Question*, 115.
29. Elsässer, *Coptic Question*, 110–21.
30. Galal, "Coptic Christian Practices," 56.
31. Elsässer, *Coptic Question*, 120–21.

Historian Vivian Ibrahim argues that assertions of national unity ultimately marginalized minority claims as either secondary or antagonistic to Egyptian affairs, which, in effect, made Coptic concerns of discrimination invisible.[32] The Mubarak regime's response to sectarian violence was to erase it entirely from the public sphere. State media often denied the existence of communal tensions,[33] and journalists even reported receiving instructions from their editor-in-chief not to cover any sectarian affairs.[34] When news media did acknowledge communal violence, it attributed disputes to reasons other than sectarianism, such as mental illness, family feuds, or even the existence of external forces set out to destroy the strong bond of unity between Christians and Muslims.[35] To counter the exclusion of Coptic affairs from mainstream media, Coptic media developed to address communal affairs and shape Coptic religious identity. This, in turn, resulted in a paradox as particularistic media further isolated Copts from the public.[36] It was not until the 1990s, with the liberalization of the press and the rise of new forms of media, that sectarian tensions transformed from being a public taboo to a sensationalist media topic.[37] Additionally, customary reconciliation councils characterized Mubarak's approach to sectarian tensions, where local representatives of Muslims and Christians, typically an imam and a priest, came together along with the implicated families to diffuse sectarian tensions. Reconciliation councils act as an alternative to the judicial system, reducing sectarian clashes to two seemingly equal parties, often absolving the perpetrating party and unfairly punishing Christians.[38] These councils were, and remain to this day, the initial step to diffusing communal clashes.

The response to the bombing of the al-Qidiseen Church on New Year's Eve Mass in 2011, in which thirty-one worshipers were killed, resembled the epitome of the empty rhetoric of national unity. Mubarak, the Ministry of Interior, and the media immediately denied that the car bombing was the responsibility of any Egyptian, blaming foreign terrorism rather than domestic sectarianism. Some commentators even argued that both Christians and Muslims were targeted, as there was a mosque across form the church. Reflecting on how the proximity of the mosque and the church meant that the blood of the martyrs spattered on both buildings, marking a "Christian

---

32. V. Ibrahim, "Beyond the Cross," 2589.

33. Iskander, "'Mediation' of Muslim-Christian Relations," 36–42.

34. Tadros, *Copts at the Crossroads*, 45–46.

35. Iskander, "'Mediation' of Muslim-Christian Relations," 36.

36. Monier, "Middle Eastern Minorities."

37. Elsässer, "Press Liberalization."

38. I. Ibrahim, *According to Which Customs*.

presence in a Muslim space," anthropologist Anthony Shenoda called it a "gruesome kind of national unity."[39] This incident catalyzed many Copts to participate in the revolution. Months later, leaked sources suggested that the attack was, in fact, orchestrated by the Ministry of Interior's State Security Investigations (SSI) to punish Shenouda III, reflecting growing tensions between the church and state during Mubarak's final years.

While visiting Pope Shenouda III to offer his condolences in the aftermath of the Qidiseen Church bombing, the grand imam of al-Azhar, Sheikh Ahmed el-Tayeb, proposed the idea of establishing an initiative that would strengthen religious unity between Muslims and Christians. Together, they founded the Bayt al-'Aila al-Masreya (Egyptian Family House) initiative in 2011 to promote an interfaith approach to citizenship, national unity, and coexistence.[40] The initiative brought together representatives from al-Azhar, as well as Protestant, Catholic, and Orthodox churches, and government ministers to work together on public policy issues to improve interreligious harmony. To ensure that the initiative created real change, they established branches throughout Egypt (sometimes even mediating sectarian tensions) and convened conferences to facilitate community building and dialogue.

The presidency of Abdel Fatah al-Sisi was marked by the return of the rhetoric of national unity, calling on Muslims and Christians to unite against the external threat of Islamism. Sisi advanced symbolic gestures to assure Copts that they would be protected under his leadership. For example, he established a mega-mosque and the largest Christian cathedral in the Middle East, the Cathedral of the Nativity of Christ, in the new administrative capital. During his inauguration speech, Sisi began by acknowledging the recent spate of terrorist attacks. He strategically represented terrorist attacks against Copts as attacks against the nation, identifying terrorism as a threat to national security: "All my greetings and respect to the souls of our Egyptian martyrs that fell. I'm saying all Egyptians. I'm not talking specifically about the military or the police, or our civilian Coptic brethren, or even from the recent attack against the mosque." He continued by declaring that no external forces could come between Muslims and Christians: "I'm not going to say sectarian strife. I don't like that term because that's not who we are. We are one. We are one. And we will remain one." The comments were met with cheers and applause from the Copts in attendance.[41]

In constructing terrorism as the ultimate threat to Egypt, the Coptic question is defined primarily as a national security concern. After the

39. Shenoda, "Reflections on the (In)Visibility."
40. Casper, "Egyptian Family House."
41. ONdrama, "كلمة الرئيس السيسي".

al-Qidiseen bombing in 2011, churches in Egypt became securitized. Security personnel guard the entrance of Churches and check people's identification cards to confirm their Christian affiliation before they walk through metal detectors. After a particularly brutal series of terrorist attacks against Copts leading up to 2018, President Sisi created a Committee to Combat Sectarianism, which was comprised of members of the armed forces, military intelligence, general intelligence, and the National Security Agency. There was no representation from the Coptic community, the legislature, the judiciary, or the human rights community.[42] A securitized approach to managing Coptic marginality has ultimately limited public religion, including participation in *mulids*, Masses, and pilgrimages.[43] This approach ignores other factors that contribute to the marginalization of Copts, including the absence of Copts in the security sector, as well as state-sponsored violence by the security apparatus itself, as illustrated by the Maspero massacre and the al-Qidiseen bombing in 2011.

Citizenship Rights as Counter-Narrative

The rhetoric of Coptic citizenship regained momentum after the Egyptian revolution of 2011. Widespread calls for equality and freedom offered a political opportunity for Coptic advocates and activists to mobilize for their rights. This framework of rights focuses on the role of the state as the grantor of rights and protector of its citizens, including minority groups.

As well as Coptic-specific organizations, human rights organizations also mobilize around Coptic affairs within a broader agenda on rights and freedoms. While the human rights movement emerged in Egypt in the 1980s, it was only in the mid-2000s that organizations started to address religious minorities.[44] In 2007, for example, the Egyptian Initiative for Personal Rights published a report on the challenges faced by religious minorities in terms of recognition and invisibilization by the state.[45] Other organizations that address religious minorities include the Egyptian Commission for Rights and Freedoms, based in Egypt, and the Tahrir Institute for Middle East Policy, based in Washington, DC. These organizations locate religious freedom and minority rights within broader conversations pertaining to human rights, citizenship, and democracy.

42. Kaldas, "Egypt's Sectarian Committee."

43. See Casper, "How the Egyptian Church"; Fallas, "What the Taming"; I. Ibrahim, "Egypt's Ban."

44. Elsässer, *Coptic Question*, 185.

45. Bahgat and Stork, *Prohibited Identities*.

Despite having distinct and, sometimes, differing approaches to the Coptic question, advocacy and rights organizations typically problematize the state's regulation of religion, arguing that it reifies, rather than neutralizes, religious difference. Through this lens, the specific challenges of identification cards, blasphemy laws, and church building laws come to the fore. On the issue of identification cards, Egypt remains one of the few countries to include religious affiliation on civil identification cards, which are required for governmental services, security checkpoints, and access to employment, health care, and education. Yet the government recognizes only the three Abrahamic religions, rendering others, including Baha'is, Quranists, Jehovah's Witnesses, and the nonreligious, invisible and stripped of their constitutional rights.[46] Additionally, blasphemy laws are often leveraged against non-Muslim and non-Sunni individuals, as well as intellectuals and critics, as a way to advance the state's hegemonic interpretation of Islam while controlling minority speech in the name of maintaining public order and security.[47]

Building and constructing houses of worship remains one of the most long-standing and controversial issues pertaining to religious freedom in Egypt. Under Ottoman rule, construction laws in Egypt subjected Christian denominations to discriminatory restrictions. For example, until the era of Mubarak, church construction and renovation required the approval of the president. Rumors that Copts are worshiping in buildings without an official license is a key source of sectarian clashes, often ending with reconciliation councils.[48] As part of initiatives to improve religious freedom for Copts in Egypt, President Sisi ratified a church construction law in 2016. This law streamlined the process for Christian denominations to submit requests for the construction or renovation of churches. While the Egyptian government and its supporters have heralded this law as a major step towards improving Coptic rights, human rights organizations have pointed to challenges in the law's content and implementation.[49] For example, the law stipulates that

46. Ezzat, *Identity Documents, Marriage Certificates.*

47. Mandour, "Egypt's Criminalisation."

48. The most notorious example of this type of incident is the sectarian violence in al-Khanka in 1972. After local Muslims learned that Copts were worshiping in the headquarters of the Bible Society Association, a building that was not officially licensed as a house of worship, they torched the building. A large group of Copts, including priests, traveled to the village to celebrate Mass and were met with further attacks on Coptic property. The pope's relationship with President Sadat continued to deteriorate. Incidents of violence around the renovation or construction of churches remain common in Egypt. The Egyptian Initiative for Personal Rights has documented seventy-four incidents between 2011 and 2016 alone; see I. Ibrahim, *Closed on Security Grounds.*

49. Farouk et al., *Report—Prayers Unanswered.*

approval by a governor be based on the size and needs of a congregation, yet Egypt has no census. This is especially challenging for smaller Christian denominations (some of which are not even legally recognized) who may not be sizable but still desire to worship in churches.[50]

Insecurity in the Face of Political Islam

While utopic and transformative, the aftermath of the revolution, especially amid rising sectarian violence, was also characterized by fear and insecurity for many Copts. Though short-lived, Mohamed Morsi's one-year rule resembled the political revival of the Muslim Brotherhood and triggered deep-seated fears among Copts about their diminishing status as citizens in Egypt. While Islamist parties initially exploited Coptic political participation to appear moderate and inclusive, they eventually grew to fear the political role of Copts, especially as Copts mobilized against the Islamization of Egypt.[51]

Between 2011 and 2014, Copts reported heightened verbal and physical assaults in their everyday lives, including teachers informally segregating classrooms by religion or women being harassed on the streets for not covering their hair.[52] Notably, Islamists targeted Copts as a form of retribution for not supporting Morsi's presidency.[53] This was especially evident after the then-commander-in-chief of the Egyptian armed forces, Abdel Fatah al-Sisi, seized power through a military coup on July 3, 2013. After six weeks of continuous pro-Morsi protests, Egyptian security forces raided the sit-in at the Rabaa al-Adawiya Mosque, resulting in a death toll of at least nine hundred protestors in what became known as the Rabaa massacre. In the aftermath of the massacre, the Egyptian government arrested leaders and supporters of the Muslim Brotherhood in an attempt to eradicate them as a political entity. Subsequently, some Islamists accused Copts of supporting the military regime in ousting Mohamed Morsi. This incited pro-Morsi supporters to retaliate by torching and looting around seventy-plus Coptic churches and Christian properties across Egypt, mostly in Upper Egypt. Lay Christians and clergy called on the security forces to intervene, but they were largely absent, facilitating the continuation of these sectarian attacks. The violence against Copts after the Rabaa massacre became emblematic of acts of retribution, further justifying Copts' feelings of insecurity. Upon

50. Casper, "Egypt's Other Churches."

51. Hager, "From 'Polytheists' to 'Partners,'" 294–302.

52. Tadros, "Decrypting Copts' Perspectives," 13–14.

53. Tadros, "Decrypting Copts' Perspectives," 12–17.

assuming power, President Sisi framed himself as the savior of Copts from the alternative of the Muslim Brotherhood.

Coptic Cultural Trauma and the Theodicy of Martyrdom

The Coptic Church frames contemporary incidents of violence as a continuation of centuries of persecution, reifying a theological conviction that the past, present, and future of the Coptic Church is one of martyrdom. Responding to violence and discrimination, the church offers a theodicy of martyrdom that transforms death into a blessing by constructing martyrdom as evidence of God's divine intervention and a pathway to heaven. In bearing witness to the faith, martyrs come to reflect deep-seated beliefs about the prophetic centrality of persecution in Christianity generally, and specifically for Coptic Christians. This theodicy of martyrdom is reinforced through rituals and traditions that glorify saints and martyrs.[54] In doing so, the church's narrative of cultural trauma represents martyrdom as indelible, affirming its identity as the church of martyrs and its adherents as the descendants of martyrs.[55]

This theodicy of martyrdom became particularly pertinent between 2015 and 2018 when Copts experienced an increase in the frequency and brutality of violence that captured the attention of the whole world. On February 15, 2015, ISIS released a video of the beheading of twenty Coptic Christian Egyptians and a Ghanaian on a beach in Libya, who later become known as the twenty-one Libya martyrs. The video offered a visual representation of the brutality of ISIS attacks against religious minorities across the Middle East. It also set the tone for future terrorist attacks against Copts. In the coming years, Copts experienced three church bombings on two different occasions, killing a total of seventy-seven people. Attacks in Northern Sinai resulted in the mass displacement of several Coptic families. During this time, ISIS released a video announcing that Coptic Christians are their "favorite prey."[56] On two separate occasions, exactly a year apart, ISIS militants attacked a convoy of pilgrims visiting the Monastery of St. Samuel the Confessor, killing a total of thirty-seven people. The relentless brutality of these massacres drove the Coptic Church to designate February 15, the anniversary of the massacre of the twenty-one Libya Martyrs, as the modern-day Coptic Martyrs Day.

54. See El-Gendi and Pinfari, "Icons of Contention"; Heo, *Political Lives of Saints*; Ramzy, "To Die Is Gain"; Tumara, "Sign of Martyrdom."

55. Alexander et al., *Cultural Trauma*; Philips, "We Love Martyrdom."

56. Correspondent in Sinai, "Christian Flee."

Copts responded to these massacres in different ways, as I have shown elsewhere.[57] While Coptic cultural trauma is characterized by an emphasis on martyrdom, the varied ways that Copts engage with this theodicy in response to violence reflects the complexity of Coptic religious and political subjectivities. First, many Copts find solace in the church's theodicy of suffering as it imbues collective suffering with meaning. Even in grief, fear, and anger, this theodicy reframes suffering as part of a continuous history of the triumph of what is righteous. Scholars have argued that this discourse of heavenly citizenship and persecution offers Copts a way to discuss their social, political, and cultural marginalization in Egypt in seemingly apolitical ways.[58]

A second group of Copts, mainly advocates and activists, have altogether rejected the interpretive framework of martyrdom and persecution in favor of citizenship and rights. These advocates are critical of the church's employment of the discourse of persecution, arguing that by encouraging Copts to accept, and even celebrate, martyrdom, the church is deterring them from mobilizing in pursuit of their rights.[59] Critical Coptic scholars have argued that the church's cultural trauma narrative of martyrdom reinforces ecclesiastical hierarchy and maintains the church's authority over Coptic identity.[60]

A third group of Copts seek to reconcile the theodicy of martyrdom with the framework of rights, offering a hybrid theology that emphasizes both life on earth and in heaven. After the 2017 Palm Sunday bombing, Bishop Raphael remarked: "We love martyrdom, but we also love life." This comment came to resemble a belief that while Copts accept martyrdom as a blessing, life itself is not disposable and is worth fighting for. In the diaspora, Archbishop Angaelos has become a leading voice of a theology of advocacy that argues that Christians have a religious duty to advocate against oppression.

OPPORTUNITIES AND CHALLENGES IN THE DIASPORA

Multiple waves of emigration since the 1950s have transformed Copts into a global community. Copts started emigrating in the 1950s during Nasser's liberalization policies in search of economic and professional success. In the 1970s, they migrated to escape growing religious discrimination facilitated

57. Philips, "We Love Martyrdom."
58. Ramzy, "To Die Is Gain," 652; Shenoda, "Politics of Faith."
59. See I. Ibrahim, "Coptic Martyrdom."
60. See V. Ibrahim, Copts of Egypt.

by Sadat's Islamization policies. The rise of insecurity, instability, and sectarian violence in the aftermath of the Egyptian revolution in 2011 also resulted in the exodus of Copts, and again in 2013 after Mohamed Morsi assumed power. The Arabian Gulf and Libya served as temporary destinations for many economic migrants, while other Copts pursued more permanent settlement in Australia and North America. To celebrate the globalization of Copts, Coptic American Nader Anise initiated Global Coptic Day on June 1, coinciding with the Holy Family's arrival to Egypt.

Copts in the diaspora have contributed significantly to Coptic politics, identity, and heritage, as detailed throughout this chapter, through political and cultural initiatives. They have also established churches, seminaries, and monasteries, transforming what was once a national church in Egypt into a transnational one. Beyond the religious sphere, they have established museums, political groups, cultural associations, and humanitarian organizations.[61] Here, I discuss two fields in particular where diasporic Copts have excelled: service and arts.

Service organizations have flourished in the diaspora, each with a unique goal and target audience. Coptic Orphans, for example, a development organization founded in 1988 and based in Virginia, United States, serves rural villages in Egypt, particularly through programming that empowers girls and improves Muslim-Christian relations. Coptic Orphans works closely with the Egyptian government and the Coptic Church to obtain access in Egypt to implement their programs. Volunteering opportunities also offer American Copts a chance to visit Egypt and connect with their heritage. SALT, based in Minnesota, United States, is a missionary organization that encourages youth to travel to Africa, Latin America, and parts of the United States to evangelize through social, spiritual, and educational services. While officially independent from the Coptic Church, SALT is led by Fr. Jacob Zaki and seeks to spread Christian values. Elmahaba Center, founded in 2019 and based in Tennessee, United States, is the first Coptic-led organization that prides itself on serving all Arabic-speaking immigrants regardless of their religion or nationality. Its programming aims to help new immigrants navigate economic immobility, segregation, isolation, and discrimination by building inclusive, intersectional, and intergenerational communities of care. Unlike the former two organizations, however, Elmahaba has a contentious relationship with the church for highlighting corruption and mismanagement within the Diocese of the Southern United States. Each of these examples illustrates how Copts, through service,

61. See Akladios, "Heteroglossia"; Akladios and Philips, "Contested Politics"; Brinkerhoff, "Assimilation and Heritage Identity"; Marzouki, "US Coptic Diaspora"; Yefet, "Coptic Diaspora."

connect with their homeland, their new communities, and with other parts of the world.

Copts have also risen to global prominence in the field of cultural production. As award-winning actors, the success of Rami Malek, an LA-born and -raised Copt, and Mena Massoud, an Egypt-born and Ontario-raised Copt, shed light on the possibilities for success in the diaspora. Mena Massoud captured the hearts of many in his charming role as Aladdin in the live-action reproduction by Walt Disney Pictures. For his role as Freddie Mercury in the biopic *Bohemian Rhapsody*, Rami Malek won an Oscar, a BAFTA, and a Golden Globe. Copts, Egyptians, and Middle Easterners more broadly celebrated these successes as their own, sparking debate about the boundaries of Coptic identity and its relationship to Arabness and whiteness.[62] It also generated discussions in Egypt and abroad about religious discrimination, homophobia, state repression, the state of film production in the Middle East, and the problems of casting Arabs as terrorists in American media.[63]

Migration has not come without its challenges. In its attempt to encompass Coptic migrants in the diaspora, the church serves as what Ghada Botros calls the consoler and helper, offering migrants material and emotional support.[64] The church's primary challenge remains in its capacity to ensure that second- and third-generation Copts remain connected to their faith. Diasporic churches now offer English liturgy, ordain priests who were born and raised in the diaspora, and offer extracurricular activities designed to build community and enhance group identity.[65] English-language services have attracted many converts, opening up conversations within the church about the possibility of forgoing its Egyptian identity in order to be more inclusive.[66] These changes and discussions have alienated first-generation Copts and new immigrants who approach the church not only as a spiritual haven but also as a cultural and communal one.[67] The variety in congregants and their needs has often resulted in the construction of several churches in one locality, each serving different groups. These divisions have stirred debates about classism and assimilation.

---

62. Dolan, "Even as Prince."

63. Asfour, "Oscar for the Arabs"; Philips, "Somebody to Love"; Riad, "Rami Malek Extravaganza."

64. Botros, "Coptic Migrant Churches," 111–18.

65. Botros, "Coptic Migrant Churches," 116–18.

66. Loewen, "Strategies of Adaptation."

67. Youssef, "Becoming Saints," 79.

CONCLUSION

The turn of the century saw rapid political transformations for Copts in Egypt and abroad. Along with the revolutionary moment of 2011, an increasingly global diaspora, an era of martyrs, rapid changes in political and religious leadership, and an oscillating entente between the church and state have all left an indelible mark on Copts. While Coptic lay movements witnessed a moment of revival during and in the aftermath of the revolution, the entrenchment of authoritarianism has largely hindered their expansion and influence. Paul Rowe argues that while the church-state entente facilitates the church's consolidation of political representation, the church is not actually threatened by Coptic mobilization, as long as it does not directly challenge or compromise its authority.[68] Tensions between the church and Copts are evident in the differential ways that the Coptic hierarchy has responded to lay initiatives calling for internal reform. While it has facilitated and even supported many development and missionary organizations such as Coptic Orphans and SALT, it has sought to delegitimize and silence the Coptic Survivor movement for challenging the church's handling of sexual abuse. The church has, at times, also responded favorably to Coptic protests such as those pertaining to divorce laws. Indeed, this new era is marked by the continued authority of the Coptic Church over Coptic affairs, yet not without legitimate attempts by Coptic laity, in Egypt and abroad, to take control of their identity, heritage, and politics.

BIBLIOGRAPHY

Akladios, Michael. "Heteroglossia: Interpretation and the Experiences of Coptic Immigrants from Egypt in North America, 1955–1975." *Histoire Sociale/Social History* 53 (2020) 627–50.

Akladios, Michael, and Miray Philips. "The Contested Politics of Coptic Diasporic Activism." Tahrir Institute for Middle East Policy, June 7, 2021. https://timep.org/commentary/analysis/the-contested-politics-of-coptic-diasporic-activism/.

Alexander, Jeffrey C., et al. *Cultural Trauma and Collective Identity*. Oakland: University of California Press, 2004.

Asfour, Nana. "An Oscar for the Arabs." *New York Times*, Mar. 2, 2019.

Asia News. "Mohammed Morsi Meets Catholic Bishops in Cairo." *Asia News*, 2012.

Bahgat, Hosam, and Joe Stork. *Prohibited Identities: State Interference with Religious Freedom*. Human Rights Watch, Nov. 11, 2007. https://www.hrw.org/report/2007/11/11/prohibited-identities/state-interference-religious-freedom.

Botros, Ghada. "Coptic Migrant Churches: Transnationalism and the Negotiation of Different Roles." In *Copts in Context: Negotiating Identity, Tradition, and Modernity*,

---

68. Rowe, "Building Coptic Civil Society."

edited by Nelly van Doorn-Harder, 107–24. Columbia: University of South Carolina Press, 2017.

Brinkerhoff, Jennifer M. "Assimilation and Heritage Identity: Lessons from the Coptic Diaspora." *Journal of International Migration and Integration* 17 (2016) 467–85.

Casper, Jayson. "The Egyptian Family House: Fostering Religious Unity." Middle East Institute, Mar. 24, 2015. https://www.mei.edu/publications/egyptian-family-house-fostering-religious-unity.

———. "Egypt's Other Churches: Smaller Denominations React to New Construction Law." Tahrir Institute for Middle East Policy, Oct. 12, 2016. https://timep.org/commentary/egypts-other-churches-smaller-denominations-react-to-new-construction-law/.

———. "How the Egyptian Church Secures Itself." Tahrir Institute for Middle East Policy, June 21, 2017. https://timep.org/commentary/analysis/how-the-egyptian-church-secures-itself/.

Christian Youth Channel. "The Word of the President of Egypt, Abdel Fattah El-Sisi, during His Surprise Visit to St. Mark." YouTube, Jan. 8, 2015. https://www.youtube.com/watch?v=_OeaXI128BQ.

CopticSurvivor. "Pope Tawadros's Response to Sexually Abusive Coptic Priests Exposed on Social Media." YouTube, Oct. 11, 2020; from interview July 25, 2020. https://www.youtube.com/watch?v=xGvxtAoB610.

Correspondent in Sinai, A. "Christian Flee North Sinai Violence." Tahrir Institute for Middle East Policy, Mar. 7, 2017. https://timep.org/commentary/analysis/christians-flee-north-sinai-violence/.

Dolan, Thomas. "Even as Prince, Rami Malek Isn't 'a White Guy.'" Egypt Migrations, Nov. 19, 2021. https://egyptmigrations.com/2021/11/19/even-as-prince-rami-malek-isnt-white/.

Dowell, Anna. "Landscapes of Belonging: Protestant Activism in Revolutionary Egypt." *International Journal of Sociology of the Family* 45 (2015) 190–205.

El-Gendi, Yosra, and Marco Pinfari. "Icons of Contention: The Iconography of Martyrdom and the Construction of Coptic Identity in Post-Revolutionary Egypt." *Media, War & Conflict* 13 (2019) 50–69.

Elsässer, Sebastian. "The Coptic Divorce Struggle in Contemporary Egypt." *Social Compass* 66 (2019) 333–51.

———. *The Coptic Question in the Mubarak Era.* New York: Oxford University Press, 2014.

———. "Press Liberalization, the New Media, and the 'Coptic Question': Muslim–Coptic Relations in Egypt in a Changing Media Landscape." *Middle Eastern Studies* 46 (2010) 131–50.

Ezzat, Amr. *Identity Documents, Marriage Certificates, and Burial: The Missing Rights of Adherents of "Unrecognized" Religions.* Egyptian Initiative for Personal Rights, Jan. 13, 2022. https://eipr.org/en/publications/identity-documents-marriage-certificates-and-burial-missing-rights-adherents-.

Fahmi, Georges. "The Coptic Church and Politics in Egypt." Carnegie Middle East Center, Dec. 18, 2014. https://carnegie-mec.org/2014/12/18/coptic-church-and-politics-in-egypt-pub-57563.

Fallas, Amy. "What the Taming of Christian Spaces Reveals about Egypt's Security Complex." Jadaliyya, Nov. 4, 2019. https://www.jadaliyya.com/Details/40190.

Farouk, Mahmood, et al. *Report—Prayers Unanswered: Assessing the Impact of Egypt's 2016 Church Construction Law*. Project on Middle East Democracy, Dec. 12, 2018. https://pomed.org/report-prayers-unanswered-assessing-the-impact-of-egypts-2016-church-construction-law/.

Galal, Lise Paulsen. "Coptic Christian Practices: Formations of Sameness and Difference." *Islam and Christian-Muslim Relations* 23 (2012) 45–58.

Hager, Anna. "From 'Polytheists' to 'Partners in the Nation': Islamist Attitudes towards Coptic Egyptians in Post-Revolutionary Egypt (2011–2013)." *Islam and Christian-Muslim Relations* 29 (2018) 289–308.

Hasan, S. S. *Christians vs Muslims in Modern Egypt: The Century-Long Struggle for Coptic Equality*. NewYork: Oxford University Press, 2003.

Henderson, Randall P. "The Egyptian Coptic Christians: The Conflict between Identity and Equality." *Islam and Christian-Muslim Relations* 16 (2005) 155–66.

Heo, Angie. *The Political Lives of Saints: Christian-Muslim Mediation in Egypt*. Oakland: University of California Press, 2018.

Hernandez, Rebecca Skreslet. "At the Borders of Identity: Reflections on Egyptian Protestant Public Theology in the Wake of the Arab Spring." *Exchange* 49 (2020) 237–56.

Ibrahim, Ishak. *According to Which Customs: The Role of Customary Reconciliation Sessions in Sectarian Incidents and the Responsibility of the State*. Egyptian Initiative for Personal Rights, June 11, 2015. https://eipr.org/en/publications/"whose-customs-role-customary-reconciliation-sectarian-disputes-and-state.

———. *Closed on Security Grounds: Sectarian Tensions and Attacks Resulting from the Construction and Renovation of Churches*. Egyptian Initiative for Personal Rights, Nov. 2017. https://eipr.org/sites/default/files/reports/pdf/closed_on_security_grounds_web.pdf.

———. "Coptic Martyrdom: Religious Identity at a Time of Persecution." Tahrir Institute for Middle East Policy, Oct. 17, 2018. https://timep.org/commentary/analysis/coptic-martyrdom-religious-identity-at-a-time-of-persecution/.

———. "Egypt's Ban on Church Trips Sends Dangerous Message." Tahrir Institute for Middle East Policy, Sept. 1, 2017. https://timep.org/commentary/analysis/egypts-ban-on-church-trips-sends-dangerous-message/.

Ibrahim, Mina. "Drinking in Times of Change: The Haunting Presence of Alcohol in Egypt." In *Alcohol in the Maghreb and the Middle East since the Nineteenth Century: Disputes, Policies, and Practices*, edited by E. Biçer-Deveci and P. Bourmaud, 163–84. Cham, Switz.: Springer International, 2021.

———. "A Minority at the Bar: Revisiting the Coptic Christian (In-)Visibility." *Social Compass* 66 (2019) 366–82.

Ibrahim, Vivian. "Beyond the Cross and the Crescent: Plural Identities and the Copts in Contemporary Egypt." *Ethnic and Racial Studies* 38 (2015) 2584–97.

———. *The Copts of Egypt: The Challenges of Modernisation and Identity*. Library of Modern Middle East Studies. Reprint, London: Tauris, 2013.

Iskander, Elizabeth. "The 'Mediation' of Muslim-Christian Relations in Egypt: The Strategies and Discourses of the Official Egyptian Press during Mubarak's Presidency." *Islam and Christian-Muslim Relations* 23 (2012) 31–44.

Kaldas, Timothy E. "Egypt's Sectarian Committee to Combat Sectarianism." Tahrir Institute for Middle East Policy, Jan. 28, 2019. https://timep.org/commentary/analysis/egypts-sectarian-committee-to-combat-sectarianism/.

Kirkpatrick, David D. "Egyptian Islamists Approve Draft Constitution despite Objections." *New York Times*, Nov. 29, 2012.

Kortam, Hend. "Morsi Meets Religious Leaders." *Daily News Egypt*, June 19, 2013. https://dailynewsegypt.com/2013/06/19/morsi-meets-religious-leaders/.

Loewen, Rachel. "Strategies of Adaptation and Survival: The Introduction of Converts to the Coptic Orthodox Community in the Greater Toronto Area." In *Copts in Context: Negotiating Identity, Tradition, and Modernity*, edited by Nelly van Doorn-Harder, 124–34. Columbia: University of South Carolina Press, 2017.

Lukasik, Candace. "Conquest of Paradise: Secular Binds and Coptic Political Mobilization." *Middle East Critique* 25 (2016) 107–25.

Mada Masr. "Coptic Activists Criticize Church's Support of Sisi's New York Visit." *Mada Masr*, Sept. 19, 2016. https://www.madamasr.com/en/2016/09/19/news/u/coptic-activists-criticize-churchs-support-of-sisis-new-york-visit/.

Mahmood, Saba. *Religious Difference in a Secular Age: A Minority Report*. Princeton, NJ: Princeton University Press, 2015.

Mandour, Mohamed. "Egypt's Criminalisation of Minority Free Speech through Blasphemy Cases." *Rowaq Arabi*, June 24, 2021. https://rowaq.cihrs.org/views-egypts-criminalisation-of-minority-free-speech-through-blasphemy-cases/?lang=en.

Marzouki, Nadia. "The US Coptic Diaspora and the Limit of Polarization." *Journal of Immigrant & Refugee Studies* 14 (2016) 261–76.

Miyokawa, Hiroko. "The Revival of the Coptic Language and the Formation of Coptic Ethnoreligious Identity in Modern Egypt." In *Copts in Context: Negotiating Identity, Tradition, and Modernity*, edited by Nelly van Doorn-Harder, 151–57. Columbia: University of South Carolina Press, 2017.

Monier, Elizabeth. "Middle Eastern Minorities and the Media." In *Routledge Handbook of Minorities in the Middle East*, edited by Paul S. Rowe, 370–82. London: Routledge, 2019.

———. *Whose Heritage Counts? Narratives of Coptic People's Heritage*. CREID Working Paper 11. Brighton, UK: Institute of Development Studies, 2021. doi: 10.19088/creid.2021.015.

ONdrama. "كلمة الرئيس السيسي في افتتاح كاتدرائية ميلاد المسيح بالعاصمة الإدارية" [Al-Sisi's statement on the occasion of the opening of the Cathedral of the Nativity in the new administrative capital]. YouTube, Jan. 6, 2019. https://www.youtube.com/watch?v=iHJYTSW9ZVo.

Philips, Miray. "Somebody to Love? Rami Malek without Freddie Mercury." *Egyptian Streets*, Feb. 17, 2019. https://egyptianstreets.com/2019/02/27/somebody-to-love-rami-malek-without-freddie-mercury/.

———. "'We Love Martyrdom, but We Also Love Life': Coptic Cultural Trauma between Martyrdom and Rights." *American Journal of Cultural Sociology* (2022). https://doi.org/10.1057/s41290-022-00162-5.

Progressive Copts. "Open Statement against the Coptic Church's Position on the LGBTQI+ Community." Medium, Jan. 15, 2020. https://medium.com/@info.progressivecopts/open-statement-against-the-coptic-churchs-position-on-the-lgbtqi-community-e89f824acf8b.

Ramzy, Carolyn M. "Singing Strategic Multiculturalism: The Discursive Politics of Song in Coptic-Canadian Protests." In *Copts in Context: Negotiating Identity, Tradition, and Modernity*, edited by Nelly van Doorn-Harder, 93–107. Columbia: University of South Carolina Press,2017.

———. "To Die Is Gain: Singing a Heavenly Citizenship among Egypt's Coptic Christians." *Ethnos* 80 (2015) 649–70.

Riad, Andrew. "A Rami Malek Extravaganza: To Queer or Not to Queer?" Medium, Mar. 8, 2019. https://medium.com/sia-nyuad/a-rami-malek-extravaganza-too-queer-or-not-to-queer-d4b37decco9d.

Rowe, Paul. "Building Coptic Civil Society: Christian Groups and the State in Mubarak's Egypt." *Middle Eastern Studies* 45 (2009) 111–26.

Salama, Pishoy. "Coptic Orthodox Spokesperson on Sexual Misconduct." Facebook, July 25, 2022. https://m.facebook.com/504365958/posts/10157509083290959/?e xtid=V8STqCxdrLxaEpJp&d=n.

Sedra, Paul. "The Copts under Morsi: Leave Them to the Church." Middle East Institute, May 1, 2013. https://www.mei.edu/publications/copts-under-morsi-leave-them-church.

Sense of Belonging, A. "لقاء مشترك للإخوان المسلمين و قيادات الكنيسة الانجيلية." A Sense of Belonging, Apr. 2012. https://asenseofbelonging.files.wordpress.com/2012/04/agreement-arabic.pdf.

Shenoda, Anthony. "The Politics of Faith: On Faith, Skepticism, and Miracles among Coptic Christians in Egypt." *Ethnos* 77 (2012) 477–95.

———. "Reflections on the (In)Visibility of Copts in Egypt." Jadaliyya, May 18, 2011. https://www.jadaliyya.com/Details/24007/Reflections-on-the-InVisibility-of-Copts-in-Egypt.

Tadros, Mariz. *Copts at the Crossroads: The Challenges of Building Inclusive Democracy in Egypt*. Cairo: American University in Cairo, 2013.

———. "Decrypting Copts' Perspectives on Communal Relations in Contemporary Egypt through Vernacular Politics (2013–2014)." Institute of Development Studies, May 21, 2015. https://opendocs.ids.ac.uk/opendocs/handle/20.500.12413/6166.

———. "Vicissitudes in the Entente between the Coptic Orthodox Church and the State in Egypt." *International Journal of Middle East Studies* 41 (2009) 269–87.

Tumara, Nebojsa. "'Sign of Martyrdom, Heresy and Pride': The Christian Coptic Tattoo and the Construction of Coptic Identity." In *Copts in Modernity: Proceedings of the 5th International Symposium of Coptic Studies, Melbourne, 13–16 July 2018*, edited by Elizabeth Agaiby et al., Texts and Studies in Eastern Christianity 22, 295–320. Leiden, Neth.: Brill, 2021.

Van der Vliet, Jacques. "The Copts: 'Modern Sons of the Pharaohs'?" *Church History and Religious Culture* (2009) 279–90.

Yefet, Bosmat. "The Coptic Diaspora and the Status of the Coptic Minority in Egypt." *Journal of Ethnic and Migration Studies* 43 (2017) 1205–21.

Youssef, Joseph. "Becoming Saints: Coptic Orthodox Monasticism, Exemplarity, & Negotiating Christian Virtue." PhD diss., University of Toronto, 2019.

Zacharia, Marcus. 2021. "Tackling Sex Education and Sexual Abuse in the Egyptian-Canadian Diaspora." Egyptian Streets, Apr. 4, 2021. https://egyptianstreets.com/2021/04/04/tackling-sex-education-and-sexual-abuse-in-the-egyptian-canadian-diaspora/.

Palestinian Christians under Israeli Rule and the Struggle to Remain

Amir Marshi and Khaled Anabtawi

INTRODUCTION

DURING THE CHRISTIAN HOLIDAY of the annunciation, April 7, 2021, at the square outside the Greek Orthodox Church of the Annunciation in Nazareth, a woman named Aida Breik shouted across the closed gate of the church's inner square: "Traitor, traitor, undeserving, undeserving!" In the inner square behind the gate and leading the celebratory procession was Theophilos III, the Greek Orthodox patriarch who has been accused by protestors of unilaterally conducting land leasing deals with Israeli settler organizations at the expense of members of the community. Breik was apprehended by the Israeli police on the spot. As she was escorted away by security personnel, she repeatedly declared: "Gheir mustahiq, gheir mustahiq, khae'n" (Unworthy, unworthy, traitor).[1] A few months earlier, Theophilos had sparked outrage after being accused of planning to sell twenty-seven acres of church property in the south of Jerusalem to two Israeli companies to build illegal settlements in the area.[2] This was just one of a series of similar controversial deals carried out by the patriarch involving numerous plots of land owned by the patriarchate, but which the Orthodox Arab community in Palestine and Jordan argues should belong to them.[3] Four years earlier, following a similar protest about the same issue, the head of

---

1. *Panet*, "Denunciations of Brik's Arrest."
2. Muaddi, "Jerusalem's Orthodox Church."
3. Swa'ed, "Al-Ba'na."

the Greek Orthodox Church Council in Nazareth, Afaf Touma, declared in an interview about Theophilos's dealings:

> These deals ultimately aim to empty the Christian and Arab presence, and this in itself is a danger and a disaster for the members of the Christian community and their sacred places and their history in this country, as well as for the Palestinian cause, given that Jerusalem is the capital of Palestine.[4]

This chapter follows the voices of Palestinian Christian community organizers in the 1948 Territories[5] with the aim of contextualizing the "Christian Arab presence" within the broader political reality that challenges and maintains it. In doing so, the chapter explores how state and church institutions interact with national and religious belonging among Palestinian Christians with Israeli citizenship, and as a colonized community undergoing a continuous history of settler-colonial dispossession.

For the Palestinians who remained on the lands upon which the state of Israel was established, and who survived the mass expulsion of most of their compatriots during the 1948 Nakba, *al-baqaa'* (remaining) on their land is an overarching theme of political and existential struggle. This struggle continues today for Palestinian Christians in the 1948 territories as they confront various state practices that result in land dispossession, disenfranchisement, exclusion, and communal fragmentation—all factors that further threaten the vulnerable presence of the community. This chapter aims to understand the struggle to remain as it is played out by Palestinian Christians in the 1948 Territories against the backdrop of the external dynamics of inclusion and exclusion operating at the levels of: (1) the Jewish state in which they are citizens, (2) the church to which they belong, and (3) the religiously diverse Palestinian community of which they are a part. We argue in the following that the relationship between the community and these dynamic layers of attachment cannot be understood outside the geopolitical and spatial formations that make up the reality of Palestinian Christians in the 1948 Territories, a community confronted by forces of

---

4. Swaed, "Activists."

5. The "1948 Territories" is the term used by Palestinians to refer to the part of historic Palestine occupied in 1948. "Behind the green line" is another term applied to the same status. The authors refrain from using the term "Palestinian Christian in Israel" in order to highlight the Palestinian worldview but also to be specific, as Israel has no official boundaries. To say "in Israel" may include Jerusalem, where members of the Palestinian Christian community live but which is not part of the focus of this study. Although part of the same community, those who live in Jerusalem were incorporated illegally into Israel in 1967 and were given "permanent residency," status as opposed to the citizenship given to Palestinians in the 1948 Territories.

uprootedness on the one hand, while constantly struggling to maintain its roots within the land on the other.

Christians in Palestine are among the oldest existing Christian communities in the world. Jerusalem, Bethlehem, Acre, and Nazareth—to name only a few of the historic Palestinian centers—are places where Christians have existed since the time of Jesus himself. This is an extensive history that the chapter does not dwell on.[6] Rather, in the following, we focus on the contemporary sociopolitical existence of the community and the modern history that forms that existence. This is an ambitious endeavor in itself that can only be accomplished to a limited extent within the scope of this chapter. However, our modest attempt is executed here with the hope that it constitutes a fresh viewpoint for future discussion and research about the Palestinian Arab Christian community, the structure of citizenship in the Jewish state, and sectarianism within colonized Arab communities.

First, we begin by reflecting on the contemporary demographic, socioeconomic, and educational status of the Palestinian Christian community in the 1948 Territories, particularly the complex dynamics of state inclusion and exclusion on all these levels. Second, we will analyze the contemporary relationship between state, church, and congregation as it pertains to the subject of landed property, reflecting briefly on the community's struggle to maintain their presence through activism aimed at gaining control over church institutions through the Arabization and democratization of church institutions. Third, we will explore how colonial state practices of fragmentation and co-optation are influencing interfaith relations in the Palestinian community in the 1948 Territories in the context of rising trends of religious Zionism in Israel, and Islamic and Christian fundamentalism in the region.

The chapter takes the point of departure that theory, methodology, and politics cannot be separated. Like every religious group that is part of a larger national group, Palestinian Arab Christians who are citizens of Israel ascribe to diverse political opinions. The authors, however, have consciously chosen to highlight the position, discourse, and practice of the Palestinian Christian community in organizing against land confiscation. The viewpoint promoted by this chapter is one that addresses the dual political context of settler-colonial dispossession and practices of indigenous decolonization.

6. See F. Farah, *Living Stones*.

I—PALESTINIAN CHRISTIANS IN 1948 TERRITORIES TODAY: FACTS AND FIGURES

Demographic Trends

Totaling some 1,575,000 (1.6 million) persons in spring 2021,[7] Palestinians in the 1948 Territories comprise 17.6 percent of the entire Israeli population. The Palestinian community in the 1948 Territories is diverse: Arab Muslims represent 84.3 percent (1,327,725), Arab Druze around 7.8 percent (123,400),[8] and Arab Christians make up almost 7.9 percent (124,623) and about 1.5 percent of the total Israeli population.[9] Around twenty different Christian denominations are active in the 1948 Territories, with ten recognized by the state.[10] Palestinian Arab Christians in the 1948 lands comprise multiple confessional denominations, including Melkite Roum (Greek) Catholic (about 38 percent), Roum (Greek) Orthodox (about 33 percent),[11] Latin Catholic (about 17 percent), Maronite (about 7 percent), and numerically smaller communities such as the Anglican, Protestant, Lutheran, and Coptic communities (comprising 5 percent all together).[12] The majority of Palestinian Christians in the 1948 Territories live in the north of the Galilee, the north of Haifa, and the central coastal area with 70.4 percent, 13.4 percent, and 9.2 percent respectively.[13]

7. Anabtawi, *Palestinian Youth in Israel*, 16–17.

8. Researchers' analysis of Central Bureau of Statistics, "Christmas 2020," 1; *Statistical Abstract of Israel* (appendices 2.1 and 2.2).

9. Both Arab and non-Arab people of Christian faith constitute some 2 percent, or 165,000, of the total Israeli population. This means that nearly 75.5 percent of Christians in the 1948 Territories are Palestinian Arabs, while 24.5 percent, or 40,600, are not. The vast majority of non-Arab Christians are descendants of people who immigrated and settled in Israel as members of Jewish families in the early 1990s under the Israeli Law of Return. In addition to Ethiopia, the former USSR is one of the most prominent countries of origin of these families. The rest originate from countries that include the Philippines, Romania, and Germany (Central Bureau of Statistics, "Christmas 2020," 3–6).

10. The Anglican denomination was the latest to be recognized by Israel as a religious sect in 1970 (Frantzman et al., "Anglican Church in Palestine").

11. The adjective *Roum* ("Roman") in Arabic refers to the heritage of the post-Byzantine Eastern Christians. Although in mainstream literature "Greek Orthodox" and "Greek Catholic" are the applied terms, in our study we will mainly use *Roum* since this is the term applied by Palestinian Christians who refrain from using Greek (*Yonani* in Arabic) when speaking about their denominational affiliation or religious identity, and prefer *Roum Arthodox* and *Roum Katholik*.

12. It is not easy to determine the demographic distribution of various Christian denominations throughout the 1948 Territories, as no entity or framework provides such a profile (Kofman, *Arab Society in Israel*, 112).

13. Central Bureau of Statistics, "Christmas 2020," 5.

A continuous decline in the percentage of Christians in relation to the broader community is a worrying trend for the community and prompts visions of a future where Christians will no longer constitute a considerable community on the land from which Christianity spread throughout the world (see appendix 1). Indeed, the percentage of Christian Palestinians in the Palestinian population present in the 1948 Territories has dropped sharply from 20 percent in 1949 following the establishment of Israel in 1948 to 7.9 percent today.[14] The stream of negative migration to Western countries by Palestinian Christians contributes significantly to this trend.

The particular history of Palestinian Christian emigration to the West and the permanency of their stay in the diaspora goes back a hundred years, with various stages of migration, each with specific push factors.[15] This history led to the existence of an expansive Palestinian Christian diaspora centered in the Americas (Canada, US, and Latin America), Europe, and, more recently, Australia—a diaspora almost five times larger than the Palestinian community existing in historical Palestine.[16] Germane to understanding the history of negative migration among Palestinian Christians in the 1948 Territories is the forced eviction from villages and cities, growing Jewish immigration, the marginalization of Palestinians in the Israeli labor market, and the continuing unstable political situation and impediments put in the way of education.[17] In the early 1990s, when the phenomenon of negative migration was becoming pronounced, al-Liqa' Center conducted a survey that illustrated that the main motive behind Palestinian Christian migration from the 1948 Territories was mostly the lack of economic opportunities and an insecure economic future.[18]

14. Close to 33,000, a quarter of these Christians (25 percent), were internally displaced persons within the 1948 Territories.

15. For an overview of the history of Palestinian Christian outward migration, see Raheb, "Palestinian Christians." (1) The migration of Christian traders during the late Ottoman period until the First World War was mostly to Latin America. Many of those who migrated wanted to return in the 1920s, but new regulations introduced by the British Mandate prevented them from their right to naturalization, while that right was given to Jews worldwide (Bawalsa, "Legislating Exclusion"). (2) The ethnic cleansing of most of Palestine in 1948 (the Nakba) was when the majority of Palestinians were forcibly displaced and scattered across the region and the world. (3) Migration from the West Bank to Jordan and the West for search of better opportunities occurred between 1949 and 1967, at a time when Palestinians in the 1948 Territories were under military rule (1948–1966) that restricted their movements (J. Mansour, *Arab Christians in Israel*, 50–54). (4) After the occupation of the West Bank and Gaza in 1967 that suffocated towns and villages, isolated them from one another, and dismantled the Palestinian economy, many Christians migrated, mostly to Europe and the Americas.

16. J. Mansour, *Arab Christians in Israel*, 50.

17. J. Mansour, *Arab Christians in Israel*, 50.

18. Al-Liqa' Center conducted a survey once in 1991 and again in 2009. Interviews showed that Palestinian Christian citizens attribute negative migration to conditions of

This is expressed by one of the interviewees who stated, "If our homeland does not provide me with a roof under which to shade, I am in no need of its skies."[19] Note that the economic struggle faced by the community is linked to the economic inequality fomented by an ethnocratic citizenry regime where privileges and opportunities are reserved for Jewish citizens.[20] Thus, the key issues prompting Christian migration are not the exclusive burden of the Christian community but are, in fact, shared by their Muslim compatriots as non-Jewish Arabs within a Jewish state.[21] The disproportionate difference in the rate of migration between the Christian and the Muslim Palestinian communities can be attributed to multiple reasons, among them the accessibility enjoyed by the former to the Western world thanks to the hundred-year-old, well-established Palestinian Christian diaspora that can be harnessed for chain migration in times of crises in the homeland.

In addition to negative migration, the fertility rates of Palestinian Christians are the lowest of the Palestinian community in the 1948 Territories. Some forty thousand Christian households live in the 1948 Territories, comprising 3.39 persons per house[22] (see appendix 2) and consisting on average of 1.97 children (up to the age of seventeen).[23] This is mediocre compared to Muslim households (2.69 children) and Druze households (2.14 children) (see appendix 3).[24] Indeed, in 2019, the birth rate among

---

political crises the inaccessibility of the labor market, the search for an academic future or a specific profession, and rejection from the Israeli labor market due to racism (J. Mansour, *Arab Christians in Israel*, 52).

To a limited yet increasing extent, the lack of religious freedom caused by rising religious fanaticism is another reason given by those who emigrate: "Three point six percent of respondents in the 2009 poll stated that religious fanaticism and sectarian conflict in a number of Galilee villages and cities constituted, and still constitute, one of the major motivators for the emigration of Arab Christians in their search for a place that guarantees their freedom of worship and the practice of their religious life without censorship or pressure. Despite the small percentage that expressed this motivation, its negative impact is far-reaching. The religious reason is related to religious manifestations becoming more widespread in a number of mixed cities and villages" (J. Mansour, *Arab Christians in Israel*, 52).

19. In an interview conducted by the al-Liqa' Center in the 1990s on the motives for Christian negative migration: "Our homeland does not provide me a support system, therefore I don't need it" (cited in E. Khoury, *Signatures on the Sand*, 10).

20. Miaari, *Do Economic Changes Affect*.

21. Central Bureau of Statistics, "Christmas 2020," 6.

22. Christian households with six persons and over made up just 7 percent, compared to 31 percent of Muslim households and 9 percent of Jewish households.

23. Central Bureau of Statistics, "Christmas 2020," 6–7.

24. Towards the end of 2018, 785 Christian couples were married, including 90 percent Christian grooms and 88 percent Christian brides. These data demonstrate that mixed marriages continue to be limited in number and uncommon in the Palestinian

Christian households was 1.76, versus 3.16 in Muslim households, 2.2 in Druze households, and 3.09 in Jewish households.[25]

Economic Status

Today, Palestinian Christians in the 1948 lands are characterized as a thriving urban and highly educated middle class.[26] This was not always the case. With the establishment of the state of Israel in 1948, the Palestinian social and economic structure was totally dismantled. However, throughout the years, largely due to the community's educational and cultural capital and various political and economic transformations, the community gained back its social mobility on an individual level and became prominent in various sectors of the Israeli economy.

Since the beginning of the century, employment and educational opportunities have transformed significantly for the Palestinian community in the 1948 Territories. Since the Israeli government established the so-called Authority for the Economic Development of the Minority Sectors in 2007 and joined the OECD in 2010, state economic policy has increasingly targeted a margin of economic development among the Arab public by focusing on greater participation in the labor market and greater academic enrollment. In 2015, Israel approved a five-year socioeconomic plan totaling 15 billion NIS in support of Arab local authorities, employment, education, and other projects.[27] These policies are driven by an ongoing Israeli shift towards, and extension of, neoliberal policies, in addition to a policy of civil pacification of Palestinian citizens through economic "integration"[28] following their participation in the second intifada around the year 2000.[29]

community in the 1948 Territories. For Christian men, the average age at marriage was 29.9 years, one year older than the Druze, two and a half years older than the Jews, and three years older than Muslim men. The average age at marriage was 26.3 years among Christian women, half a year older than Jewish women, one year older than the Druze, and three and a half years older than Muslims.

25. Central Bureau of Statistics, "Christmas 2020," 6.

26. Mack, "Christian Palestinian Communities."

27. Israeli Prime Minister's Office, "Government Activity."

28. The Or Committee: A committee of inquiry appointed by the Israeli government to investigate the events of Oct. 2000 (during the second Palestinian intifada) in which twelve Palestinian citizens of Israel and one Palestinian from Gaza were killed by Israeli police in the 1948 Territories. The committee published its recommendations in 2003. One of the recommendations promoted the pacification of the Palestinian community through "bridging economic gaps." See Or Committee, "Or Committee Recommendations."

29. Israeli Prime Minister's Office, "Government Activity."

Despite a margin of economic relief in the Palestinian community in general, and particularly Palestinian Christians, economic gaps continue to be significant in comparison with Jewish citizens.[30] Discrepancies in population density and space remain considerable, and although fertility and birth rates are dropping among Palestinian Christians in the 1948 Territories, household density is higher among Christians than among Jews.[31] Population density and housing are specifically linked to land, a key theme of the conflict and restrictions on Christians, along with all Palestinians, across the 1948 Territories, to which we will turn later in the chapter.

Ecclesiastical Schools, State, and Community

"Schools are the basis of our churches."

—ARCHBISHOP GREGORIOS HAJJAR[32]

For the Palestinian Christian community in the 1948 Territories, education has long been an essential means for social and economic progress. A total of forty-seven ecclesiastical schools exist in the 1948 Territories and are run by Catholic, Orthodox, Anglican, and Baptist churches and organizations.[33] The vast majority of Arab Christian students attend these schools, which serve thirty-five thousand students from Christian and non-Christian backgrounds. Given the fact that almost 60 percent of the Christian school population is Muslim and 40 percent Christian, ecclesiastical schools have been widely regarded as leverage for the Palestinian community at large rather than for Christians alone.[34]

Given the political realities referred to above, Christian ecclesiastical schools, which do not fall within the Israeli category of so-called informal but recognized schools, have historically graduated a considerable number of Palestinian intellectuals and political leaders. Even according to general Israeli standards these days, Christian schools remain outstanding

30. Some 56.1 percent of Palestinian Christians (above fifteen years) are in the labor market, in comparison to 67.8 percent of Jewish participants. The gap is more striking among Christian women in contrast with Jewish females, with 66.1 percent and 48.8 percent respectively (Central Bureau of Statistics, "Christmas 2020," 13).

31. One person per room, compared to 0.79 persons per room respectively (Central Bureau of Statistics, "Christmas 2020," 13).

32. From the statement of Archbishop Gregory Hajjar and his declaration on the construction of the Catholic School in Shefa Amr in 1924. The document was obtained by the researcher from the archive of the Shefa Amr municipality.

33. Amborozelly, "Israeli Ministry of Education."

34. Sha'lan, "Excellence in Strike"; Zoubi, "Private Schools, National Fortresses."

educational facilities.[35] Some view these schools as a national cultural hub and space for non-curricular education premised on the value of fostering a sense of community among students.[36] The president of the Haifa-based Orthodox Arab College School—with the word "Arab" in the name to emphasize its national character—asserted that the "Orthodox College is not only concerned with the content of education, but it also adopts a myriad of educational projects to achieve its goals and give students a sense of belonging to their school and people."[37] It is worth noting that some 65 to 70 percent of Arab students in Haifa attend ecclesiastical schools. The Orthodox Arab College School in Haifa is no exception. Nazareth is home to nearly fifteen Christian community schools. The best known of these are the Saint Joseph Seminary and High School (est. 1886) and the Don Bosco School (est. 1896). These schools serve the Nazareth community as a whole. Muslim students account for as much as 70 percent of the general student population in some community schools in Nazareth.[38]

In the 2019–2020 academic year, twenty-four thousand Arab Christian students were enrolled in primary and secondary schools.[39] Comparatively high levels of education are found among Arab Christians, as demonstrated by data collected over the past eight academic years (2010–2011 to 2018–2019) on students who completed secondary education. In addition, Arab Christian student outcomes are relatively higher than others.[40] Some 51.6 percent of Arab Christian students received a bachelor's degree within eight years following completion of secondary education, compared to 33.7 percent among the overall Arab student population. The majority of Christian students complete their education at academic universities rather than at colleges or educational colleges (see appendix 4).

The proportion of Arab Christian students enrolled in higher education is higher than in the broader population.[41] Moreover, there is a relatively

35. Amborozelly, "Israeli Ministry of Education."

36. Sha'lan, "Excellence in Strike"; Zoubi, "Private Schools, National Fortresses."

37. *Haifanet*, "Mr. Edward Sheiban."

38. Amborozelly, "Israeli Ministry of Education."

39. Central Bureau of Statistics, "Christmas 2020," 8.

40. Some 71.2 percent of Christian students were eligible for the Israeli matriculation (*bagrut*) certificate that qualifies them for admission to university, compared to 71.4 percent of students in the Jewish community (excluding Haredi Jews), 64.5 percent of Arab Druze students, and 45.1 percent of Arab Muslim students (Central Bureau of Statistics, "Christmas 2020," 8–9).

41. Some 2.3 percent of all students at Israeli universities and colleges are Arab Christians (approximately 6,100 students). Of these, 72.8 percent are studying for a bachelor's degree, 21 percent for a master's degree, and 3.6 percent for a PhD. The percentage of women among Christian students was also higher than among overall

specific pattern of education among the Arab Christian student community as higher numbers of educated Christian youth enroll in the fields of high tech, medicine, and law (see appendix 5).

However, as scholars have demonstrated, education has also been used as a key tool for political control and surveillance by Israel over the Palestinian community.[42] Having divided the educational system into Druze, Bedouin, and Arab subsystems, the Arab education apparatus is under the complete control of the Israeli Ministry of Education (MoE), which determines budget appropriations and oversees educational materials, ultimately censoring Palestinian narratives while seeking to advance Zionist narratives. In addition, the educational system is designed in the contemporary Israeli neoliberal context and produces individualistic values among students. So, while it is important to note that there has been a consistent increase in educational attainment by Palestinian students, in many cases it is seen as a tool for individual advancement rather than communal development.[43]

Unlike Israeli religious or Haredi schools, which are almost 100 percent funded by the MoE, Christian schools were only partially financed by the ministry. In 2015, the Israeli government announced its intention to reduce its financial support for Christian schools from 75 percent funding to as low as 29 percent of school budget allocations. Furthermore, the MoE declared it would restrict the collection of registration and tuition fees from parents, which are the main funding source for Christian schools.[44] In protest against the ministry's decision, at the start of the 2015 school year, the General Secretariat of Christian Schools declared an open-ended strike in which forty-seven schools serving thirty-three thousand students participated. For the community, the ministry's decision was seen as "declaring war on Christian schools" and seeking to dry up resources in an attempt to convert these facilities into government schools under the full control of the Israeli MoE. Protests were not confined to Christian schools, and the National Committee of the Heads of Arab Localities also declared a strike throughout Arab governmental schools in solidarity with Christian community schools.[45] The strike lasted about a month, during which schoolchildren, rather than attending their regular classes, attended

---

students in the 2019–2020 academic year. Compared to 59.7 percent of all students, 62.4 percent of Arab Christian students were women (Central Bureau of Statistics, "Christmas 2020," 9).

42. See Jiryis, *Arabs in Israel*; Al-Haj, *Education, Empowerment, and Control*; Agbaria and Jabareen, "Minority Educational Autonomy Rights," 25.

43. Agbaria, "Neoliberalism in Arab Education."

44. B. Mansour, "Christian Schools in Israel."

45. Bakri, "Acre: Arab Schools."

protests and demonstrations to save their schools. It was called off after the General Secretariat and MoE reached a temporary agreement to transfer emergency funding (some 50 million NIS) to Christian community schools, and a joint committee was to be established to discuss remaining contentious matters.[46]

The agreement was not satisfactory to the whole community and sparked many debates. It was criticized particularly by students' parents because it did not deliver on the demands that had prompted Christian schools to declare the strike in the first place. Furthermore, some parents felt that they were excluded from the decision-making process. It subsequently turned out that the ministry's decision was a delaying tactic either to back out of the agreement or to link the transfer of funds to what the government described as "promoting Christian content in schools."[47] These practices clearly reflected Israel's colonial and neoliberal vision and policy.

The strike and the protests created a space for heightened awareness by the parents of students of their key role in the struggle for the future of their children against a state that consistently marginalizes them and also against the institutional approach of church-run institutions. Many parents who were committed to, supported, and took part in the strike saw it as an opportunity not only to realize the rights of Christian schools but also to expand their role as a community in both exerting pressure on the ministry and influencing the decision-making process within the General Secretariat and the educational facilities in general. During and after the strike, parents continued to emphasize the need for elected parent committees in Christian schools to create an enabling environment for parents to exert an influence over their children's future.[48]

Broadly speaking, the problem of Christian schools was left unresolved indefinitely. The dynamics and ramifications of the crisis, along with the heated debates that followed, demonstrate the tension-ridden trinity of state, church, and community as a lens to trace the wider context of the *baqa'a* struggle among Palestinian Christians, a subject to which we will now turn in relation to the subject of church landed property.

46. *i24 News*, "Private Schools Strike Ends."
47. J. Khoury, "Crisis of Private School."
48. Baransy, "Private Schools in Israel."

II—DISPOSSESSION OF LAND: CHURCH LANDS AND THE ONGOING NAKBA

God has become a refugee, oh sir, confiscate then the carpet of the mosque
And sell the church, as it is his property, and sell the muezzin[49] in the black auction

—RASHID HUSSEIN

By the second part of the nineteenth century, Ottoman constitutional re-forms were being put in place, and global, regional. and local Christian churches of the Catholic, Orthodox. and Anglican denominations began to purchase land all over Palestine. They constructed parishes, churches, monasteries, orphanages, housing projects, schools, hospitals, and hospices, as well as saving tracts of land for future expansion.[50] This process contin-ued well into the first half of the twentieth century, paving the way for the educational and economic advancement of Palestinian Christians and con-tributing to the flourishing of the broader community.[51] Indeed, largely due to the initiation of various Christian churches buying land outside the walls of Jerusalem, the Old City expanded into the "New City," which until 1948 was a modern urban center made up of middle-class neighborhoods such as Qatamon, Talbiyeh, and Malha, in which both Christian and Muslim Jerusalemites lived.[52] The New City also harbored the Palestinian political elite and intelligentsia.[53] During the 1948 Nakba, the New City of Jerusalem was violently and completely emptied of its original inhabitants, who were prevented from returning to their homes and deprived of their land and properties; Jerusalem's New City became, as Salim Tamari described it, a "phantom city."[54]

What befell the Jerusalem community was the same as for most Pales-tinians in the 1948 Nakba, whereby 800,000 Palestinians were forcibly dis-placed from their homeland and became refugees. Some became internally

49. Muezzin: The imam who gives the call to prayer at a mosque.

50. Katz and Kark, "Church and Landed Property," 383.

51. Katz and Kark, "Church and Landed Property," 384.

52. The New City also hosted the Jewish community, which was growing rapidly due to the initiation of the Zionist movement that moved settlers into newly built settle-ments (*yeshuvs*) (Davis, "Growth of Western Communities").

53. Among them was the renowned Arab Christian Orthodox intellectual and educator Khalil al-Sakakini. A politically active and outspoken Arab nationalist, al-Sakakini was imprisoned by the Ottoman authorities and ostracized by the Orthodox Church because of his political ideals. See Hadid, "Khalil Sakakini."

54. Tamari, "Phantom City," 2.

displaced persons (IDPs) (accounting for 450,000 today),[55] with most of their villages occupied, either settled by Jewish immigrants or partially or completely destroyed.[56] The minority of Palestinians who could remain, anywhere from 60,000 to 156,000, among whom 32,000 were Christian,[57] became strangers within their own homeland, with no political or religious leadership, alienated from their lands, their collective rights, and their civil institutions, and put under military rule that restricted their movement. The Absentee Property Law of 1950 issued by the state of Israel transferred ownership over Palestinian property of those who became refugees in neighboring states, or of those who remained within the borders but became IDPs, to the Custodian for Absentee Property,[58] which, in its turn, transferred ownership to the state.[59] This included the Roum Catholic and mostly Maronite villages of Iqrith and Birim located on the Lebanese border, which were evacuated by the military in 1948. Despite ongoing legitimate appeals by the residents to return to their homes, both these villages were demolished completely by the use of planted and air-dropped bombs: Iqrith on Christmas Day 1951 and Kfur Birim on the day of Exaltation of the Holy Cross in 1953. In both villages, the churches are the only structures left standing.[60]

Although 1948 was the most catastrophic year for Palestinians, the displacement, alienation, and dispossession of land did not stop with the Nakba, nor did it begin there. Since it was founded, the Zionist political movement adopted the slogan of "a land without a people for a people without a land." As more Jews migrated to Palestine during the nineteenth century, Zionists created multiple institutions to accrue land with the logic

55. According to a survey by BADIL Resource Center for Palestinian Residency and Refugee Rights on Palestinian refugees and internally displaced persons, by the end of 2018 roughly 8.7 million people were designated as forcibly displaced persons (66.7 percent of the entire worldwide Palestinian population of 13.05 million) (BADIL, *Survey*, 22). Some 7.94 million Palestinians are designated as refugees, among them 5.54 million registered by the United Nations Relief and Works Agency (UNRWA), which tends specifically to the needs of Palestinian refugees in camps (BADIL, *Survey*, 25). There are also approximately 760,000 internally displaced persons: about 415,000 of them are citizens of Israel who live close to their original home town but are not allowed to return (BADIL, *Survey*, 22).

56. See W. Khalidi, *All That Remains*.

57. Mack, "Christian Palestinian Communities," 284.

58. Adalah, "Absentees' Property Law."

59. Lehn, "Jewish National Fund."

60. Ryan, "Refugees within Israel." Al-Mansura is another Christian village that was completely emptied. Other mixed Christian and Muslim villages and cities that were emptied include al-Barwa, Suhmata, Maʿalul, Sireen, al-Bassa, Safad, Tiberias, Bisan, Haifa, and Ramleh.

of "land redemption" as the core value,[61] i.e., the "purchase, *reclamation* and settlement of land in Eretz Israel (Palestine),"[62] also called "Judaization." These institutions received substantial help from land reforms implemented by the British Mandate aimed at facilitating Jewish settlement.[63] The most prominent of these organizations is the Jewish National Fund (JNF),[64] which is the biggest owner of land today after the state. The public lands and settled territories under the supervision of the JNF are still regarded as exclusively Jewish, and land-leasing deals to non-Jews are prohibited.[65]

While military rule over Palestinian citizens officially ended in 1966, practices of land dispossession were embodied within legislative and bureaucratic practices. In 1976, for instance, the Israeli government announced a plan to expropriate twenty-one thousand dunams of land in the Galilee as part of its policy to Judaize the Galilee, where Arab presence and land ownership is considerable. This plan failed due to Palestinian popular resistance.[66] Today, Palestinian citizens of Israel make up around 17 percent of the population and own less than 2 percent of the land.[67] Municipalities and councils of Arab cities and villages are generally restricted from expanding their jurisdiction.[68] While hundreds of localities have been built for Jewish citizens since 1948, none have been constructed for Arabs,[69] and more than thirty-five Palestinian Bedouin villages are unrecognized.[70] In all matters

61. Such as the Jewish Colonization Association founded in 1891, the Palestine Land Development Company founded in 1908, the Jewish Colonization Association (PICA) founded in 1923, and the Jewish Agency founded in 1929 (Greenwood, "Immigration to Israel").

62. Greenwood, "Immigration to Israel" (emphasis added).

63. Forman and Kedar, "Colonialism, Colonization."

64. Founded in 1901 by the World Zionist Organization, the JNF continues to this day to secure territories for the Jewish public and is the second largest owner after the state.

65. Shahar, "Is the JNF Racist?"

66. On Mar. 30, 1976, Palestinian citizens organized marches in all of the villages and cities, from the north to the south, and went on a national strike. The uprising was costly for the Palestinians as six young men were shot dead by police and became martyrs, but it was successful in putting pressure on the Israeli government about land confiscation. March 30 marks the commemoration of these events each year, known to Palestinians as Land Day, when Palestinians gather to march as they did back in 1976 from the village of Deir Hanna to Arraba, and then to Sakhnin. See Mossawa Centre, *Land Day.*

67. Kayyal, "Under the Policy"; Y. Jabareen, "National Planning Policy."

68. Y. Jabareen," National Planning Policy."

69. Y. Jabareen, "National Planning Policy."

70. Yiftachel et al., *Alternative Master Plan,* 14.

relating to *collective* ownership of land, Palestinians in the 1948 Territories are still essentially without rights.

Landed Property: Between Church, State, and Congregation

Most land in the 1948 Territories (93 percent) is considered public land, defined as Jewish.[71] For the Palestinians who remained, putting aside the individual properties that they were able to retain, Christian and Muslim endowments (waqfs) were the closest thing they had to public land. However, most Islamic waqf properties in what became Israel, estimated to comprise a sixth of the country's land, were expropriated under the Absentee Property Law.[72] Disputes over the ownership of these estates continue to the present day, with Israel completely disregarding all religious decrees and civil rights appeals, and proceeding to confiscate, destroy, and desecrate sacred Islamic sites such as mosques and cemeteries in Jerusalem, Jaffa, Haifa, and elsewhere to build state institutions and profit-based facilities.[73] For land registered to the Christian church, largely due to Israel's interest in maintaining its alliance with the Western Christian countries on which it depends, the state could not simply expropriate church property as it did Muslim endowments.[74] This did not mean that church-owned land was completely in the hands of the Christian community itself. Ultimately, a large portion of this land was alienated from the community and transferred to the Israeli state, albeit mostly through land sales and land leasing agreements conducted between the church and the state.

The Israeli state dealt with the different churches and their landed property in accordance with the policy of segregation it inherited from the British Mandate. Each church was treated based on different negotiations and agreements that depended on multiple factors: the power of the international entity responsible for the church, the extent of Arabness of the

---

71. Kedar, "Legal Transformation," 947.

72. Suleiman and Home, "God Is an Absentee."

73. For instance, between 2011 and 2015, most of the Sheikh Muwannes Islamic cemetery was desecrated and destroyed. In its place, Tel Aviv University built a student dorm, shopping center, and parking lot. After appeals by al-Aqsa Institute against the university's actions, the Israeli Supreme Court confirmed the right of the university to proceed with the construction (*Arab48*, "Israel's Supreme Court). Another example is the ancient Ma'man Allah Cemetery in Jerusalem, parts of which were destroyed and turned into a mall, while another part is to be covered by the construction of a "museum of rolerance." For a critical analysis of both cases, see Shalhoub-Kevorkian, "Necropolitical Debris."

74. Ramon, *Christians and Christianity.*

church, and the size of the denominational community in question.[75] While there are many churches operating in the 1948 Territories, for the purpose of this chapter, we will demonstrate the case of church landed property primarily in the Greek-dominated Orthodox Patriarchate of Jerusalem and the Arab Melkite Greek Catholic Archeparchy of Acre, Haifa, and all of the Galilee. These two churches rule over 33 percent and 38 percent of Palestinian Christians in the 1948 Territories respectively.

The Orthodox Patriarchate of Jerusalem

In 1534, the Ottoman Empire removed the last Arab indigenous patriarch of Jerusalem. Since then, control has been exclusively endowed to the predominantly Greek clergy, or the so-called Brotherhood of the Holy Sepulchre, which rules over a predominantly Arab laity that lives in the region of Jordan and historic Palestine (the West Bank, Jerusalem, and Israel). Since the nineteenth century, members of the Orthodox community have waged a struggle for Arabization and liberation from the authority of the Greek clergy, which has monopolized church properties, endowments, appointments, and promotions within the ecclesiastical hierarchy.[76]

After 1948, although the patriarchate was located in the Old City of Jerusalem in what was considered "enemy territories," Israel recognized the holdings of the Greek Patriarchate. This happened only after Israel pressured the patriarchate in 1952 to lease a large portion of its properties in West Jerusalem to the state at a very low price. Since then, the patriarchate—until recently the largest owner of land after the Israeli state[77]—has either sold estate or leased it for long periods of time to the state or to settler organizations, in contravention of established Ottoman, British, and Jordanian agreements,[78] and completely disregarding the numerous decrees produced by Orthodox congregation councils in Jordan and historical Palestine. This resulted in the forfeiture of church estates to the Israeli state and Zionist settler organizations in Jerusalem, Jaffa, Tiberias, Nazareth, Caesarea, and

75. Mack, "Christian Palestinian Communities," 291; Ramon, *Christians and Christianity*, 6.

76. For a brief history of the struggle, especially in the years before the establishment of the state of Israel, see S. Khoury and Khoury, "Brief History."

77. Chabin, "Greek Orthodox Church."

78. This is not to say that the relative compromises completely fulfilled the desires of the communities. These agreements include: the 1856 Hatt-i Humayun reforms, the 1875 Katastatikon, the Ottoman Orders of 1910 and 1912, the 1941 Law under the British Mandate, and the 1957 Jordanian law, which was later reformed in 1958 to suit the desires of the patriarchate. See S. Khoury and Khoury, "Brief History."

Bisan—many of them areas from which Palestinians were displaced in 1948. The patriarchate, influenced by a nationalist discourse, considers these estates as national Greek property.[79]

Tensions worsened with the election of Theophilos III in 2005, who, since his election, has been involved in numerous land deals with Israel that lost the congregation tens if not hundreds of plots of lands, especially in Jerusalem (West and East). These include land in Sheikh Jarrah north of Jerusalem, a key area of the Old City next to Jaffa Gate, the vast Mar Elias monastery land south of Jerusalem, and land in Talbiyeh, today's Rehavia and Beit Shemesh in West Jerusalem.[80] The latest deal to be exposed was one between the patriarchate and a fabricated Israeli settler company of more than 110 dunams of land between Bethlehem and Jerusalem, where Israel plans to construct an illegal settlement that will completely cut off Bethlehem from Jerusalem, to the detriment of the Palestinian community in the region.

Melkite Greek Catholic Archeparchy of Acre, Haifa, and the Rest of the Galilee

Contrary to the Orthodox and Latin Churches, the Melkite Greek Catholic Archeparchy of Akka, Haifa, and the rest of the Galilee is a distinctly Arab and autonomous institution. By the end of the nineteenth century, the archeparchy had little property and real estate.[81] However, according to Palestinian historian Johnny Mansour, following the election of Gregorias Hajjar as archbishop in 1901, "the endowment sector began to flourish, as the diocese gained tracts of land offered by members of the congregation or gained by purchase."[82] Referred to as "Mutran al-Arab" (bishop of the Arabs), the young and charismatic Arab nationalist bishop was able to widen the network of endowments registered in his personal name and some in the name of local councils in various villages.[83] Throughout the mandate years, the archeparchy became a thriving institution that managed a vast network of schools, hospitals, and many other institutions intended to serve the community.

---

79. Abu Raya, "Most Disputed Land."
80. Abu Raya, "Most Disputed Land."
81. Frantzman and Kark, "Catholic Church," 381.
82. J. Mansour, *New Vision of Life*, 56.
83. J. Mansour, *New Vision of Life*, 61.

Although the Palestinian church was devastated by the 1948 war, in the 1950s it managed to restore some properties from the state,[84] and the tradition of communal responsibility and activism was carried forward by later church leaders and archbishops. We mention two of them here. Archbishop Joseph Raya (1968–1974), who was involved in the civil rights movement in the US, was also involved in a hunger strike to obtain justice for the Palestinian Christian villages of Iqrith and Birim.[85] Archbishop Raya was also known to sell land to peasant Muslims as restitution for past injustices. He believed that after they had worked on the land for seventy years, they had earned the right to own it.[86] Elias Chacour was born in Kufr Birim and was displaced along with his family and the rest of the villagers when he was a child. After he became a priest, he was one of the key people who helped the Kufr Birim community to organize camps in the village, demand their right to return, and restore the church.[87] His biggest achievement is the Mar Elias school in Ib'ilin. This became a respected school attended by children from seventy different Palestinian villages and cities.

The Roum Catholic Church was known for its significant contribution to the evolution of the Arab community and educational institutions that have played a role in Palestinian community development and survival in times of hardship across the 1948 Territories. In some sense, it contributed to solving a housing shortage by creating residential neighborhoods (e.g., Shikon Alarab in Nazareth) and schools (e.g., St. Joseph School).[88] However, during the late 1980s and up to the early 2000s, the archeparchy underwent financial crises. Members of the congregation criticized the church leadership and voiced concerns over the lack of transparency in the handling of financial matters, corruption, and the selling of land at nominal prices to Israeli companies without the consent of the congregation, particularly land and property in the city of Haifa.[89]

The Struggle of the Congregation

Congregation council members and sizeable segments of the Palestinian community believe that the church endowments and properties should be

84. Kaufman, *Arab Society in Israel*, 113.

85. See Sabada, "Religious Peacebuilding."

86. Sabada, "Archbishop Joseph Raya."

87. See Chacour and Hazard, *Blood Brother*.

88 Kaufman, *Arab Society in Israel*, 113.

89. For a full history of the association written by the founder, see E. Khoury, *Signatures on the Sand*.

used and invested in community services, development, economy, housing, and education. Indeed, Palestinian churches, especially those that successfully underwent a process of Arabizing the clergy, were able to provide the congregation with means for communal social and educational progress, and, at times of hardship, means of survival. At times, the presence of the church saved the community from outright displacement; for example, Nazareth was salvaged in 1948 and became a refuge for Palestinians forcibly displaced from surrounding villages mainly because Israeli leaders feared the Vatican's response.[90] However, the potential of the church to assist the Palestinian Christian community was curbed by several factors.

This explains the reason why movements formed to mobilize the community into holding the church leadership accountable, to Arabize the church and the patriarchate, and to hand control of land and property over to the local congregational councils. This is especially, but not exclusively, the case with the Greek Orthodox Patriarchate. Palestinian Christians across their denominational lines have criticized both clergy and state and have risen up in a long-term struggle to Arabize and democratize the church. The well-known struggle for the Arabization of the Orthodox Church has been the most influential factor in the social and political formation of the Orthodox community, and is dialectically linked to the construction and maintenance of the Palestinian identity.[91] In fact, it contributed to shaping patterns of Palestinization and Arab nationalism in the Palestinian community early in the twentieth century.[92] Many local members of Orthodox congregation councils were active proponents and pioneers of nationalist and commmunist political parties.[93] They saw the liberation of religious endowments and the church as part of the struggle for land restitution to the Palestinians in general. The unilateralism of Theophilos and his disregard for the community's concerns have sparked outrage among Palestinians and prompted renewed action from the congregation. Councils have called for the boycott and isolation of Theophilos,[94] and new grassroots congregational movements have been formed by Palestinian Christians in the 1948 Territories such as "The Orthodox Truth Movement—No to the Forfeiture of Church Property."

90 Abd al-Jawad, "Why We Cannot Write"; Ghanim, "Nakba," 1:16.

91. Bowman, "Nationalizing the Sacred."

92. Robson, "Communalism and Nationalism."

93. Robson, "Communalism and Nationalism"; see Kaufman, *Arab Society in Israel*, 113.

94. Melhem, "Are Days Numbered."

The cause of democratizing and opening church institutions for communal management was also taken up by the Roum Catholic *Jamyiat Abnaa' Abrashiyat al-Jalil* or the Society of the Sons of the Archeparchy of Galilee, which was founded in 1989 by a group of prominent Palestinian Christians within the congregation.[95] Concerns about the well-being of the community and increasing migration led to attempts to strengthen and develop it through the institution of the archeparchy. Members of the foundation sought to address the controversial land management of the archeparchy through letters to the archbishop, open letters in the media, letters to the Vatican, and, ultimately, through demonstrations. Their demands were for the formation of laity-clergy councils to conjointly manage the affairs of the archeparchy with the aim of developing the community through the institution of thecChurch by, among other things, providing hospitals, family and student housing, college funds, and the creation of an Arab university. After multiple broken promises by the church leadership who disregarded an official report on the subject, many institutions such as orphanages and monasteries were given up. The activities of the foundation waned with the election of Elias Chacour as archbishop in 2006.[96]

Of course, other Palestinian churches such as the Anglican, Latin, and Maronite churches went through their own particular struggles with the state as pertains to landed property. While we will not be able to cover these within the limited scope of this research, it is important to note that these struggles were contiguous with the efforts of the Orthodox congregation's communal cause and the Palestinian national cause in general. The story of the Anglican Church in particular is quite enlightening in this respect. Introduced in Palestine a little over 150 years ago, the Anglican mission evolved quickly among proselyting Palestinian Christians to become an Arabized church by the late 1940s. Church leadership, in its Arab and non-Arab (mostly English) components, were advocates of the struggle of Palestinians against Zionism. Mostly due to the church's anti-Zionist views, most of the church's property was expropriated by the Israeli state in 1948 through the Custodian of Absentee Property. The struggle to gain back these estates began in the 1950s and lasted until 2005, when the church was able to repossess most, but not all, of its original holdings.[97]

The Latin Catholic Church is another prominent church in Palestine. One of the most prosperous and powerful, it has benefited the community in several ways by operating schools, three major hospitals, institutions for

---

95. E. Khoury, *Signatures on the Sand*.
96. E. Khoury, *Signatures on the Sand*.
97. Frantzman et al., "Anglican Church."

persons with special needs, etc. Since the 1960s, the Vatican has taken action to Arabize or centralize the Latin Church locally. To this end, in 1964, the Vatican appointed an Arab patriarchal exarchate, Hanna Kildani.[98] Later, in 1987, the first Arab Palestinian patriarch, Michel Sabbah, was ordained. Most recently however, the Latin Church decided to cover debts accumulated in a university project it embarked upon in Jordan by selling 270 dunams of land in Nazareth, a city particularly desperate to provide housing for the young generation. This sparked many protests and condemnations by members of the laity and gave birth to a short-lived revolt by the Latin Catholic community. Weekly protests took place under the Church of Annunciation to demand transparency and the use of estate for the benefit of the community, under the banner *ard al-bishara mish lal tijara* or "the land of annunciation is not for sale."[99]

While nationalism does not necessarily penetrate every aspect of the struggle to democratize the church, such as in this case of the Latin Church, activities by Christian Palestinians promoting church reformation and communal control over collective property cannot be seen outside the community's struggle against a reality of land dispossession, the right to be within the land of Palestine, to own land in it as a full citizen, and to be able to determine their destiny on it.

III- PALESTINIAN CHRISTIAN BELONGING: BETWEEN THE NATION AND THE JEWISH NATION-STATE

The Palestinian Christian community is often treated in research from the viewpoint of an endangered religious "minority within a minority," highlighting their disposition as a Christian minority within a mostly Muslim society, existing within a dominant Israeli Jewish majority.[100] This stance correlates with researchers' focus on internal identitarian dynamics when analyzing Palestinian Christian belonging and affiliation.[101] Such an outlook attracts attention in a contemporary regional environment in which different strands of religious fundamentalism are on the rise. The research

---

98. McGahern, *Palestinian Christians in Israel*, 120–21.

99. Hassa, "Why Does Latin Church."

100. See R. Farah, "Identity and Culture."

101. These insights concur with other recent research highlighting the liquidity of Christian identity within Israel. For instance, see Fakhoury, "Christian Arabs in Israel." Fakhoury states that Christian Arabs in Israel adopt contradictory boundary strategies; a contraction strategy from the Arab category in favor of the Christian category on the one hand, and a strategy of equalization with the Jewish-Israeli majority by emphasizing the Arab component of their identity on the other hand.

of Kårtveit Bård, for instance, on Palestinian Christians in the West Bank explores the community's "dilemmas of attachment."[102] Multilayered affiliations are germane to the historically richly diverse region of which Palestine is a part and where national, regional, familial, and religious affiliations have coexisted in relative harmony throughout its history.[103] However, as scholars of the Arab world have shown, the decline of Arab nationalism in the region and the absence of unified national leadership have given rise to sectarian attitudes among communities administered by postcolonial nation-states.[104]

In order to understand this multilayered dynamic of attachment among Palestinian Christians in the 1948 Territories, it is important to locate internal communal conflict, religious or otherwise, within the structure of citizenship maintained by the settler-colonial Jewish state. In this section, we will analyze various state political practices involved in the shaping and reshaping of religious, communal, and national affiliations among Palestinian Christians in the 1948 Territories. We categorize these state practices into three types of colonial interaction with the community: (1) *elimination*, i.e., practices aimed at the physical and symbolic negation of non-Jewish presence on the land; (2) *fragmentation*, i.e., practices aimed at politically dividing the colonized community based on religious affiliation; and (3) *co-optation*, i.e., practices aimed at promoting separatist leadership among religious groups.

(1) Elimination: Settler Colonialism and Jewish Fundamentalism

First and foremost, Christians have faced institutional racist discrimination since 1948 as part of an indigenous Palestinian group within a Jewish state increasingly working to cement Jewish ethnocracy.[105] Discrimination against Palestinian Christians is part of Israel's discrimination against the Palestinian minority as a whole due to the Zionist ideology (religious and nonreligious) that does not recognize the existence of other national groups. We can see this policy taking shape with the 1952 Law of Return that granted Jews worldwide the right to settle and become citizens within the state, while taking away the same right from Palestinians who were displaced. In 2018, Israel enacted the Basic Law: Israel as the Nation-State of the Jewish People (aka the Nation-State or Nationality Law), which reasserted the

102. Bård, *Dilemmas of Attachment.*

103. For more about Palestinian identity and its history as a site of multilayered attachments, see R. Khalidi, *Palestinian Identity.*

104. Bishara, "Matters of Identity."

105. Yiftachel, *Ethnocracy.*

ideological pennants of the basic Zionist principle of exclusive Jewish sovereignty.[106] So while Palestinians in the 1948 Territories are citizens, they are denied recognition of a right to belong to the land or any claim to collective rights within it. The law explicitly constitutionalizes Jewish exclusivity and significantly downgrades the status of the Arabic language of Palestinian citizens[107] and "construct[s] the Palestinians, through legal means, as an alien population."[108] As Israeli historian Ilan Pappe claims, the law is "a natural, almost inevitable, product of the Zionist project in Palestine."[109]

Israeli scholar Oren Yiftachel argues that "ethnocracy" is the model by which settler-colonial societies must be understood. He describes how the Israeli nation-state uses ethnicity as the primary criterion for the distribution of power and resources.[110] However, "ethnic stratification" does not suffice to coherently comprehend the legal, constitutional, and institutional structure of the settler-colonial state. Nadim Rouhana and Areej Sabbagh, in their study, point out that the model through which the relationship between Israel and its Palestinian citizens should be read is that of settler colonialism. In the settler-colonial political-economic structure, as Patrick Wolfe argues, settler-colonial social formations are based on "elimination," on the "irreducible element" of accessing and appropriating indigenous lands in a process of further accumulating and centralizing the capital on which all colonial systems operate.[111] Hence, Rouhana and Sabbagh describe Palestinian citizenship in Israel as "settler-colonial citizenship" within an economic and political structure that facilitates Jewish exclusive control over Palestinian land; the Judaization of Palestinian space; the elimination of history; and the suppression of demographic growth, national identity, and collective political will.[112] This reasserts what we have already argued in the last section, that

---

106. The law states that: "(a) The Land of Israel is the historical homeland of the Jewish people, in which the State of Israel was established; (b) The State of Israel is the nation state of the Jewish People, in which it realizes its natural, cultural, religious and historical right to self-determination; (c) The exercise of the right to national self-determination in the State of Israel is unique to the Jewish People. This law—which has distinct apartheid characteristics—guarantees the ethnic-religious character of Israel as exclusively Jewish and entrenches the privileges enjoyed by Jewish citizens, while simultaneously anchoring discrimination against Palestinian citizens and legitimizing exclusion, racism, and systemic inequality. For more on the legal consequences of the nation-state law, see Adalah, "Israel's Jewish Nation-State Law."

107. H. Jabareen and Bishara, "Jewish Nation-State Law."

108. Sa'di, "Nation State," 172.

109. Pappe, "Israeli Nationality Law."

110. Yiftachel, Ethnocracy.

111. Wolfe, "Settler Colonialism."

112. Rouhana and Sabbagh-Khoury, "Settler-Colonial Citizenship."

is, despite Palestinian Christians in the 1948 Territories being designated as citizens of the state, their collective rights over land and space are absolutely denied. Indeed, dispossession and Judaization of their land have defined their history.

In addition to the various discriminatory measures that Palestinian citizens are subject to, the emphasis on the Jewishness of the state and the land gave birth to a religious Zionism that began in the 1970s with Jewish fundamentalist groups and political parties promoting the cleansing of the land of all non-Jewish elements. Scholarship has highlighted the significant changes in Zionism since the end of the 1967 war. This process can be traced back to the growth of the settler project in the 1967 territories and the theological messianic aspects embedded in it.[113] After 1967, the Zionist project became more aligned to religion, while in parallel, Orthodox Judaism in Israel was more aligned to the Zionist project.[114] Thus, we have witnessed drastic sociological and political changes within Israeli Jewish society, notably within the political spectrum where prominent actors have emerged, such as the Orthodox and Religious Zionist movements.

In spite of Israel's efforts on the international stage to present itself as the protector of religious minorities, state institutions have not been spared the impact of religious Zionist agendas. Over the last two decades, there has been a marked rise in instances of institutional restriction of religious freedoms. For example, some institutions of higher education placed restrictions on setting up Christmas trees to celebrate Christmas: the University of Haifa turned down a request from the Arab Student Committee to set up a Christmas tree in 2004.[115] In 2016, the rabbi of the synagogue at the Technion-Israel Institute of Technology in Haifa prohibited a Christmas tree from being put up in the student house on the basis that this would "impinge on the Jewish identity on campus."[116]

Attacks against Christians and Christian sites by fanatical right-wing Jewish organizations (such as so-called "price tag" attacks) have been on the rise during the last two decades. Given the lack of a dedicated monitoring center, there are no accurate data on the number and nature of these attacks.

---

113. For instance, Kimmerling, Bishara, and Ghanem have asserted that in the post-war period, the settler project shifted dramatically and was a watershed in the relationship between Zionism and Judaism. In his ground-breaking work, Kimmerling substantiated that Zionism became more embedded with Judaism, and Judaism and Orthodox denominations more connected with Zionism. See Kimmerling, "Religion, Nationalism and Democracy"; Abu-Irshaid, "Dr. Ghanem: Deep Changes."

114. Abu-Irshaid, "Dr. Ghanem: Deep Changes."

115. Adalah, "Request."

116. Shpigel and Khoury, "Rabbi of the Technion."

The most prominent attack involved the arson of the Loaves and Fishes Church in Tabgha, Tiberias, in June 2015. Two extremist Orthodox Jews were accused of starting a fire and causing severe damage to the church. Other attacks have included offensive graffiti against Christianity.[117] This was not the first attack against the Tabgha church; it had been vandalized one year earlier.[118] Monasteries and churches in the city of Jerusalem are also subjected to attacks.[119] Last year, a Jewish extremist attempted to set fire to the Church of All Nations, also known as the Church or Basilica of the Agony. In 2015, an attack on the Benedictine Abbey of the Dormition in Jerusalem involved sabotage of the church as well as offensive and racist graffiti against Christians and Christianity.[120] Among many other assaults, a Catholic monastery near Beit Shemesh was vandalized in 2013.[121] Often, these attacks end without arrests or the release of suspects in court. This was the case in the 2015 attack on the Benedictine church in Jerusalem, where the key suspect was released without being punished.[122]

Scholars have described religiously motivated attacks as natural ramifications of Israeli colonial policies that sanctify Jewish supremacy.[123] As indicated above, many state policies are not overt or visible, but examination of the background of offenders lays bare incitement from religious, political, and spiritual Jewish circles and leaders against Christians. These groups provide a cover for these offences. For example, the leading extremist, right-wing activist Itamar Ben-Gvir (now a member of Knesset for an extreme right-wing party) represented a defendant in the case of the Tabgha church incident.[124] In a similar vein, amid increasing fascist attacks on Christians, in 2012, an Israeli extremist MK burned a copy of the Bible publicly in his Knesset office.[125]

Incitement is not limited to extremist politicians or personalities but has involved religious leaders and institutions. In 2019, *Yad L'Achim* (A Hand for Brothers), a Haredi Orthodox organization, released a statement

117. Rapad and Zitoon, "Accusation of Setting Fire."

118. Ashkenasi and Khoury, "Unknown Individuals."

119. Goldech and Predeson, "Attempt to Set Fire."

120. Yoruvsky, "Hate Crime."

121. J. Khoury et al., "Catholic Church on Arson."

122. J. Khoury et al., "Catholic Church on Arson."

123. Shalhoub-Kevorkian and David, "Is the Violence." Shalhoub-Kevorkian identifies acts of violence by groups as a direct result of a sacralized state and settler-colonial violence that sanctifies Jewishness and marks Palestinians as targets of elimination (Shalhoub-Kevorkian, "Sacralized Politics").

124. Rapad and Zitoon, "Accusation of Setting Fir."

125. King of Glory Jerusalem, "MK Michael Ben Arie."

warning of so-called "Christian symbols invading Israeli education institutions." The warning referred to festive events celebrating Christmas in
the public space or putting up a Christmas tree in some establishments or
mixed cities.[126] Extremist Orthodox incitement was apparent in 2019 when
Rabbi Shlomo Aviner published an article against the backdrop of the Notre
Dame de Paris fire, labeling Christianity as polytheism and implying that
the fire may have been divine retribution that was deserved by Christians.
Indeed, Aviner described Christians as the "number one enemy of Judaism
over the course of history."[127]

(2) Fragmentation: Sectarianism and the Shihab al-Din Affair

Since Zionism is based on the concept of an exclusively Jewish homeland,
Palestinian Arab national identity is officially and politically suppressed.
Palestinian citizens are perceived by the state through secondary layers of
affiliations and documents in formal Israeli institutions describing them as
"religious sects," "minorities," "non-Jews," and so on.[128] While Palestinian
Christians were at the forefront of Palestinian national politics in the early
twentieth century, they began to be legally defined as a religious minority
during British rule over Palestine. Arabs were treated legally and politically
as "religious communities" at the same time as the British administration
officially treated Jews as a national group, carrying forward the ethos of the
Balfour Declaration.[129] These policies can be traced back to the "divide and
conquer" strategies used by colonial powers historically to maintain control
over colonized native populations. Indeed, the Zionist movement during
the mandate years, as a utilitarian argument for colonization, sought to
portray itself as a "modern" national agent in Palestine vis-à-vis the "pre-
modern" scattered communities plagued by a history of sectarian division
and strife.[130]

Since its inception, Israel has operated a policy of fragmentation towards Palestinian citizens with the aim of dismantling Arab national unity
and dividing Palestinians into "minorities" according to ethnic, familial,
and religious affiliations.[131] As Lustick demonstrates in his 1980 study, in

---

126. Bhol,"Yad Laachim Warns."

127. Shlomo, "Christian Church."

128. Jamal, "Nationalizing States and Constitution"; Lustick, *Arabs in Jewish State* .

129. Robson, "Communalism and Nationalism."

130. Sa'di, "Modernization as Explanatory Discourse."

131. Lustick, *Arabs in Jewish State*; Bauml, *Blue and White Shadow*, 82; Jamal,
"Nationalizing States and Constitution"; Jiryis, "Arabs in Israel"; Zureik, *Palestinians*

the first two decades of its establishment, when it came to the Palestinains who were given citizenship, Israel applied a mechanism of control and surveillance with three "functional requisites": segmentation, dependence, and co-optation, all reinforced through structural, institutional, and programmatic dimensions of power.[132] In addition to the suppression of national Palestinian leadership and representation, fragmentation is achieved by actively fostering internal divisions and sectarian and *hamulian* (lineage) tensions within Palestinian villages.[133]

In Palestine, political Islam began to rise in the 1980s, as part of the same wave that was taking place in the rest of the Arab world, except that in Palestine it was mostly focused on resisting Israel and giving services to the Muslim community. Religious extremism *did* have a base in the eruption of multiple cases of sectarian violence in various Palestinian villages and cities. Several events related to sectarian disputes unfolded within Palestinian society, specifically in multireligious towns such as Kufr Yassif, Shefa Amr, Nazareth, Mghar, Tur'an, Abu-Snan, and I'bilin. With the exception of Kufr Yassif, all these events occurred between 1998 and 2015.[134] The most significant events were in Mghar and Nazareth, where there were many wounded civilians, destruction of property, and an impact that has lasted to the

---

in Israel. Israeli governmental protocols illustrate multiple attempts to bring the fragmentation process to realization. For instance, an Israeli politician (Mordechai Namir) said in a government meeting: "We must attempt to divide the unity of the Arabs . . .we need to sustain an internal political division." In the same meeting, Barket Sha'al proposed to "reinforce sectarian interests in each sect through positive discrimination and providing benefits differently . . . in order to be contrary to each other . . . so that they will not merge together into a whole unit" (Bauml, *Blue and White Shadow*, 83). In addition, Moshe Dayan suggested: "*In* the matter of the Arabs, the existing divisions are urban, rural and Bedouin settlements. There should be more divisions" (Bauml, *Blue and White Shadow*, 8). Various studies show how the Zionist leadership posed the idea of isolating the Druze from the Palestinian struggle during the Palestinian uprising of 1936–39 (see Cohen, *Army of Shadows*, 254–56). The so-called Prime Minister's Adviser for Arab Affairs, Toledano, proposed to deal differently with the religious groups. He suggested prioritizing some benefits for the Druze, then for the Catholic Christians, then for the Orthodox Christians, and finally for Muslims (Benzamin and Mansour, *Sub-Tenants*, 82). To maintain sectarian interests, one of the MAPAI conclusions was to set up a list of Christians running for elections and two separate Muslim lists (Benzamin and Mansour, *Sub-Tenants*, 82). Also, a government report that included recommendations for the treatment of Palestinians stated, "Government policy for the last decade has striven to divide the Arab population into sects and regions . . . the sectarian policy and the *hamulian* divisions in villages aimed to prevent the formation of Arab unity" (Benzamin and Mansour, *Sub-Tenants*, 82).

132. Lustick, *Arabs in Jewish State*, 77; McGahern, *Palestinian Christians in Israel*, 4.

133. Jamal, "Nationalizing States and Constitution"; Bauml, *Blue and White Shadow*.

134. McGahern, *Palestinian Christians in Israel*, 126.

present day. While symbolic religious factors played a part in the dispute, they cannot be understood outside the reality of dispossession and economic crisis suffered by these communities in the face of neoliberal policies.[135] We examine the events that unfolded in Nazareth for elaboration.

Between 1997 and 1998, tensions between Muslims and Christians played out in the city of Nazareth over the fate of a six-thousand-square-foot plot of land in the city center.[136] The source of conflict was the "Nazareth 2000" project launched by the municipality in the 1990s (then led by the Communist Party), which aimed at renovating areas of the city. However, the right-wing coalition led by the Likud Party in alliance with ultra-Orthodox parties such as Shas, which had strong anti-Christian sentiments, took control of the Israeli government in 1996, and funding was withheld. The municipality was granted permission to pursue the project only on a limited scale, particularly in the plaza in front of the Latin Basilica Church, which was under the control of the Israeli Land Administration.[137] The project was opposed by the Islamic Movement of the local council, which argued that this space was an Islamic waqf (endowment) where an ancient Muslim leader by the name of Shihab al-Din is believed to have been buried. The Islamic movement, and later, Muslim protesters, demanded that a mosque be constructed on the site.[138] The Islamic Movement erected a tent and established a camp over the site, while proclaiming its intention to build Shihab al-Din mosque on it. Hundreds of Muslim protesters began to visit the camp, in which they also conducted their weekly Friday prayers.

Tensions increasingly escalated within the city, culminating in conflicts between Christian and Muslim protesters in April 1998. Dozens were injured, with homes, property, and vehicles extensively damaged. A year later, representatives of Likud and other religious parties in the government ruling coalition visited the tents that still stood in the disputed square and publicly expressed their support for the building of the mosque.[139] Indeed, the government's handling of the incident prompted many Palestinians

135. In many of these cases, especially in Mghar, members of the Druze community were undergoing an economic downturn and perceived Christians as monopolizing the economy. This was expressed through violence.

136. McGahern, *Palestinian Christians in Israel*, 131.

137. A commission of inquiry into the Shihab al-Din affair headed by Professor Raphael Israeli showed that one of the reasons why funding was halted was because the new government coalition, of which the ultra-Orthodox Sephardic Shas Party was a part, loathed Christians and Christianity. The plaza was the only project that could move forward (Tsimhoni, "Shihab al-Din Mosque Affair").

138. McGahern. *Palestinian Christians in Israel*, 132.

139. Tsimhoni, "Shihab al-Din MosqueAaffair," 208.

(Christian and non-Christian) to claim that authorities were not interested in resolving the dispute but were engaged in a policy of "divide and rule." This event and various others like it raise questions about the relationship between the Palestinian Christian community and the broader, predominantly Muslim community of which it is a part, in light of Israeli state policies towards Palestinian citizens, whether Christian, Muslim, or Druze.

The Shihab al-Din affair is a clear example of how the rise of Islamic political movements affected Christian-Muslim relations in Palestine. However, as many scholars have indicated, the incident cannot be viewed outside the broader context that harbored it and the role played by the government.[140] The fact that the Islamic Movement was able to rally support among Muslims in Nazareth against the municipality is partly due to the alienation felt on the part of Muslim-majority neighborhoods in the east of the city in areas significantly marginalized by the Nazareth 2000 project, which was aimed mostly at tourist spots, i.e., Christian sectors of the city. Despite the involvement of the Vatican and various Catholic churches from around the world, and the opposition of moderate Muslims and even Arab Islamic states, the government insisted on supporting the construction of the mosque in the square. Two ministerial investigations were conducted by two consecutive governments in 1999, with one proposing to set up a new police station next to the square in order to maintain order. After substantial pressure, subsequent governments decided to block the construction of the mosque. It is clear that the right-wing government had an interest in the dispute between the nascent Islamic Movement and the secular Communist-led municipality, in line with the interest of dismantling the infrastructure for a national Arab leadership. Twenty years later, the wounds of the affair have yet to heal, breeding dormant sectarian sentiments among Christian and Muslim communities.[141]

This interpretation has been confirmed in a study in which local Islamic leaders stated that they used the case of Shihab al-Din as a tool to reorganize what they called "Muslim society" in the city by building schools, youth community centers, a hospital, libraries, and so on.[142] Therefore, as Azmi Bishara argued, Shihab al-Din was not a religious-based conflict but, rather, a political endeavor to reshape sectarian identities. However, Bishara and other critical scholars seem to have overlooked the spatial aspects of the case. In a field study on sectarian perceptions in Palestine, a number of interviewees posed the issue of the huge disparities between the Christian

140. Abu-Irshaid, "Nazareth from Shihab al-Din."
141. Tsimhoni, "Shihab al-Din Mosque Affair," 208.
142. Anbatawi, "Perception of Sectarianism," 70.

and Islamic endowments in favor of Christians.[143] This sectarian discourse surrounding endowments cannot be understood outside the spatial Israeli policies of expropriating land from Nazareth to build Jewish settlements, in addition to maintaining Christian endowments while expropriating those of Muslims. Israel's repressive land policy towards Palestinian citizens thereby maintains and consolidates the internal sectarian conflict between religious groups.[144]

(3) Co-optation: The Case of Christian Nationalism

The policy of encouraging the recruitment of targeted Palestinian groups into the Israeli army is seen as a pivotal tactic in isolating some groups from the rest of the Palestinian population, as well as reinforcing sectarian division. A case in point is the Druze community, defined by Israel as a distinct non-Arab national group in 1956 and forced into mandatory Israeli military service. Archived government reports show that Moshe Sharon (advisor to the prime minister 1978–1984) suggested that the government also consider Christian enlistment in the army. Benjamin Arieh, who later replaced Sharon, suggested allocating some benefits to the Druze sect and encouraging the recruitment of Bedouins and Catholics into the army.[145] In the contemporary era, new attempts to enlist Christians into the Israeli army have emerged, especially after the Arab uprising and the eruption of religious-based violence that legitimized dormant sectarian sentiments in the community (Muslims and Christians) and paved the way for a marginal, yet rising, trend of Christian nationalism.[146]

The Christian Nationalist movement within the Palestinian Christian community is represented by the personalities of Jubrael Naddaf, an Orthodox priest based in Nazareth; and Shadi Khalloul, an Arab Maronite and an Israeli politician and activist based in the Galilean Palestinian Christian-majority village of Jish. Commonly referred to as the "spiritual father" of the Israeli Christians Recruitment Forum, the Orthodox priest from Nazareth founded an association to encourage the drafting of Palestinian Christians into the Israeli military. A resident of Jish and self-proclaimed representative of the Free Christian Voice, Shadi Khalloul has dedicated his life to Aramaic Nationalism and is a political member of the far-right Zionist nationalist

---

143. Anbatawi, "Perception of Sectarianism," 70.

144. Anbatawi, "Perception of Sectarianism," 70.

145. Benzamin and Mansour, *Sub-Tenants*, 82–83.

146. Felsch, "Christian Political Activism."

party, Yisrael Beiteinu (Israel Is Our Home).[147] In 2014, Khalloul founded the Israeli Christian Aramaic Association (ICAA), which primarily aims to revitalize and preserve Aramaic Syriac as a language and "heritage" among Palestinian Maronite Christians, and to educate Jews and Christians around the world about the Aramaic culture and history.[148] The main objective of his educational work with Christian-Jewish youth, as Khalloul puts it, is to teach them about their "common roots" as "Christians that developed from Judaism."[149] His efforts have been controversial among Christian Palestinians and Palestinians in general, and much like Jubrael Naddaf, he has been criticized for promoting Israeli interests and stirring up new divisions within the Palestinian community. In 2014, through the efforts of Khalloul and his organization, the Ministry of Internal Affairs made what Naddaf referred to as a "historical decision" to officially recognize Aramaic as a legitimate nationality.[150]

Naddaf and Khalloul's self-identification as Aramaeans is based on an interpretation of Christian tradition that self-excises Christian belonging from the broader Arab national belonging. Aramaean-ness as an ethno-religious national belonging bases its legitimacy on biblical narratives in the same way that Jewishness is understood according to Zionist interpretations. The assertion of common ancestry between Aramaean-ness and Jewishness serves the Aramaic movement politically as it strategically positions the imagined Christian sect within an ethnocratic political hierarchy in which the Jewish people are the only group entitled to collective national rights on the land. The narrative focuses on Palestinian Christians as an endangered minority due to its existence within the Muslim majority and their need for protection from the Israeli state, and the view that Jews and Christians share a common cause against Eastern culture and, hence, recruitment.[151]

The ideological projection of this movement puts the resurgence of the Aramaean identity, unpolluted by the 1,400-year-old history of illegitimate and still ongoing Islamic "invasion," at the center of collective aspiration.[152]

---

147. Dillon, "Meet the Christian Israeli."

148. Khalloul himself served as a paratrooper in the Israeli army in 1993 and actively works to encourage the drafting of Christians into the military. He founded the Christian-Jewish Pre-Army Preparatory Program to "prepare Christians and Jews for the IDF by giving them training and education on navigation, leadership, Christianity, Judaism, Aramaic and the history of Israel" (Dillon, "Meet the Christian Israeli").

149. Dillon, "Meet the Christian Israeli."

150. Nabulsi, "Palestinian Youth."

151. Nabulsi, "Palestinian Youth."

152. As Khalloul nostalgically exclaims as he recollects the life of Arameans in the seventh century, "In these high valleys they could preserve their religious and national

The quest for the collective good becomes based on a salvage mentality where the ideal future envisions a place where the community can once again be untainted by Islamic invasion. This is achieved through the state-sponsored reeducation of Christians into a supposed ancient culture.[153] This political ideology of self-preservation, as posited by the Aramaic nationalists, is tied to a moral/political commitment to integrate into the Israeli state security institutions. "Assimilation" and "loyalty" seem to be key values espoused by Naddaf to be upheld by the Christian community. The vision, Naddaf proclaims, is "moving forward to prove our loyalty [to the state], to accept our duties and receive our rights, with the hope that the state will want, and support us as well."[154] It is through this form of assimilation that the community could achieve equality with the Jewish people, through the sharing of the "rights and duties" of that state or what Rhoda Kanaaneh calls "conditional citizenship."[155] In other words, the recruitment of Christians to the army—whatever such service may provide for the individual members of the group—will never address the fundamental basis on which the settler state is built with exclusive territorial and collective rights for only one ethnic group. Under such a system, no matter how hard they may try and wish it could be otherwise, Christian Arabs are destined to remain non-Jews in a Jewish state.

It is important to stress here that support for the movement among Palestinian Christians is very low. A recent study among Palestinian youth in the 1948 Territories showed that 65 percent of Palestinian Christians have a sense of belonging to the Palestinian nation, 82.6 percent believe that

peculiarity as an Aramaic population" (Israeli Christian Aramaic Association, "Never Again").

153. Khalloul went as far as to propose building an isolated Christian Maronite town (Dillon, "Meet the Christian Israeli").

154. Liaison Committee, "Israel Christian Recruitment Forum."

155. Kanaaneh, *Surrounded Palestinian Soldiers*, 31. This discusses the false promises of "equal rights" made by the state to Arabs who joined the Israeli army. Kanaaneh writes: "Judaization policies target all Arabs—whatever their loyalties, military service or political affiliations—and largely override any attempt to co-opt, Israelize or integrate small groups within the Arab population" (Kanaaneh, *Surrounded Palestinian Soldiers*, 77). The ethnocratic structure that privileges Jews over non-Jews will remain intact, and this is why Arab recruits are very rarely rewarded as promised. Kanaaneh notes: "These cases are the result of the supremacy of one set of goals—of creating a homogeneous nation-state of and for Jews, and promoting their particular demographic, economic, linguistic, cultural and political interests. The individual Palestinian soldier may be able to achieve certain material and symbolic gains as long as these do not conflict with the ethnic goals of the state. In the end, the military, like all other state institutions, is a tool the dominant majority wields to preserve Jewish privilege" (Kanaaneh, *Surrounded Palestinian Soldiers*, 77) .

Israel is not a democratic state for Jews and Arabs, and the absolute majority (90.9 percent) reject Arabs having to perform civic service, which means that they also reject military service.[156] Our analysis of the voting patterns of Christians proves that the overwhelming majority back the Joint List, which is composed of Arab parties.[157] Hence, we see the attempts represented by Naddaf and Kahlouol as embodying the interests and discourse of the Israeli nation-state, yet shaped through narratives of salvation in which the community is engaged in its struggle to remain.

IV—A STRUGGLE FOR LAND, IDENTITY, AND UNITY: AL-BAQAA'

The struggle to remain, i.e., *al-baqaa*, for Palestinian Christians in the 1948 Territories faces a multifaceted reality that facilitates the uprooting of the Christian Arab presence. This reality is embedded within the political structure that dominates the community as: (1) non-Jewish citizens within a Jewish state, (2) a colonized indigenous population undergoing a history of dispossession, and (3) a Christian community within a broader multifaith national community. Maintaining that presence entails a struggle against forces of uprootedness emanating from the settler state as it embodies the ideological pillars of Zionism. We have located these forces of uprootedness within three dimensions that define the Palestinian Christian presence: (1) the demographic, economic, and educational standing of the community; (2) the community's control of and ownership over collective land and space (both national and church-based); and (3) the Palestinian Christian sense of belonging and affiliation.

First, the denial of collective rights for the Palestinian community at large exacerbates the demographic and economic challenges already faced by the Arab Christian community. Despite having a relatively higher educational and economic status than the rest of the Palestinian community, the community as a collective is still subject to discriminatory policies as

---

156. Anabtawi, *Palestinian Youth in Israel*, 93–94.

157. Our analysis is based on the election results for the twenty-third Knesset in Arab cities composed of a high percentage (relatively) of Christians. For example, 92 percent of voters in Kufr Yassif voted for the Joint List, 96 percent in Nazareth, 80 percent in Fassouta, 84 percent in Shefa Amr, 78 percent in E'laboun, 92 percent in Iblin, and 74 perecnt in Jish (the hometown of Khaloul) (Central Election Committee for the 23rd Knesset, "True Results"). Notwithstanding, we have witnessed a retracting of the Christian presence in the formal political elite in the 1948 Territories since the 1970s in line with the increase in the number of Muslim and Druze politicians engaged in the local and central elite. See McGahern, *Palestinian Christians in Israel*, 52–53.

non-Jews within a Jewish state. Before and after the Nakba, education has historically been a means for survival and *baqaa'* for the Arab Christian community in the 1948 Territories, as it constitutes a primary cultural capital for Palestinian Christians in the country. Cuts to the budgets of Christian schools by the state—while the state heavily invests in Jewish religious schools—illustrate how ministerial policy actively drains Palestinian Christian institutions of learning, and thereby imposes forms of dispossession that deprive the community of its most essential means to remain and develop and progress within the homeland. We have argued that these processes cannot be understood in isolation from the citizenry structure that maintains collective Jewish rights on the land based on ethno-religious identity, while granting non-Jews rights only as individuals in a neoliberal economy and whose collective institutions of empowerment are targeted.

Second, Palestinian Christians find themselves in the context of a coherent history of Nakba that begins with their disposition as Palestinians who are dispossessed of the right to return, the right to their homeland, and the right to administer their own destiny. Land has been at the center of the Palestinian-Zionist conflict and has become the main pillar of Palestinian political struggle. Over the years, Israel has accumulated as much territory as possible with the aim of accruing as few Arabs as possible. Our findings suggest that the marginalization of communal control by the church cannot be seen outside the political context of Israel's settler-colonial ambitions. Israel benefits greatly from the reinforcement of traditional hierarchical power within the Arab Christian church to avoid scrutiny from Western allies, while at the same time suppressing the church's potential as a resource of power for the Palestinian community. The campaign by Orthodox Palestinians to Arabize and assume control of church institutions has been at the forefront of Palestinian national politics precisely because of the connection of land to the Christian presence and the Palestinian struggle for self-determination. The sentiment is shared by the different movements that have arisen against church hierarchies as they see that both the state and state corruption are damaging the prospects of a continued Christian presence on the land.

Third, state practices involved in the shape and reshape of communal boundaries based on sectarian-religious grounds fall within three categories: *elimination, fragmentation,* and *co-optation.* The eliminatory mechanism takes shape through state bureaucratic policies that deny recognition of national affiliation while encouraging extreme forms of Jewish fundamentalism that target the non-Jewish physical and symbolic presence on the land—for example, direct attacks against Christian places of worship that are not addressed properly by the state. Fragmentation occurs in internal communal conflict within the religiously diverse Palestinian community and is produced by competition over resources due to the dispossession that the entire community is undergoing. Co-optation is a function intended to subdue the community and in which a separatist Christian leadership, supported by the state, promotes "conditional rights" based on uprooting the religious community from the broader national community and proving its loyalty to the nation-state through military conscription.

Let us dwell briefly on this last point. The self-identification of Palestinian Christians as Arab Palestinians is challenged in multiple ways by state institutions that have created competing identifications and narratives. The phenomenon of rising sectarian tendencies gave rise to forms of separatism that claim to protect the Christian presence through acts of self-preservation. Here the practice of *baqaa'* is inverted as it adopts state ideological discourses that uproot the community from its broader sphere of belonging. This prompts Palestinian Christian activists to emphasize their Palestinian and Arab identities, and to oppose isolationist or sectarianist approaches, including those of the Greek Patriarchate, which has often rejected Arab claims to the church. Palestinian Christian opposition to sales of land by the church, and attempts to stress their Palestinian Arab identity and the Arab identity of the church, are intended not only to rectify the historical and national self-identification of the community as one that is undergoing an ongoing Nakba.[158] Rather, they are also attempts to draw a specific vision of a future that ties national liberation to the salvation of the land and, hence, the salvaging of Christian presence on that land. They deliberately center Palestinian Arab identity and extend it to spheres unmitigated by state borders or colonial segmentation and unbounded by state-centered bureaucracy, not as a "minority within a minority" seeking self-preservation but as part of a national group seeking self-determination.

We end this chapter with another event that took place one month after the scene we described at the beginning of the chapter, and in a nearby location. On May 18 in Nazareth, there was a national day of strike (aka Strike of Dignity) against Israeli aggression on Gaza and the ethnic cleansing of the Jerusalem neighborhood of Sheikh Jarrah (where land was also sold by the Greek Orthodox Patriarchate).[159] Young Palestinians, Christians, and Muslims took to the streets at noon and marched towards al-Madina square under the Latin Basilica of the Annunciation, also known as Shihab al-Din Square, where the violent events took place between Christians and Muslims in 1998. There, at the Shuhada Fountain (Martyrs' Fountain), the Palestinian

158. Bowman, "Nationalizing the Sacred."
159. Aslan, "New Deal by Theophilos"; *Sama News*, "New Leaked Deal."

flag waved high over the faces carved in stone and the names of three young Nazarene martyrs who fell during the second intifada. This is how a single space in Nazareth can simultaneously embrace the wounds of sectarian strife and the healing power of national unity. This scene, along with that at the beginning of the chapter, took place in one city in a matter of a month and illustrates how members of the Palestinian community who are of Christian faith share the same fate and will of their non-Christian compatriots as Palestinians determined to maintain their roots and remain in their homeland despite all attempts at exclusion, dispossession, and division.

BIBLIOGRAPHY

Abd al-Jawad, Saleh. "Why We Cannot Write Our Modern History without Using Oral Sources." [In Arabic.] In *Towards a Historical Narrative of the* Nakba, edited by Mustafa Kabha, 25–55. Haifa: Mada al-Carmel, 2006.

Abu-Irshaid, Suliman. "Dr. Ghanem: Deep Changes within Israeli Society Lead to a Shift to the Right." [In Arabic.] *Arab48*, Jan. 9, 2021. https://bit.ly/3FvUIFt.

———. "Nazareth from Shihab al-Din Crisis to the 'Who Is the President' Crisis." [In Arabic.] *Arab48*, Jan 16, 2014. https://bit.ly/3lqre3T.

Abu Raya, Jihad. "The Most Disputed Land on Earth: How the Greek Orthodox Church Sold Off Palestinian Plots." [In Arabic.] *Middle East Eye*, Dec. 6 2017. https://bit.ly/3euAqQz.

Adalah. "Israel's Jewish Nation-State Law." Adalah, Dec. 20, 2020. https://bit.ly/3O2RJEl.

———. "Absentees' Property Law." Adalah, n.d. https://bit.ly/3AdgNb8.

———. "A Request to Set Up a Christmas Tree in the Main Building at Haifa University." Adalah, Sept. 20, 2021. https://bit.ly/3aj56Sr.

Agbaria, Ayman. "Neoliberalism in the Arab Education System in Israel: The Hard State, the Soft State and the Surveillance." [In Arabic.] Mada al-Carmel, Jan. 2021. https://bit.ly/3OO9vW6.

Agbaria, Ayman, and T. Yousef Jabareen. "Minority Educational Autonomy Rights: The Case of Arab-Palestinians in Israel." *Virginia Journal of Social Policy & the Law* 24 (2017) 25–55.

Al-Haj, Majid. *Education, Empowerment, and Control: The Case of the Arabs in Israel.* Albany: State University of New York Press, 1995.

Amborozelly, Meryam. "The Israeli Ministry of Education Ranks Christian Schools among the Best Educational Institutes in the Country." [In Arabic.] Latin Patriarchate of Jerusalem, Aug. 22, 2016. https://bit.ly/2YAwLvx.

Anabtawi, Khaled. *Palestinian Youth in Israel: Perceptions, Attitudes, and Needs in a Complex Reality.* Haifa: Baladna-Association for Arab Youth, 2021.

———. "Perception of Sectarianism, Political Sectarianism and Sectarian Identity among Palestinians in Israel." [In Hebrew.] Master's thesis, University of Haifa, 2016.

Arab48. "Israel's Supreme Court Allows Tel Aviv University to Continue Violating Sheikh Muwanness Cemetery." [In Arabic.] *Arab48*, Aug. 14, 2012. https://bit.ly/3zeQX4E.

Ashkenasi, Eli, and Jacky Khoury. "Unknown Individuals Vandalized a Cross and Benches in the Courtyard of the Tabgha Church in Tiberias." [In Hebrew.] *Haaretz*, Apr. 29, 2014. https://bit.ly/3lot8BQ.

Aslan, Hiba. "A New Deal by Theophilos Selling Land in Jerusalem." [In Arabic.] *Al-Jazeera*, Nov. 19, 2017. https://bit.ly/3eyuzcY.

BADIL Resource Center for Palestinian Residency & Refugee Rights. *Survey of Palestinian Refugees and Internally Displaced Persons 2016–2018.* Survey of Palestinian Refugees and Internally Displaced Persons 9. Bethlehem: Al-Ayyam, n.d.

Bakri, Kasem. "Acre: Arab Schools Are Committed to the Solidarity Strike with Private Schools." [In Arabic.] *Arab48*, Sept. 7, 2015. https://bit.ly/3CNX9RA.

Baransy, Samir. "Private Schools in Israel: Between Parents' Demands and Government 'Discrimination.'" *i24News*, May 9, 2018. https://bit.ly/3BGNoVn.

Bård, Kårtveit. *Dilemmas of Attachment: Identity and Belonging among Palestinian Christians.* Social, Economic and Political Studies of the Middle East and Asia 112. Leiden, Neth.: Brill, 2014.

Bauml, Yair. *A Blue and White Shadow: The Israeli Establishment's Policy and Actions among Its Arab Citizens: The Formative Years: 1958–1968.* [In Hebrew.] Haifa: Pardis, 2007.

Bawalsa, N. Nadim. "Legislating Exclusion: Palestinian Migrants and Interwar Citizenship." *Journal of Palestine Studies* 46 (2017) 44–59. https://doi.org/10.1525/jps.2017.46.2.44.

Benzamin, Uzi, and Atallah Mansour. *Sub-Tenants: Israel's Arabs, Their Situation and Policy towards Them.* [In Hebrew.] Jerusalem: Koter, 1992.

Bhol. "Yad Laachim Warns: Significant Christian Signs Flow to Educational and Public Institutions in Israel Sponsored by 'New Year's Celebrations.'" [In Hebrew.] *Bhol*, Jan. 1, 2019. https://bit.ly/3bRkSIP.

Bishara, Azmi. "Matters of Identity." [In Hebrew.] In *Between "I" and "We" in the Construction of Identities and Israeli Identity*, edited by Azmi Bishara, 7–16. Jerusalem: Van-Leer, 1999.

Bowman, Glenn. "Nationalizing the Sacred: Shrines and Shifting Identities in the Israeli Occupied Territories." *Royal Anthropological Institute of Great Britain and Ireland* 28 (1993) 431–60. https://www.jstor.org/stable/2804234.

Central Bureau of Statistics. "Christmas 2020—Christians in Israel." [In Hebrew.] CBS, Apr. 19, 2020. https://www.cbs.gov.il/he/mediarelease/DocLib/2020/419/11_20_419b.pdf.

———. *Statistical Abstract of Israel 2020.* [In Hebrew.] CBS, 2020. https://www.cbs.gov.il/he/publications/DocLib/2020/Shnaton71.pdf.

Central Election Committee for the 23rd Knesset. "The True Results of the Elections to the 23rd Knesset: National Results." [In Hebrew.] Central Election Committee for the 23rd Knesset, Mar. 2, 2020. https://votes23.bechirot.gov.il/nationalresults.

Chabin, Michelle. "Greek Orthodox Church Faces Israeli Homeowners' Ire after Land Sales." *Religious News Service*, Jan, 15. 2019. https://bit.ly/3eN1737.

Chacour, Elias, and David Hazard. *Blood Brothers—The Dramatic Story of a Palestinian Christian Working for Peace in Israel.* Grand Rapids: Baker, 2013.

Cohen, Hillel. *Army of Shadows: Palestinian Collaboration with Zionism, 1917–1948.* Berkeley: University of California Press, 2008.

Davis, Rochelle. "The Growth of the Western Communities." In *Jerusalem 1948: The Arab Neighbourhoods and Their Fate in the War*, edited by Salim Tamari, 30–68. Jerusalem: Institute of Jerusalem Studies and Badil Resource Center, 2002.

Dillon, Kassy. "Meet the Christian Israeli Who Is on a Mission to Create the First Aramaean Christian Town In Israel." *Daily Wire*, Aug 28, 2018. https://bit. ly/3BU9UwO .

Fakhoury, Amir. "Christian Arabs in Israel: Guardians of Israeli Borders or Keepers of Arab Identity?" [In Hebrew.] Master's thesis, University of Haifa, 2014.

Farah, Fouad. *Living Stones: Arab Christians in the Holy Land*. [In Arabic.] Nazareth: Ministry of Science, Culture and Sports, 2003.

Farah, Rima. "Identity and Culture of Israeli Christians in the Face of Islamic Resurgence: Cultural Distinctiveness of a Minority within a Minority." *Levantine Review* 2 (2013) 138–58. https://bit.ly/3zPDwc2.

Felsch, Maximilian. "Christian Political Activism in Lebanon: A Revival of Religious Nationalism in Times of Arab Upheavals." *Studies in Ethnicity and Nationalism* 18 (2018) 19–37. https://doi.org/10.1111/sena.12262.

Forman, Geremy, and Alexandre Kedar. "Colonialism, Colonization, and Land Law in Mandate Palestine: The Zor al-Zarqa and Barrat Qisarya Land Disputes in Historical Perspective." *Theoretical Inquiries in Law* 4 (2003) 491–539.

Frantzman, J. Seth, and Ruth Kark. "The Catholic Church in Palestine/Israel: Real Estate in *Terra Sancta*." *Middle Eastern Studies* 50 (2014) 370–96. https://doi.org/ 10.1080/00263206.2013.871266.

Frantzman, J. Seth, et al. "The Anglican Church in Palestine and Israel: Colonialism, Arabization and Land Ownership." *Middle Eastern Studies* 47 (2011) 101–26. https://doi.org/10.1080/00263201003590482.

Ghanem, Honaida. "The Nakba." In *Palestinians in Israel: Readings in History, Politics and Society*, edited by Nadim N. Rouhana and Areej Sabbagh-Khoury, 1:16–25. Haifa: Mada al-Carmel, 2011. https://bit.ly/3ADINlv.

Goldech, Haiem, and Yaell Predeson. "Attempt to Set Fire to the Holy Church on the Mount of Olives: Luckily the Fire Did Not Spread." [In Hebrew.] *Ynet News*, Dec. 4, 2012. https://bit.ly/3AjYzSc.

Greenwood, Naftali. "Immigration to Israel: 'The Redeemers of the Land.'" Ministry of Foreign Affairs, Oct. 18, 1999. https://www.jewishvirtuallibrary.org/quot-the-redeemers-of-the-land-quot.

Hadid, Subhi. "Khalil Sakakini, a Revolutionary Educator Who Carried the Arab Identity of Palestine." [In Arabic.] *Al-Jazeera*, June 18, 2008. https://bit.ly/3sE28Cq.

Haifanet. "Mr. Edward Sheiban." [In Arabic.] *Haifanet*, Sept. 12, 2009. https://haifanet. co.il/archives/2453.

Hassa, Zakaria. "Why Does the Latin Church Want to Sell Land in Nazareth and for Whom?" [In Arabic.] *Arab 48*, June 15, 2020. https://bit.ly/3sE19SK.

i24 News. "The Private Schools' Strike Ends in Israel." [In Arabic.] *i24 News*, Sept. 27, 2015. https://bit.ly/3AL10OR.

Israeli Christian Aramaic Association. "Never Again Is Not Enough. We Request Actions as our Syriac Aramaic Christian Maronite Forefathers Did in Kfar Baram and Lebanon." Israeli Christian Aramaic Association, n.d. https://bit.ly/3bPznwO.

Israeli Prime Minister's Office. "Government Activity for Economic Development towards Minorities in the Years 2016–2020." [In Hebrew.] Israeli Prime Minister's Office, Dec. 30, 2015. https://bit.ly/3alC3On.

Jabareen, Hassan, and Suhad Bishara. "The Jewish Nation-State Law: Antecedents and Constitutional Implications." *Journal of Palestine Studies*, Dec. 18, 2019. https://bit.ly/3drIswh.

Jabareen, Yousef. "National Planning Policy in Israel." In *The Palestinians in Israel: Readings in History, Politics and Society*, edited by Nadim N. Rouhana and Areej Sabbagh-Khoury, 2:73–84. Haifa: Mada al-Carmel, 2018. https://bit.ly/3SJoux7.

Jamal, Amal. "Nationalizing States and the Constitution of 'Hollow Citizenship': Israel and Its Palestinian Citizens." *Ethnopolitics* 6 (2007) 471–93. https://doi.org/10.1080/17449050701448647.

Jiryis, Sabri. *The Arabs in Israel*. London: Monthly Review, 1976.

———. "The Arabs in Israel, 1973–79." *Journal of Palestine Studies* 8 (1979) 31–56.

Kanaaneh, A. Rhoda. *Surrounded Palestinian Soldiers in the Israeli Military*. Stanford, CA: Stanford University Press, 2008.

Katz, Itamar, and Ruth Kark. "The Church and Landed Property: The Greek Orthodox Patriarchate of Jerusalem." *Middle Eastern Studies* 43 (2007) 383–408. https://doi.org/10.1080/00263200701245969.

Kayyal, Muhammad. "Under the Policy of Racial Discrimination: Arab Village and Municipal Councils Are without Authority or Influence." [In Arabic.] *Jaridat Haq al-Awda* 36 (2009) 9–10. https://badil.org/ar/publications-ar/periodicals-ar/haqelawda-ar/item/1321-art-8.html.

Kaufman, Ilana. *Arab Society in Israel*. Vol. B. [In Hebrew.] Ra'ananna, Isr.: Open University, 2014.

Kedar, Alexandre. "The Legal Transformation of Ethnic Geography: Israeli Law and the Palestinian Landholder 1948–1967." *Journal of International Law and Politics* 9 (2001) 932–1000. https://bit.ly/3AguNRG.

King of Glory Jerusalem. "MK Michael Ben Arie Tore the Bible He Had Received in the Mailbox." [In Hebrew.] King of Glory Jerusalem, n.d. https://bit.ly/2WXlipF.

Khalidi, Rashid. *Palestinian Identity: The Construction of Modern National Consciousness*. New York: Columbia University Press, 1997.

Khalidi, Walid. *All That Remains: The Palestinian Villages Occupied and Depopulated by Israel in 1948*. Washington, DC: Institute for Palestine Studies, 2015.

Khoury, E. Hattem. *Signatures on the Sand: The Story of the Diocese of Galilee Members Association's Relationship with the Church Leadership*. [In Arabic.] Haifa: N.p., 2014.

Khoury, Jacky. "The Crisis of the Private Schools: Demanding a Meeting with Netanyahu." [In Arabic.] YouTube, July 26, 2016. https://bit.ly/3FH5okT.

Khoury, Jacky, et al. "The Catholic Church on the Arson in the Kinneret: Continuation of Aggression That Did Not Receive a Response from the Government." [In Hebrew.] *Haaretz*, June 18, 2015. https://bit.ly/3DvbWkX.

Khoury, Shehadeh, and Nikola Khoury. "A Brief History of the Orthodox Cause in Palestine and Jordan 1925–1992." In *A History of Jerusalem's Orthodox Church*, edited by Arab Orthodox Nahda Charity Association, 391–446. [In Arabic.] Jerusalem: Bayt al-Maqdis, 1992.

Kimmerling, Baruch. "Religion, Nationalism and Democracy in Israel." *Zmanim: A Historical Quarterly* 50/51 (1994) 116–31.

Lehn, Walter. "The Jewish National Fund." *Journal of Palestine Studies* 3 (1974) 74–96. https://doi.org/10.2307/2535450.

Liaison Committee. "The Israel Christian Recruitment Forum—Fr. Garbriel Naddaf (Hebrew)." YouTube, Oct 14, 2013. https://bit.ly/3vUVdpy. Video in Hebrew with English subtitles.

Lustick, Ian. *Arabs in the Jewish State, Israel's Control of a National Minority.* Austin: University of Texas Press, 1980.

Mack, Merav. "Christian Palestinian Communities in Israel: Tensions between Laity, Clergy and State." In *Sacred Space in Israel and Palestine,* edited by J. Marshall Berger et al., 284–310. London: Routledge, 2012. https://doi.org/10.4324/9780203137925-21.

Mansour, Bader. "Christian Schools in Israel Are in Danger of Being Shut Down." Come and See, Sept. 9, 2015. https://bit.ly/3oPTYoG.

Mansour, Johnny. *Arab Christians in Israel: Facts, Figures and Trends.* Bethlehem: Diyar, 2012.

———. *A New Vision of the Life & Works of Bishop Gregorios Hajjar.* [In Arabic.] Haifa: Al-Hakem, 2013.

McGahern, Una. *Palestinian Christians in Israel: State Attitudes towards Non-Muslims in a Jewish State.* Durham, UK: Durham University Press, 2011.

Melhem, Ahmad. "Are Days Numbered for Jerusalem's Greek Orthodox Patriarch?" *Al-Monitor,* Oct. 12, 2017. https://bit.ly/3QBXM7D.

Miaari, H. Sami. *Do Economic Changes Affect the Political Preferences of Arabs in Israel?* Haifa: Mada al-Carmel, 2020. https://bit.ly/3Dx7It8.

Mossawa Centre. *Land Day: A History, A Struggle, and a Memorial.* [In Arabic.] Haifa: Mossawa Centre, 2008.

Muaddi, Qassam. "Jerusalem's Orthodox Church Accused of Selling Off Land for 'Settlement Belt.'" *Middle East Eye,* Jan. 5 2021. https://bit.ly/3oI1msG.

Nabulsi, Razi. "Palestinian Youth: 'Aramaic Nationalism—A Clear Israeli Agenda.'" [In Arabic.] *Arab 48,* Sept. 21, 2014. https://bit.ly/3qQd5Qt.

Panet. "Denunciations of Brik's Arrest . . . and a Sharp Attack on Patriarch Theophilus: He Is Still Selling Properties." [In Arabic.] *Panet,* Apr. 7, 2021. https://bokra.net/Article-1460553.

Pappe, Ilan. "The Israeli Nationality Law—A Blueprint for a 21st Century Settler Colonial State." *Nuovi Autoritarismi e Democrazie* (NAD-DIS) 1 (2019) 75–86. https://doi.org/10.13130/2612-6672/11836.

Raheb, Mitri. "Palestinian Christians in Modern History: Between Migration and Displacement." In *Palestinian Christians: Emigration, Displacement and Diaspora,* edited by Mitri Raheb, 9–28. Bethlehem: Diyar, 2017.

Ramon, Amnon. *Christians and Christianity in the Jewish State: Israeli Policy towards the Churches and the Christian Communities (1948–2010).* Jerusalem: erusalem Institute for Israel Studies and Jerusalem Center for Jewish-Christian Relations, 2012.

Rapad, Ahia, and Yoav Zitoon. "An Accusation of Setting Fire to the Church: Jews Committed a Hate Crime against Christianity." [In Hebrew.] *Ynet News,* July 29, 2015. https://bit.ly/3ajDNYr.

Robson, Laura. "Communalism and Nationalism in the Mandate: The Greek Orthodox Controversy and the National Movement." *Journal of Palestine Studies* 41 (2011) 6–23. https://www.palestine-studies.org/en/node/42506.

Rouhana, Nadim N., and Areej Sabbagh-Khoury. "Settler-Colonial Citizenship: Conceptualizing the Relationship between Israel and Its Palestinian Citizens."

Settler Colonial Studies 5 (2014) 205–25. https://doi.org/10.1080/2201473x.2014
.947671.

Ryan, L. Joseph. "Refugees within Israel: The Case of the Villagers of Kfur Bir'im and Iqrit." *Journal of Palestine Studies* 2(1973) 55–81. https://doi.org/10.2307/2535631.

Sabada, Lesya. "Archbishop Joseph Raya—Apostle of Peace and Love." Arab America, Nov. 13, 2014. https://bit.ly/3Ag6D9V.

———. "Religious Peacebuilding: The Life and Work of Archbishop Raya as a Model for Religious Peacebuilding." PhD diss., Saint Paul University, 2016.

Sa'di, Ahmad H. "Modernization as an Explanatory Discourse of Zionist-Palestinian Relations." *British Journal of Middle Eastern Studies* 24 (1997) 25–48.

———. "The Nation State of the Jewish People's Basic Law: A Threshold of Elimination." *Journal of Holy Land and Palestine Studies* 19 (2019) 163–77. 10.3366/hlps.2019 .0213.

Sama News. "A New Leaked Deal under Which the Orthodox Patriarchate Sold Land in Sheikh Jarrah." [In Arabic.] *Sama News,* Nov. 4, 2017. https://bit.ly/3qpwWEo.

Sha'lan, Hasan. "Excellence in Strike: A Look at Church Schools." [In Hebrew.] *Ynet News,* Sept 18, 2015. https://bit.ly/3Ap4MMQ.

Shahar, Ilan. "Is the JNF Racist?" *Haaretz,* July 25, 2007. https://www.haaretz.com/1.49 55233.

Shalhoub-Kevorkian, Nadera. "Sacralized Politics: The Case of Occupied East Jerusalem." In *When Politics Are Sacralized Comparative Perspectives on Religious Claims and Nationalism,* edited by Nadim N. Rouhana and Nadera Shalhoub-Kevorkian, 134–58. Cambridge: Cambridge University Press, 2021.

———. "Necropolitical Debris: The Dichotomy of Life and Death." *State Crime Journal* 4 (2021) 49–65. https://doi.org/10.13169/statecrime.4.1.0034 (pages numbered 1–18 in online version).

Shalhoub-Kevorkian, Nadera, and Yossi David. "Is the Violence of Tag Mehir a State Crime?" *British Journal of Criminology* 56 (2016) 835–56. https://doi.org/10.1093/bjc/azv101.

Shlomo, Avniery. "The Christian Church Is on Fire." [In Hebrew.] *Srugim,* Apr. 16, 2019. https://bit.ly/3mGOr19.

Shpigel, Noa, and Jacky Khoury. "Rabbi of the Technion Banned Entering the 'Student House' Due to the Christmas Tree: 'Violation of Jewish Identity on Campus.'" [In Hebrew.] *Haaretz,* Dec. 20, 2016. https://bit.ly/3FrFzF7.

Suleiman, Haitam, and Robert Home. "'God Is an Absentee, Too': The Treatment of *Waqf* (Islamic Trust) Land in Israel/Palestine." *Journal of Legal Pluralism and Unofficial Law* 41 (2019) 49–65. https://doi.org/10.1080/07329113.2009.10756629.

Swa'ed, Rabea'. "Activists: The Leaking of Endowments Aims to Strike the Heart of the Arab Christian Presence." [In Arabic.] *Arab48,* Jan. 16 2018. https://bit.ly/3ctoBJ8.

———. "Al-Ba'na: Movement to Save the Orthodox Endowments." [In Arabic.] *Arab48,* Jan. 20, 2018. https://bit.ly/3FoiBxG.

Tamari, Salim. "The Phantom City." In *Jerusalem 1948: The Arab Neighbourhoods and Their Fate in the War,* edited by Salim Tamari, 1–10. Jerusalem: Institute of Jerusalem Studies and Badil Resource Center, 2002.

Tsimhoni, Daphna. "The Shihab al-Din Mosque Affair in Nazareth: A Case Study of Muslim-Christian-Jewish Relations in the State of Israel." In *Holy Places in the Israeli-Palestinian Conflict: Confrontation and Co-Existence,* edited by Marshall J. Breger et al., 193–230. New York: Routledge, 2010.

Or Committee. "Or Committee Recommendations." [In Hebrew.] Government of Israel, Oct. 2003. https://www.gov.il/BlobFolder/generalpage/official_inquiry_committees_october/he/הקדמה.pdf.

Wolfe, Patrick. "Settler Colonialism and the Elimination of the Native." *Journal of Genocide Research* 8 (2006) 387–409. https://doi.org/10.1080/14623520601056240.

Yiftachel, Oren. *Ethnocracy: Land and Identity Politics in Israel-Palestine*. Philadelphia: University of Pennsylvania Press, 2006.

Yiftachel, Oren, et al. *Alternative Master Plan for the Unrecognized Bedouin Villages in the Negev*. Abridged ed. N.p.: Bimkom, 2012. https://bit.ly/3BZGey7.

Yoruvsky, Anat. "Hate Crime: Court Acquitted the Accused of Setting Fire to Dormition Church for Lack of Evidence." [In Hebrew.] *Davar*, Mar. 11, 2019. https://bit.ly/3vXRYNY.

Zoubi, Munqeth. "Private Schools, National Fortresses That Must Be Preserved." [In Arabic.] *Panet*, June 7, 2015. https://bit.ly/3SEY2EZ.

Zureik, Elia. *The Palestinians in Israel: A Study in Internal Colonialism*. London: Routledge & Kegan Paul, 1979.

Christians in Jordan[1]

Paolo Maggiolini

THE SOCIOPOLITICAL AND ECONOMIC CONTEXT

FOR JORDAN, THE LAST two decades have been a period of growing challenges at both the domestic and the regional levels. Although Jordan is distinctive for its resilience and capacity to endure amid wars, revolutions, and instability, the kingdom has registered divergencies between its geopolitical commitments and geoeconomic interests. It is important to stress that among the many dynamics and vicissitudes that have challenged Jordanian stability, none have specifically targeted Christian Jordanians. This is also due to the constant commitment of national authorities to defusing any possible tension or process of polarization that could foster division between Muslim and Christian Jordanians. This policy was particularly important during the escalation of violence in Iraq (2005–2008) and Syria-Iraq (after 2011), with the rise of the jihadist threat that targeted Jordan as one of its enemies, as the terrorist attacks that hit the country confirm.

Accordingly, Christian Jordanians' attachment to and level of trust in the Crown and the kingdom remain high. They appreciate the efforts undertaken by official authorities to defend pluralism and the stability of the country. Compared with the situation of countries such as Iraq, Syria, Egypt, and, more recently, Lebanon, Christian Jordanians feel fortunate to live in the kingdom. Nevertheless, geopolitical turbulences and new forms

1. This chapter is based on a series of interviews undertaken in Jordan during Sept. 2021 with both Muslim and Christian Jordanians. The names of the interviewees have been anonymized to respect their requests. I am most grateful to all the people who supported and made this fieldwork possible.

of extremism from both Muslims and Christians still exert a negative impact on Christian perceptions of their future in the region.[2]

Since the accession to the throne of King Abdullah II in 1999, Jordan has sought to capitalize fully on its geopolitical position within the Middle East, aspiring to become a sort of lynchpin for US and Gulf interests in the region.[3] It has also invested heavily in integrating into the international market by joining the WTO and implementing economic reforms inspired by neoliberal principles. Since 2004, the "War on Terror" and neoliberal reforms became the two strategic policies for mitigating Jordan's vulnerability to regional spillover, and for gathering new aid and revenues from the international community. External aid is particularly necessary given the weaknesses of the Jordanian economy and its lack or scarcity of natural resources. Although these policies have achieved some important payoffs in the short term, Jordan's economic conditions have not structurally improved. It remains subject to a high budget deficit, high unemployment rates, and increasing poverty levels.

Furthermore, in recent years, its economic inefficiency has worsened. External revenues have not been used to reform the Jordanian system but have amplified its dysfunctions and structural limits. To date, this remains one of the main weaknesses of the Jordanian system and is a structural limitation to its reform. In fact, foreign aid is still considered the main propeller for the country's economic development rather than domestic production and trade. Jordan's commitment to neoliberal reforms has not made the country more autonomous and protected from external negative spillover. Quite the contrary, it has increased its dependency and exposure. This becomes clear looking at the impact of the main regional and international crises on Jordan's economy. The downturn in oil prices in 2005 reduced external aid to Amman, imposing a rapid economic adjustment. Similarly, the financial crisis of 2008–2009 amplified the negative performance of the Jordanian economy.[4]

Since 2011 Jordan has experienced recurrent periods of political and economic crises, fostering protests and demonstrations. Fiscal dysfunction, budgetary pressure, rising unemployment, the inability to cope with high rates of subsidies, and an overexpanded public sector have gradually weakened Jordanian institutions and their legitimacy.

This negative trend has been amplified by the emergence of new socioeconomic and spatial divides, increasingly eroding the Jordanian middle

2. This opinion was widely shared by those interviewed.

3. See Ryan, *Jordan in Transition.*

4. Ryan, "Jordanian Foreign Policy," 144–45.

class, a phenomenon begun much earlier during the late 1980s.[5] An increasing number of Jordanians have gone from middle class to lower class. Moreover, emigration has increased, not only abroad but also towards Amman. Given their demographic outlook, Christians feel particularly touched by these dynamics. Local communities in areas outside Amman have decreased in number, if not almost disappeared in locations such as Zarqa. This creates apprehension and disorientation for many Christians who have seen their traditional environment transform rapidly over the span of few decades.[6]

Although Jordan has not experienced the same dynamics as countries such as Tunisia, Egypt, and Syria since 2011, the rate of protests and demonstrations over the last decade is an alarming wake-up call.[7] Until today, the kingdom has been able to defuse internal tensions by implementing a mix of promises of political reforms and delays in structural economic reforms, especially in the field of subsidies. This has been possible thanks to external revenue from its traditional allies in the region and the international community. However, more recently, this balance has become more difficult to preserve. The Jordanian state has become stricter towards forms of protest and demonstrations. Traditional allies in the Gulf have constantly reduced the amount and quality of their aid to the kingdom, while US foreign aid has predominantly been used in the security sector and the military.[8]

During recent years, Trump's approach to regional politics added further concerns. His administration's stance toward regional politics, particularly the Israeli-Palestinian conflict, increased Jordan's suspicions that it was being sidelined and excluded from the main geopolitical and geoeconomic dynamics involving its traditional allies. This was coupled with the worsening of the country's relationship with Israel.

Concerns were amplified in early 2020 when Washington presented its "vision" for a resolution of the Israeli-Palestinian conflict, totally ignoring Amman's interests and position. In the summer of 2020, the Abraham Accords were viewed by Jordan with suspicion, although Jordan was unable to criticize them because of the significance of Jordan's relationship with the Gulf states.

These events unfolded while Jordan was experiencing a revival of protests and demonstrations, especially after 2018. In 2020, Jordan's economic outlook was particularly concerning. The national deficit reached 1.5 percent, the highest since 2018. Jordanian public debt scaled up to 99.1 percent,

---

5. Schwedler, "Spatial Dynamics of Arab Uprisings," 230–31.

6. Information collected through personal interviews.

7. Yom, ""New Landscape," 284–85; Tell, "Early Spring in Jordan."

8. Muasher, "Jordan: Fallout."

while national economic growth remained very limited at not more than 1.9 percent.[9] To this should be added the constant increase in unemployment rates to 19 percent, or more probably 23 percent.[10] Conditions worsened with the COVID-19 pandemic that imposed not only direct costs for dealing with the health emergency and all the economic damage it caused but also forced the government to cope with a parallel reduction in remittances from the Gulf and the return of a considerable number of workers from that region.[11]

Today, Jordan is working to reestablish its traditional role as the mediator of US interests in the region. The election of Biden and the formation of a new coalition government in Israel have been viewed positively. At the same time, the kingdom is seeking to diversify its diplomatic relationships both within the region and abroad. The trilateral relationship with Iraq and Egypt is seen to carve out new margins of maneuver, while dialogue with Russia and China can provide new sources of revenue and support. Furthermore, the country is trying to overcome its political and economic impasse by discussing reforms and confirming its commitment to reducing corruption, one of the focal points of Jordanian protests and demonstrations since 2011.

Nevertheless, the combination of socioeconomic and geopolitical challenges, especially those raised by the Israeli-Palestinian context, has revived previous and still unresolved issues in Jordan, namely questions of nationality and national identity. The country is engaged in an intense debate on the principle of equality and the importance of granting equal citizenship to all Jordanians, effectively implementing Jordanian laws that already recognize these principles. In Jordan, subnational identities, demographic representation, and geographical factors are still considered contentious topics of discussion that prevent the development of a comprehensive Jordanian national identity.[12]

Finally, an analysis of Jordan's socioeconomic context during the last two decades cannot ignore the issue of refugees. Without ignoring the impact of Palestinian refugees in the history of the country, during the early 2000s the kingdom experienced two waves of Iraqi refugees: in 2003, during the fall of Baghdad, and in 2014, after the fall of Mosul and the Nineveh

9. World Bank, "Jordan's Economic Update—April 2020."

10. World Bank, "Jordan's Economic Update—April 2021."

11. Department of Statistics, "-2.2% GDP Decrease Rate."

12. Muasher, "Jordan's Identity Question."

Plain. These waves came after those of 1991, during the first Gulf War, and in 1996, after the second Gulf War.[13]

The Iraqis of the 1990s wave (Muslims and Christians) were wealthy people. Most of them quickly moved elsewhere outside the country, while others stayed in Jordan and continued to run businesses. Some have even taken Jordanian nationality. The Iraqis of the last two waves were poorer, especially those of 2014 who arrived after being stripped of everything and persecuted. Furthermore, with the outbreak of the war in Syria, the kingdom also witnessed the arrival of Syrian refugees. Hundreds of thousands of Syrians left their country, with many heading to Jordan. Among them, some seventeen thousand Christians passed through Jordan.[14] After a few months, almost all of them left for Germany, Australia, Canada, and the United States. It is also important to mention thirty-five thousand Armenians from Aleppo that the Consul General of Armenia sent through Jordan to bring them to Armenia. Currently, there are a few Christian Iraqi and Syrian families in Jordan awaiting papers to emigrate.[15]

The wars in Iraq and Syria not only damaged Jordan's economy and security but gave the kingdom a challenging humanitarian burden as one of the main regional hubs for refugees. For a country with a structural lack of resources and a severe water shortage, the arrival of an increasing number of refugees has posed great challenges. It has had a detrimental impact on Jordan's limited economy, increasing the inflation rate and the cost of living. This has been partially mitigated by new aid from the region and the international community, but these new resources have not made it possible to defuse internal tensions at the socioeconomic level. In this framework, the arrival of new refugees has had a double effect on Christians in the country. On the one hand, by meeting and exchanging firsthand accounts of their experiences, Christians have grown concerned about their condition and situation in the region.[16] They have also reinforced their identity and relationship with other Christians of different traditions. On the other, by assisting refugees, church and community institutions have performed an important role for the whole country.

The role of local churches has been particularly important, especially in the case of Iraqi refugees. During their stay on Jordanian soil, these refugees were offered everything by Caritas in Jordan: rent, schooling for children, medical care in two Catholic hospitals in Amman, and monthly food

13. Lahham, "Être chrétien en Jordanie."
14. Lahham, "Être chrétien en Jordanie."
15. Lahham, "Être chrétien en Jordanie"; see Caritas Jordan, "Emergency Response."
16. Information collected through personal interviews.

coupons. Our Lady of Peace Center hosted dozens of Syrian Christian families until their departure. In 2014, Caritas Jordan worked with a turnover of almost $30 million.[17] These sums came from a number of Caritas organizations worldwide, especially in Germany, the United States, the Vatican, Denmark, France, and Belgium. The Iraqi Christians who arrived in Jordan belonged to the Syrian Catholic Church (the majority) or the Chaldean Church, with a few Assyrians. The Catholic Church, of the Latin and the Byzantine rites, opened its places of worship to its Iraqi brethren. Eighteen Catholic parish centers welcomed Iraqi brethren for a year in parish halls before providing them with more dignified accommodation.

DEMOGRAPHIC FACTS AND FIGURES: RELIGIOUS AND DENOMINATIONAL COMPOSITION

At first glance, the Christian presence in Jordan seems to perfectly mirror some of the main features and challenges that distinguish Christian landscapes within Middle Eastern countries, particularly multivocality/ecclesiastical fragmentation and decreasing demography. Nevertheless, the case of Jordan is also very different due to the specific history of Christianity in the country, and the origins and development of the Jordanian state to date.

In Jordan, the multivocal character of local Christianity is particularly evident. With a community that makes up just 3 to 4 percent of the total population, there are a considerable number of churches and denominations, both from Eastern and Western rites. In Jordan one can find at least seventeen different churches, namely Greek Orthodox, Roman Catholic (Latin), Greek Catholic (Melkite), Armenian Orthodox, Maronites, Assyrians, Copts, Anglicans, Lutherans, Seventh-Day Adventists, Presbyterians, Baptists, Free Evangelicals, Nazarene Church, Assemblies of God, Christian and Missionary Alliance, and the Church of Jesus Christ of Latter-day Saints. The United Pentecostals and Jehovah's Witnesses are registered as societies. This multivocal landscape has been enriched during the last decades thanks to the arrival of refugees from Iraq, plus the development of charismatic and evangelical movements.

While the Orthodox Church is the oldest presence within the country, in today's Jordan the Greek Orthodox account for almost 50 percent, while the Catholics number approximately 40 percent, half of them affiliated with the Roman Catholics (Latin) and the other half with the Greek

17. Information collected through personal interviews. See Caritas Jordan, "Emergency Response."

Catholics (Melkites). The rest are made up mainly of Anglicans and Lutheran Oriental Christians.[18]

At the social and familial level, such ecclesiastical diversity has never represented a challenge per se. Christian Jordanians have fluidly joined different denominations and churches within the same family or extended kin group. This pragmatic attitude towards church multivocality still endures today and is corroborated by the strong attachment to Arabness, to this land, its traditions and customs. This characteristic has played an important role in fostering conversions from one denomination to another.[19]

Christian Jordanians (especially the Orthodox) have constantly reiterated their Arabness in the public sphere, calling for the full indigenization of local church ecclesiastical hierarchies to show their attachment to the Arab and Jordanian dimension, and vice versa. This remains the case today.[20] In essence, when Christian community spheres and boundaries have been contested and politicized, these dynamics have remained within the Christian dimension. Therefore, they have never questioned Christian belonging to the Jordanian state and their positive relationship with the Crown and Muslim Jordanians. On the contrary, Christian Jordanians have sought support from them against what they consider an unjustified or anachronistic external control over local churches and their institutions. This is particularly the case for the Orthodox in the country. Far from being an old dynamic now exhausted, indigenization and Arabization are still important factors characterizing the life of local churches in the country, especially within the context of the established churches. The tensions experienced by the Orthodox in 2014 after the decision of the Holy Synod of the Greek Orthodox Patriarchate to target Jordanian and Palestinian clerics is an example.[21]

The positive relationship between Christian Jordanians and state authorities is also favored by the recognition of a dedicated quota system. This has been particularly useful in winning the support of Christian elites who have been able to develop and progress in the country. Jordanian law grants them 9 seats (out of 130) reserved for Christians in the House of Representatives, while traditionally the Jordanian Senate (nominated by the king) always includes some Christians. The same can be said for local government. This quota system was confirmed in the recent revision of the electoral law in 2016, and it secures Christian overrepresentation in comparison with their demographic weight.

18. Lahham, "Être chrétien en Jordanie."
19. Maggiolini, "Christian Churches," 37–38.
20. Information collected through personal interviews.
21. Hager, "Orthodox Issue in Jordan," 218–19.

At the ecclesiastical and community level, multivocality has potentially represented a challenge to Christian visibility and participation in the public domain. Multivocality has easily taken the shape of ecclesiastical fragmentation, dividing and separating the local Christian presence. It has fostered competition between churches and missionary institutions. It has also undermined Christians' capacity to speak with a single voice in the Jordanian public space, pushing them to seek refuge within the limits of their communities. Moreover, according to the various traditions and attitudes of the many church presences in the country, this has produced different modi vivendi, especially in the relationship between clergy and laity and the church-state relationship, further fragmenting the position of Christians in the public space.

This situation has partially improved, especially since the 1990s, thanks to greater ecumenical dialogue and cooperative relationships between the established churches in the country. The creation and development of the Council of Heads of Churches in Jordan had a positive effect. Nevertheless, this institution still needs further development in terms of internal procedures, legal recognition, and reaching out to Christians in the country who are not necessarily well informed on issues pertaining to the life and organization of the church.[22]

In Jordan today, one of the main issues affecting the intra-Christian dimension is not competition between established churches as in the past but the development of new Christian movements. This new phenomenon is a concern to both the traditional Christian hierarchies in the country and to a considerable number of Christian Jordanians. They fear that messianic and evangelical movements could damage the image of Christianity in the country, seeding at the grassroots level and within government negative perceptions regarding their relationship with Islam, their presence, role, and attachment to Jordan and the Middle East.[23] Christian Zionists and their role in the context of Israel-Palestine raise recurrent fears of weakening the image of Christianity and the level of integration of Christians in the country's social fabric.[24]

The number of Christians living in Jordan remains uncertain, as most available data are either out of date or come from the churches. Therefore, they are not fully reliable. As for the rest of the Middle East, state authorities do not provide updated statistics and simply disseminate figures that show that Christrians make up between 2 and 4 percent of the total population.

22. Information collected through personal interviews.
23. Information collected through personal interviews.
24. Information collected through personal interviews.

Today, in Jordan there are probably 200,000 to 250,000 Christians out of almost ten million Jordanian citizens.[25]

The uncertainty of the data is also because Christians living in Jordan have received scant attention from academia and international organizations. Most studies confirm that Christians in Jordan enjoy greater protection and rights than in other countries in the Middle East, but without providing new information about demographic trends and the reasons for the fall in numbers.

Although no updated data are available, Christians feel that their numbers are steadily decreasing, especially during the last ten years.[26] The reasons for this downward trend are multiple. Almost unanimously, Christians point out the lack of economic opportunities and the role of networks with family members who have already emigrated. These are traditional push factors. At the same time, politics plays a role, as well as growing extremism and the enduring geopolitical turbulence in the region. In essence, the mounting perception of insecurity pushes an increasing number of Jordanians, no matter what their faith, to plan to move abroad.[27]

RELIGION (CHURCH) AND STATE RELATIONS

In Jordan, church-state relations have always been based on a mutually cooperative foothold. This is particularly true for the established churches. The kingdom has granted legal recognition of their presence and institutions since the foundation of the emirate.[28] The established churches have endowed Jordanians with material and symbolic capital through their activities and initiatives, especially in the field of education.

This relationship has been established and developed according to a precise vision. The Jordanian political scene was not established in opposition to religious spheres but by bureaucratizing and controlling them, giving religious and community actors room for maneuver, albeit within defined limits and red lines.[29] This is true for both Muslims and Christians despite their differences and specificities. This policy has inspired the relationship between church and state in Jordan as a precise normative and

---

25. "Jordan," in Johnson and Zurlo, *World Christian Encyclopedia*, 141.

26. Information collected through personal interviews.

27. Information collected through personal interviews.

28. Maggiolini, "Christians of the Emirate," 25–26.

29. See Wiktorowicz, *Management of Islamic Activism*; see Lucas, *Institutions and the Politics*.

constitutional framework.[30] Jordanian law recognizes Islam as the religion of the state and the king (articles 2 and 28) but grants full equality to all its citizens before the law regardless of their religion, language, or race (article 6). It also recognizes the right to freedom of worship and religious belief in accordance with the customs and traditions of the country (article 14). Therefore, the right to religious freedom is not granted fully according to international standards, but Christian religious communities have the right to create their own educational institutions (article 19) and are entitled to judge issues relating to the personal status of their members through their community courts (articles 108 and 109).

In essence, the church-state relationship in the kingdom is based on a delicate balance between legal recognition and communal autonomy. This balance still inspires their relationship today. For example, recognized non-Islamic religious communities are not eligible for state subsidies, and are financially and administratively independent from the state. In fact, Christian institutions and activities can operate only if granted full recognition by the state authorities. The level of autonomy and capacity to operate in the country differs according to the level of recognition. This approach inevitably creates internal imbalances between the diverse Christian presences depending on their status as a fully recognized community or a simple society.

Nevertheless, this normative framework has allowed churches in Jordan to stabilize their presence and be active in their community fields and in Jordanian society at large. Discrepancies and differences derive from the peculiar Jordanian Christian landscape and from its ecclesiastically fragmented facet.[31] Catholics have traditionally sought to preserve their autonomy within the field of church and community activities, counting on the diplomatic mediation of the Holy See. In this framework, the establishment of cooperative diplomatic relations between the Holy See and Jordan has been an important achievement for the local Catholic Church, which has increased its diplomatic leverage. The Orthodox recurrently petitioned the Jordanian state authorities for their support in the struggle to control their local church. In fact, they have invited the state to engage with their internal affairs. For example, in 2005, Jordan refused to recognize the new Greek Orthodox patriarch of Jerusalem, Theophilos III, unless he first implemented the 1958 law promulgated by the Jordanian government by the request of Orthodox laity to establish the national character of the patriarchate.[32]

---

30. See https://cco.gov.jo/en-us/Jordanian-Constitutional for the official constitution, to which the following article numbers refer.

31. Chatelard, "Constitution," 480–81.

32. See Hager, "Orthodox Issue in Jordan."

Since the accession to the throne of Abdullah II in 1999, the Jordanian state has sought to further standardize and regulate its relationship with the churches in the country, especially in the fields of education and charities. This goal has not always been achieved due to divergent positions between the churches in Jordan.

At the same time, the Crown and the government have increasingly invested in cultural and religious diplomacy, especially within the field of interreligious dialogue. This has enhanced their cooperative relationship with the local churches. Since 2004, the Jordanian authorities have heavily promoted the image of the country as a safe location for Middle Eastern religious diversity. The Amman Message initiative of 2004 and the commitment to Islamic-Christian dialogue (for example, with the initiative of the "Common Word between Us and You" of 2007[33]), confirmed the Hashemite family's desire to foster the country's international status, presenting itself as the guarantor of a moderate interpretation of Islam in a world increasingly dominated by the rhetoric of the "War on Terror."[34]

In this framework, the apostolic visits of Pope Benedict XVI and Pope Francis were important events for projecting a positive image of the country at the regional and international levels. They were significant not only for Christian Jordanians but for the whole country, receiving widespread attention beyond the diplomatic implications of the visits. They also provided Christian Jordanians and their churches with greater visibility in Jordanian public space.

Of equal importance, over the last two decades, Jordan has begun to invest in religious tourism, opening a new field in the church-state relationship.[35] The Jordanian government transferred the management of Christian religious sites to the Ministry of Tourism and Antiquities, while Islamic "heritage" and "patrimony" were kept under the responsibility of the Ministry of Awqaf. On the one hand, this move can be criticized because it could create new imbalances between Muslim and Christian presences within the country, subjecting their properties to different legal regimes. On the other, the decision gave Christian institutions broader margins of autonomy to develop their religious sites and patrimony according to their interests. Within this framework, two sites have been developed during recent years: the baptismal site on the Jordan River, where an annual pilgrimage has been organized every January 10, and Mount Nebo (*Syagha* in Arabic).

---

33. See https://www.acommonword.com.

34. Al Shalabi and Alrajehi, "Amman Message," 1376–77.

35. See Maggiolini, "Christian Churches."

FREEDOM OF RELIGION AND SOCIAL STATUS

Christians constitute an important and stable component of Jordanian society. Tribal affiliations and practices are common in Jordan, where family, large or small (the tribe), is the receptacle of values and the guarantor of social and political order. Christians—especially those of Jordanian descent—are as likely as some Muslims to be receptive to this tribal identification discourse because they share with Muslims the same social structures and, largely, the same social values—for example, patriarchal values in which solidarity between individuals and families is built based on kinship.[36] This common heritage has established a solid memory of dialogue of life that binds together Muslims and Christians beyond their religious diversity.

The Jordanian "model" for managing religious pluralism contrasts with that of other countries in the region that have adopted a secularist ideology (Syria, Baathist Iraq, or Turkey). Jordan is characterized by an institutionalized pluralism that legally grants spaces of expression, organization, and activities to religious groups (namely, Sunni Muslims and a dozen Christian denominational communities) but also to ethnic groups like the Circassians and Chechensm, resulting from waves of immigration from the Caucasus, and to the Bedouin tribes of the arid regions.[37]

Religious communities are institutionalized as integral parts of social functioning. However, communitarianism is effectively stemmed by channeling political expression into other spaces and by guaranteeing the access of the Christian "minority" to citizenship and social, cultural, and economic resources.

Christian Jordanians are not a "compact" minority and are scattered over much of the country in both urban and rural areas. Jordanians prefer to speak of a "numerical minority" or "components of society" to emphasize that Christians may be few in number but are not a minority. The presence of Christians is not reduced to percentages but to a quality of presence,[38] and rights and duties have their foundation in the dignity of the human person apart from his or her numerical weight.[39]

The concept of minority is understood pejoratively by Christian Jordanians for more than one reason: the first is related to the concept of numbers of a tribe in Arab Bedouin culture and which is a source of pride and power; the second is the understanding of the term as used in other places in the

---

36. Information collected through personal interviews.

37. Chatelard, "Chrétiens en Jordanie," 41–44.

38. Lahham, "Être chrétien en Jordanie."

39. Information collected through personal interviews.

world and in the collective memory of Jordanians. Minority also refers to a newly arrived group not originally from Jordan (the Armenians, for instance). This idea was enhanced by some social movements after the Gulf wars when it was argued that Christians were relics of the Crusades and were not real/original Arabs or Jordanians. Finally, there are concerns that a minority might receive minor status or receive less representation in society than the majority.[40]

Christian Jordanians have no experience of intercommunal violence. They participate actively in all areas of social life to the point that the economic, intellectual, cultural, and even political elite have a proportion of Christians far greater than their proportion in the total population.

As stated above, Jordanian law recognizes the right to freedom of worship and religious belief in accordance with the customs and traditions of the country (article 14), yet the right to religious freedom is not granted fully according to international standards. Although Christian religious communities are entitled to judge issues relating to the personal status of their members through their community courts (articles 108 and 109), they still have to follow Sharia law in matters such as inheritance, marriage, and child custody, where women and children are not treated equally. Adoption is an issue because Christian families are not allowed to adopt, since orphans are considered Muslim and should take the religion of their adoptive parents. The only chance for a Christian family to adopt is if the orphan can be considered Christian beyond any possible doubt.[41] For several years, women's and other social movements have advocated a revision of the personal status law. Special committees have been formed by several churches, including priests, lawyers, and jurists, to review questions of inheritance, custody, marriageable age, and alimony to guarantee equality between Christian men and women.[42]

In a press release, Christoforos Atallah, the Greek Orthodox metropolitan of Jordan, said that the Orthodox Church had formed a legal committee to update and reform religious laws, including the personal status law regarding marriage. He indicated that it would be approved by the Holy Synod within a few months. Archbishop Christophoros indicated that the current laws date from the Byzantine era and require updating to create a modern status law commensurate with the challenges facing the Christian family today. He also said that Greek lawyers specializing in family law would participate in the legal committee formed by the church to assist in

---

40. Information collected through personal interviews.
41. Information collected through personal interviews.
42. Information collected through personal interviews.

reviewing and updating the law. He noted that the update would include marriage issues, inheritance, and the possibility of equality in inheritance between males and females.[43]

The Latin Patriarchate is also reviewing its personal status law, according to the Ecclesiastical Court judge, Father Dr. Shawky Batarian. He said that a legal committee is preparing a draft personal status law for the Latin community, the most prominent features of which are equality of inheritance for males and females, and limiting inheritance to daughters and wives in the absence of a male brother. Other amendments include the issue of adoption and the rights arising from it within the Christian family. Batarian indicated that the draft personal status law will include custody, witness issues, and conditions related to marriage. He pointed out that the church has followed the provisions of Jordanian state law regarding the age for marriage for some twenty-five years, and stressed that it is forbidden for those under the age of eighteen to marry except in very rare and special cases, and only with the approval of the bishop in person.[44]

Nevertheless, the reform of personal status remains a controversial issue, and resistance to reform comes from within the Christian community. Patriarchal culture remains dominant and poses strong limitations on the recognition of equality between men and women. Moreover, there are many doubts about the labeling of such reforms as specifically Christian, as this could create division and distance between Christian and Muslim Jordanians.[45]

SOCIOCULTURAL IMPACT OF CHRISTIAN COMMUNITIES

Christians are very well represented at all levels of the public sector: diplomacy, public finances, and even army command. Seats are reserved for Christians in electoral districts where their numbers are significant. (A similar phenomenon is observed for Caucasians and Bedouins. Studies in electoral sociology show that a significant number of Christian voters vote for Muslim candidates.)[46]

The desire of Christians (and of other religious or ethnic minorities) to maintain their particularism does not close their access to economic and political resources, nor does it "minoritize" them by limiting their rights as citizens.

43. *Ammon News*, "الأول مرة."
44. *Ammon News*, "الأول مرة."
45. Information collected through personal interviews.
46. Chatelard, "Chrétiens en Jordanie."

The work of Arab Christians is present in all domains of life in their countries—for example, as journalists and editors in the press and in publishing, as represented by a multitude of Christian publishers, particularly in Lebanon. In the arts, there are many Christian actors, film directors, singers, musicians, and producers.

Although this presence is proudly presented by Christians as proof of their qualitative contribution to the sociocultural life of Jordan and the region, most of them prefer to highlight their work without any underlying religious factor.[47] In fact, Christian Arabs have played a role, alongside their Muslim compatriots, in promoting a powerful cultural movement of Arab national identity since the time of the Arab revolution against the Ottoman Turks.

The political role of Christians in defending Arab nationalism was very notable in countries like Syria and Palestine.[48] At this level, there are many efforts by Christians to modernize the political and social life of their countries through their positions of responsibility in the state as presidents (in Lebanon), ministers (in Jordan and Lebanon), heads of political parties (in all three countries), and government spokespersons (Jordan).[49]

Another key aspect that illustrates the crucial work of Arab Christians and coexistence with Arab Muslims is related to teaching. Since the time of the Nahda, the teaching of different languages, scientific subjects, and, above all, the Arabic language, started in many cases from seminaries, churches, and Christian religious schools. Today, these are the most advanced educational institutions and include both Christian and Muslim students. Due to their reputation for discipline and quality education based on Christian teachings, the Christian schools are the most prestigious and desired by Christian and Muslim parents for the education of their children. Education is still an important field of activity for the churches in the kingdom. It provides important services to Jordanian society as a whole and holds a strategic place in the kingdom's public domain. More recently, education has become an issue widely discussed within the Christian domain and on the Jordanian level. Christians understand the importance of providing modern education updated to meet current needs and not merely traditional education. Christians also ask their religious and community authorities to make their schools more accessible to all strata by increasing the number of scholarships.[50] This aspect leads to a second important debate. In Jordan, the public school curricula pay scant attention to Christian heritage

47. Hamarneh, "Christians in Jordan."

48. Ibn Ṭalāl, *Christianity in Arab World*, 133.

49. See Labaki, "Chrétiens dans modernité arabe."

50. Information collected through personal interviews. See Hamarneh, "Christians in Jordan."

and history in the kingdom and the country. This is viewed negatively by Christian families obliged to enroll their children in public schools. It is also counterproductive to the development of a shared culture based on the importance of diversity in the kingdom, and full recognition of equal status for Christians among both the country's elite and at the grassroot level, especially among youth.[51]

ON IDENTITY

Many Christians behave in a way that does not correspond to the spirit of their religion or do not know enough about the teachings of Christianity. These Christians consider themselves Christian by tradition but do not know enough to transmit ideas or dialogue with people of other religions. For Christians from the Middle East who live in the countries of the Islamic Arab world, the context of life significantly dictates their situation and their way of living their faith. In essence, two groups of Eastern Christians can be perceived: on the one hand, devout followers who seek to save their Christian religious identity and protect their freedom of expression of faith in an Islamic society that is more orthodox every day, and on the other, people distant from their religion for many different reasons.[52]

Their situation resembles that of many Muslims who distance themselves from their religion as a reaction to Islamist radicalism in countries with a Western liberal model in which religion is a personal choice and not a compulsory way of life for the whole country. The failure to practice a Christian life in the context of a Muslim majority manifests itself in many ways. For example, not receiving Christian religious instruction in public schools, not being able to attend Mass on Sunday (a working day in the Islamic world), or being obliged to respect Ramadan (which entails closing alcohol businesses and not drinking, smoking, or eating in public during the day under threat of jail or a fine for noncompliance). In extreme cases, Christians can face persecution in some countries in the region.

Jordanian Christians do not make any distinction between being a Christian and being an Arab, nor do they perceive conflict in the relationship between their religion and their nationality. However, it is true that on several occasions in history and due to different influences and political interference, Arab Christians have been excluded from certain spheres. This is essentially due to the connection between Arab culture and Islam promoted by numerous national movements, especially after the wars with Israel under

51. Information collected through personal interviews.
52. Information collected through personal interviews.

the banner of Pan-Arabism.[53] Thus, many Arab Christians deny their Arab identity and seek their Christian roots (such as the Syriacs or the Copts) or ethnic references from the ancient world (such as the Phoenicians).[54]

In terms of linguistic identity, the language spoken by Muslim and Christian Arabs forms the basis of a common Arabic linguistic identity. For Christians, Arabic is their mother tongue, which dates from pre-Islamic times and which reflects many aspects of their life, as reflected in the poetry of the desert in Arabia. Arabic is currently becoming the language of worship in its different forms and holds the same sacred dimension as the language does for Muslims. Therefore, Arabs of both religions are proud of their language as it reflects their common culture, customs, and values. Both have defended it on many occasions and have united around it as an Arab people, regardless of professing one faith or another.[55]

However, beyond the sense of attachment to traditional local culture, the lack of proper information on the history of Christians in the country and in the region is seen as detrimental. It exerts a potentially negative impact in daily and social life, as it not only sidelines the history of Christian contribution to the kingdom, but it also conceals their presence and allows stereotypical biases and misconceptions to be perpetuated.

MAJOR INSTITUTIONS AND MOVEMENTS WITHIN CHURCHES

Since the late nineteenth century, the established churches have dedicated themselves to developing a wide network of initiatives and institutions. These networks of schools, NGOs, and hospitals are open to Muslims and Christians alike. In Jordan, the established churches run thirty-two secondary schools and twenty-eight primary schools. The Catholic Church (the Latin Patriarchate, the Greek Catholic Melkite Church, and Catholic monastic congregations) has forty-eight schools, eleven health centers, a university (the American University of Madaba), and three cultural centers.[56] The Greek Orthodox Church has nine schools, two health centers, and one cultural center, while the Reformed Churches have three schools and two health centers.[57] In the early 1990s, the General Secretariat for the Christian Educational Foundation (GSCEF) was founded to represent

53. Galal, "Pan-Arabism in Context."
54. See Hattar, "Sacred Oriental Music."
55. Hattar, "Sacred Oriental Music."
56. Information collected through personal interviews.
57. Information collected through personal interviews.

Christian schools in the country. It is open to all Christian schools, and it encompasses fifty-five institutions.[58] Given the number and diversity of Christian activities in the country, the church is the second employer after the state and plays a major role in the humanitarian field. This is particularly important given the weak state of the national economy and the presence of many refugees. The role of Caritas is exemplary from this standpoint.

During the last decades, ecumenism and intra-church cooperation have also had important effects on the development of new initiatives. For example, the creation of the Council of Heads of Churches in Jordan has the potential to allow Christians to speak with a single voice on the most important issues affecting their life and that of the country. Nevertheless, the challenges ahead are numerous. The council still needs to improve its procedures and structures, while many Christians still lack a clear understanding of its role, status, and function.[59]

More generally, churches in Jordan are discussing how to develop new initiatives that address youth and young couples. The Orthodox Church has begun to organize youth groups and meetings for young couples wishing to marry, like those of the Latins and Protestants. There are two main concerns behind these initiatives: first, to promote a new Christian understanding of the importance of engaging with Jordanian society and participating as Jordanian citizens with their duties and rights; and second, it is seen to be of strategic importance to promote a new spiritual education among young people.[60]

MAJOR CHALLENGES AND FUTURE PROSPECTS

Christian Jordanians are proud of their role and contribution to state-building in Jordan and to Jordan's socioeconomic and political life. They appreciate the Hashemites' defence of the country's diversity and their efforts in promoting pluralism. Therefore, Christians not only feel that they are citizens of the country but believe they are able to have a role in it.

Given Jordan's complex economic situation, Christians experience the same challenges as their Muslim brethren. Emigration is part of the history of both communities in Jordan. Clearly, their demography exposes their presence, and falling numbers are of particular concern to Christian

58. GSCEF is composed of schools from the Latin Patriarchate (twenty-five), the Rosary Sisters (six), Latin congregations (three), the Armenian Catholics (one), Evangelists (two), and six schools owned by Christian individuals.

59. Information collected through personal interviews.

60. Information collected through personal interviews.

Jordanians. They have already seen the impact of this dynamic in many villages and towns in rural areas of Jordan where local community life has suffered considerably. There are concerns about some of their traditional guarantees, such as the quota system, and these concerns feed the perception that their role in the country is losing traction.[61]

Clearly, such opinions are prompted not only by challenges affecting Jordan or life in the kingdom. Regional instability, prolonged geopolitical turbulence, the worsening of the situation in Palestine, and the experience of refugees from Iraq and Syria are powerful multipliers of anxieties and disorientation. To this should be added the impact of growing extremism within both the Muslim and Christian dimensions. While extreme forms of political Islam are generally listed among the issues feared by today's Christians in the region, Christians in Jordan (like their Palestinian brethren) are also perturbed by the growth of Christian Zionism. They fear being associated with that philosophy and having their credentials as citizens in the country and the region questioned.[62]

In this framework, the church needs to make an extra effort to reconfigure and update its role and pastoral activities in both material and spiritual services. Stronger and more structured collaboration among churches is considered necessary to turn ecclesiastical fragmentation into an asset rather than a limitation. At the same time, new concrete initiatives and proposals in the field of rights, education, and youth care and mentorship are vital for the future Christian presence in the country.[63]

BIBLIOGRAPHY

Al Shalabi, Jamal, and Menawer Bayan Alrajehi. "The Amman Message: Arab Diplomacy in the Dialogue of Civilizations." *Journal of US-China Public Administration* 8 (2011) 1375–92.

Ammon News. "أول مرة . . . تعديلات على قانون الأحوال الشخصية للمسيحيين" [For the first time . . . personal status amendments for Christians.] *Ammon News*, Apr. 3, 2019. https://www.ammonnews.net/article/450082.

Caritas Jordan. "Emergency Response for Iraqi Refugees." Caritas Jordan, Dec. 2017. https://www.caritasjordan.org.jo/emergency-response-for-iraqi-refugees.

Chatelard, Géraldine. "Les chrétiens en Jordanie, dynamiques identitaires et gestion du pluralism." *Cahiers de l'Orient* 1 (2009) 41–56.

——. "The Constitution of Christian Communal Boundaries and Spheres in Jordan." *Journal of Church and State* 52 (2010) 476–502.

61. Information collected through personal interviews.
62. Information collected through personal interviews.
63. Information collected through personal interviews.

Department of Statistics. "-2.2% GDP Decrease Rate at Constant Prices in the Third Quarter of 2020." Department of Statistics, Jan. 4, 2021. http://dos.gov.jo/dos_home_e/main/archive/GDP/2021/Q3_2020.pdf.

Galal, Nassar. "Pan-Arabism in Context." *Al-Ahram Weekly*, Dec. 2009. http://weekly.ahram.org.eg/2009/976/op6.htm.

Hager, Anna. "The Orthodox Issue in Jordan: The Struggle for an Arab and Orthodox Identity." *Studies in World Christianity* 24 (2018) 212–33.

Hamarneh, Saleh. "Christians in Jordan." *Politeja* 9 (2012) 443–52.

Hattar, Renee H. "Sacred Oriental Music: Preserving the Identity of Middle Eastern Christians." *Parole de l'Orient* 44 (2018) 301–10.

Ibn Ṭalāl, Ḥasan. *Christianity in the Arab World*. London: SCM, 1998.

Johnson, Todd M., and Gina A. Zurlo, eds. *World Christian Encyclopedia*. Edinburgh: Edinburgh University Press, 2019.

Labaki, Boutrus. "Les chrétiens dans la modernité arabe." *Médium* 4 (2007) 80–93.

Lahham, Maroun. "Être chrétien en Jordanie aujourd'hui, de Mgr Maroun Lahham (1/2)." Œuvre d'Orient, Feb. 2016. https://oeuvre-orient.fr/actualites/etre-chretien-en-jordanie-aujourdhui-de-mgr-maroun-lahham-12/.

Lucas, Russel E. *Institutions and the Politics of Survival in Jordan, Domestic Responses to External Challenges, 1988–2001*. Albany: State University of New York Press, 2005.

Maggiolini, Paolo. "Christian Churches and Arab Christians in the Hashemite Kingdom of Jordan: Citizenship, Ecclesiastical Identity and Roles in the Jordanian Political Field." *Archives de sciences sociales des religions* 171 (2015) 37–58.

———. "Christians of the Emirate: The Citizenship Process, Confessionalisation and Minoritisation." In *Minorities and State-Building in the Middle East: The Case of Jordan*, edited by Maggiolini Paolo and Idir Ouahes, 25–56. Cham, Switz.: Palgrave Macmillan, 2015.

Muasher, Marwan. "Jordan: Fallout from the End of an Oil Era." In *As Gulf Donors Shift Priorities, Arab States Search for Aid*, edited by Michele Dunne. Carnegie Endowment for International Peace, June 9, 2020. https://carnegieendowment.org/2020/06/09/jordan-fallout-from-end-of-oil-era-pub-82008#comments.

———. "Jordan's Identity Question." Diwan, Aug. 2021. https://carnegie-mec.org/diwan/85140.

Ryan, Curtis R. "Jordanian Foreign Policy and the Arab Spring." *Middle East Policy* 21 (2014) 144–53.

———. *Jordan in Transition: From Hussein to Abdullah*. Boulder, CO: Rienner, 2002.

Schwedler, Jillian. "Spatial Dynamics of the Arab Uprisings." *PS: Political Science & Politics* 46 (2013) 230–34.

Tell, Tariq M. "Early Spring in Jordan: The Revolt of the Military Veterans." In *Renegotiating Civil-Military Relations in Arab States: Political and Economic Governance in Transition*. Carnegie Middle East Center, Nov. 2015. https://carnegieendowment.org/files/ACMR_Tell_Jordan_Eng_final.pdf.

World Bank. "Jordan's Economic Update—April 2020." World Bank, Apr. 16, 2020. https://www.worldbank.org/en/country/jordan/publication/economic-update-april-2020.

———. "Jordan's Economic Update—April 2021." World Bank, Apr. 2, 2021. https://www.worldbank.org/en/country/jordan/publication/economic-update-april-2021.

———. "Overview." https://www.worldbank.org/en/country/jordan/overview.

Wiktorowicz, Quintan. *The Management of Islamic Activism: Salafis, the Muslim Brotherhood, and State Power in Jordan.* Albany: State University of New York Press, 2001.

Yom, Sean L. "The New Landscape of Jordanian Politics: Social Opposition, Fiscal Crisis, and the Arab Spring." *British Journal of Middle Eastern Studies* 42 (2015) 284–300.

Christians in Lebanon

Antoine Salameh and Roula Talhouk

LEBANON WAS AWARE OF Christianity from the very first centuries, during the Roman and Byzantine eras.[1] Monks, disciples of Saint Maron, preached Christianity to some of the residents of the Lebanese mountains between the fifth and the sixth century, bringing to them the core of Maronite spirituality. Christianity then spread in a wider way through Maronite groups who migrated gradually from northern Syria, then known as Second Syria, to live in Lebanon during the middle of the seventh century.[2] They sought protection and freedom, which are values rooted in Maronites religiously and

---

1. According to Acts of the Apostles (21:3–5; 27:3), the apostle Paul met twice with the Christian communities in Tyre and Sidon, and lived with them. The Lebanese philosopher Kamal Youssef El Hajj (1917–1976) attributes the early spread of Christianity in Lebanon to the original inhabitants (Canaanites or Phoenicians) who saw in the life of Jesus Christ a convergence and resemblance to the myth of their god Baal or Tammuz or Adonis, who was killed and raised from death. According to El-Hajj, they were prepared to accept and understand the new evangelization (El-Hajj, *Christ and Lebanon*, 17, 19, 24; al-Hourani, *Lebanon in the Values* [Arabic: الحاج، المسيح ولبنان، ص ١٧، ١٩، ٢٤؛ الحوراني، لبنان في قيم تاريخه، ص ٩٧، ص ص ٢٢٣-٣٢].).

2. The Maronites, or the Maronite Church, are affiliated with Saint Maron, who lived in the fourth century in northern Syria, inventing at that time a new method of asceticism, which is asceticism or living in the open. After his death, around the year 410, his followers built a monastery near the city of Apamea (Qalaat al-Madiq). The followers of this monastery, both monks and believers, were called Maronites, and later they were organized in an independent patriarchal framework from within the Syriac Antiochene churches. And between the seventh and eighth centuries, and due to the various ideological persecutions that the Christian East witnessed and that led to the division of the "universal church" in the fifth century, the Maronites began to gradually migrate from Syria to Lebanon, where they organized, multiplied, and spread, and where their monks preached Christ to the pagans.

socially.[3] Due to Lebanon's severe nature and the atmosphere of freedom,[4] Lebanon welcomed other Christian communities from the Eastern church, especially during the sixteenth century,[5] and the number of Christian communities grew to twelve, divided into three Churches: Catholic, Orthodox, and the Reformed Churches or Protestants.[6]

Among these three Churches, Christians are divided as follows: a majority of Maronites, followed by the Greek Orthodox, then the Greek Catholics, the Armenian Orthodox, Armenian Catholics, the Syriac Orthodox, Syriac Catholic, Protestants, the Chaldeans, the Assyrians, the Latins, and the Coptic Orthodox.[7] They are distributed in almost all the governorates

3. The Maronite scholar Father Michel Hayek (1928–2005) said that the Maronites, from the first massacre of their monks in 517 until the famine imposed on them by the Turks between 1916 and 1918 during the First World War, continued to search for two concepts: land and freedom. According to Hayek, the idea of land and freedom was introduced by the Maronites to the East, where the idea of empire replaces the idea of the homeland, and where the concept of the sacred community is absorbed by individual consciousness (Hayek, *Writings* [Arabic: الحايك، كتابات، ص], 218).

4. Hitti, *History of Lebanon* (Arabic: حتّي، تاريخ لبنان، ص), 9.

5. Starting in the sixteenth century, some of the Christian communities joined the Catholic Church, where the Maronite Church has a major role. The Eastern missionaries of Franciscans, Capuchins, Jesuits, and Dominicans faced huge difficulties in directly contacting those communities. Therefore, Maronites made their mission easier and made their churches and monasteries a starting point to this united preaching work. However, when Armenian, Byzantine, and Syriac communities joined the Catholic Church, the Orthodox communities persecuted them in agreement with Ottoman emperors. They sheltered on Mount Lebanon and sought protection from the Maronite Church, which helped them financially, spiritually, and morally (El-Helou, *Church History in Brief* [Arabic: الحلو، موجز تاريخ الكنيسة، ص], 222).

6. The Reformed churches currently in Lebanon include the Presbyterian Church, the National Evangelical Church, the Anglican Church, and the Armenian Evangelical Church, all of which follow the Supreme Council of the Evangelical Community in Syria and Lebanon. This is an evangelical umbrella representing the various evangelical churches in Syria and Lebanon before the civil authorities. In addition to the Reformed churches, there are conservative churches such as the Baptists, Adventists, the Church of God . . .

7. The Coptic Orthodox community (Christians from Egypt) is a recent presence in Lebanon and was constitutionally recognized during the era of President Elias Hrawi (1989–1998). Its followers built a church in Beirut and a large monastery in the Barbara region in northern Lebanon.

and districts of Lebanon, in addition to the Muslim sects of Sunnis, Shiites, Alawites, Ismailis,[8] the Muwahidun Druze,[9] and some Jews.[10]

As time passed, Lebanon emerged as a country of openness and a beacon in the midst of an Arab and Islamic sea. The status of Christians remained acceptable compared with that of Christians in neighboring countries. Christians became associated with the name of Lebanon, especially since they formed the basis of the Lebanese entity that began to emerge in the early seventeenth century following cooperation between the Maronites and Druze princes, which was formalized in 1920 after France declared the state of Greater Lebanon,[11] in addition to the role played by the Maronite patriarch Elias Howayek (1843–1931) in this achievement.

However, a drop in the number of Christians has been noted from their making up half of the Lebanese population in the early twentieth century to just 30 percent of the population. Since 1990, Christians have felt increasingly frustrated and that they are living in a country that no longer resembles them, especially after the civil war that ended in 1975 and was

8. Sunni Muslims are distributed in the coastal cities, especially in Beirut and Sidon (in the south) and Tripoli (in the north), in addition to the villages of the Akkar district. Shiite Muslims are distributed in the south, in the southern suburbs of Beirut, and in the Baalbek-Hermel region in the Bekaa. The Alawites are spread in the Jabal Mohsen area in the east of the city of Tripoli and in the villages of the Akkar district.

9. The Druze are spread in the Chouf and Aley districts in the Mount Lebanon governorate, and in the villages of the Hasbaya district and Marjayoun district in the south, and the Rashaya district in the western Bekaa. To learn about the Druze monotheism approach that some of the Islamic communities and others consider an independent faith, refer to Khuri, *Being a Druze.*

10. Most of the Lebanese Jews are of Mazrahi origin, i.e., from the descendants of the Jews of the Middle East and some Islamic countries, especially Morocco. In Lebanon at the beginning of 1948, there were twenty thousand Jews distributed in Beirut and its suburbs. Today, after the Nakba of Palestine in 1948 and the war in Lebanon, they number about one hundred and live in disguise in Christian areas. To learn more about the Jews in Lebanon, see Abdel Samad, *Wadi Abu Jamil* (Arabic: وادي الصمد، عبد (أبو جميل; Hendler, "Beirut's last Jews."

11. On Sept. 1, 1920, France announced the establishment of the state of Greater Lebanon after the end of the rule of the Ottoman Empire (1516–1918) and following the Sykes-Picot agreement in 1916, which had divided the states ruled by the Ottoman Sultanate in the Middle East into two British and French regions. Accordingly, Lebanon was put under the authority of the French mandate. The declaration of the state of Greater Lebanon was accompanied by a series of administrative changes that included increasing its size to 10,452 square kilometers, transforming Beirut into its capital, dividing it into governorates and districts, establishing laws and constitutions, and organizing the state administration and institutions. The French mandate over Lebanon did not end until 1943 after a series of demands from the Lebanese and several international and regional changes. For more information on the modern history of Lebanon, refer to al-Salibi, *Modern History of Lebanon.*

sparked by both internal and external causes. Thus, some call it the civil war, others the "war in Lebanon" or "the war of others on our land."[12] The frustration of Christians is due to many reasons: the effects of a long war with material and human losses, immigration and emigration, fights and ruptures tagged as Christian-Christian[13] and Christian-Muslim, the Syrian tutelage imposed on their country,[14] the imprisonment and exile of Christian leaders,[15] and the emergence of Sunni Prime Minister Rafic Hariri

12. For more information about this war and its causes, refer to Khazen, *Breakdown of the State*; Hiro, *Lebanon Fire and Embers*; Tueini, *Guerre pour les autres*.

13. This Christian-Christian rupture was originally due to war in Lebanon, specifically the period of 1988 and 1990 when Christians were divided between the Lebanese Army (who were also split) led by General Michel Aoun and the Lebanese Forces Party led by Samir Geagea. Despite the end of the war, the Lebanese continue to suffer from this rupture in politics between the Free Patriotic Movement (FPM) led by Michel Aoun and the Lebanese Forces Party led by Samir Geagea. The rupture can be by blood, even between brothers of the same family. Second, Christians did not pursue true reconciliation on a popular and religious basis. Even men of religion are divided between these two parties, which aggravates the situation because each party gives itself more accreditation and legitimacy than the other. Third, Sunni-Shiite clashes in the region have increased splits among Christians, especially in decision-making regarding those who are pro-Hezbollah and the Shiites on one side, and pro-future movement that represents Sunnis on another. However, this attitude provides a formula equally in the political game, which has caused more weaknesses, in fact.

14. The Syrian army entered Lebanon in 1976 with the aim of supporting the Palestinians in their war against Israel. Instead of withdrawing following the Taif Agreement, the Syrian army remained on Lebanese territory, and Syrian rule continued to dominate all aspects of politics in Lebanon, especially between 1990 and 2005.

15. These leaders are General Michel Aoun and Dr. Samir Geagea. The former was the commander of the army before being appointed by the president, Amin Gemayel, as prime minister in 1988. When the presidential term ended, the parliament failed to elect Aoun as a successor. He led the "war of liberation" against the Syrians in 1989, and the "war of abolition" against the Lebanese Forces Party. After the Taif Agreement, he was exiled to France and continued his struggle from there against the Syrian presence in Lebanon. He returned in 2005 and established the Free Patriotic Movement, which included his followers and supporters. On Feb. 6, 2006, he made an understanding between him and Hezbollah that was known under the name of the Mar Mekhael Agreement. This discussed the differences and common goals between the two parties, such as consensual democracy, a proportional election law, Lebanese foreign relations, and a plan for weapons removal. Following this understanding, an alliance was created, which led to Aoun supporting Hezbollah in the war of 2006, while Hezbollah adopted the candidacy of Aoun in the presidential elections of 2014–2016. Samir Geagea has been the executive chairman of the Lebanese Forces since 1986. He participated in the war in Lebanon with the Phalangists (Kataeb Party) first, then with the Lebanese Forces, and was known for his struggle against the Syrian occupation. He was imprisoned in 1994 after being accused of assassinations during and after the war. Once released from prison in 2005, he continued his political work through his parliamentary and ministerial bloc.

as the de facto ruler of Lebanon at that time.[16] In addition, the power of Christians in the government decreased after the Taif Agreement, especially the powers of the president, and the terms of this agreement were not fully implemented, especially the disarmament of all groups.[17]

At the dawn of the third millennium of Christ's birth, Maronites and other Christians in Lebanon bore psychological wounds and were awaiting a new resurrection that would return them to the golden age when the Maronites were the "royal community" in politics, economics, the military, and culture. Have they achieved their goals, or have they ended up more frustrated and broken? What was their reality between the years 2000 and 2021, and the reality of the country in which they live? What are the key challenges they face at this stage? What are their future prospects and desired aspirations? Pope John Paul II described Lebanon as being more than just a country. It is a "message." Lebanon is the perfect example of coexistence of various and multiple religions where you can find Christians, Muslims, and Druze in one nation who are trying to live in peace above all odds. Will they remain loyal to the "country-message" described by Pope John Paul II?[18]

16. Rafic Hariri (1944–2005) was a prominent businessman holding both Lebanese and Saudi nationalities. He played a mediating role in ending the war in Lebanon and served as prime minister between 1992 and 1998, and 2000 to 2004.

17. The Taif Agreement was concluded in the city of Taif in Saudi Arabia in 1989 with the aim of stopping the fighting in Lebanon. The parliament was turned into a constituent assembly, and deputies studied the document of reconciliation known as the Document of National Accord, made some amendments, and voted on it. This document consisted of four articles. The first affirmed Lebanon's independence, its Arab identity, and its political form as a democratic parliamentary republic. The second stated the need to extend the sovereignty of the Lebanese state over the entire Lebanese territory. The third called for the liberation of Lebanon from the Israeli occupation, and the fourth outlined Lebanese-Syrian relations. The most significant content of the document was a series of administrative and political reforms, including the distribution of seats in the House of Representatives equally between Muslims and Christians, especially as the Maronites had held a distinguished position under the French mandate. Despite the advantages of this document at the national and political levels, and its consolidation of the foundations of coexistence, it weakened the Taif Agreement and the post of president, which is the key Christian position in the state. The agreement retained the top three posts in the state for the Maronites (the presidency of the republic), the Sunnis (prime minister), and the Shiites (the presidency of the parliament), but redistributed powers between the three posts. It transferred the executive powers from the president of the republic to the Council of Ministers collectively, and strengthened the powers of parliament by requiring the appointment of the prime minister by the president of the republic after conducting binding consultations with members of parliament. Previously, the president of the republic used to appoint the prime minister without consulting the parliament.

18. The wording that Lebanon is a "country-message" appeared many times in the sermons and homilies of Pope John Paul II (1920–2005). He intended to remind us that Lebanon's core message is one of peace, thanks to its cultural and religious pluralism

LEBANON BETWEEN SOCIETAL, POLITICAL, AND ECONOMIC VARIABLES

Despite the withdrawal of Israeli and Syrian forces from its land, Lebanon has not introduced anything new into its social and political context during the first twenty years of the current century. The country remains reliant on outside sponsorship and interference, particularly as it is a small country with limited economic resources, surrounded by larger countries and dependent on regional support.[19] The sectarianism that has marked social and political history is explained by the absolute loyalty given to the sect before the homeland and the state.[20] Politicians' engagement in public affairs is based on their foreign alliances or the traditional political practice of serving their own narrow interests in a partisan manner.

---

and the characteristics of openness, dialogue, and cooperation inherent in it (Paliki, "Two Speeches" [Arabic: ص ,"خطابان") ، (تعريب) باليكي], 720.

19. Khalaf, *Lebanon in the Middle* (Arabic: ص ,لبنان ,خلف), 11.

20. The roots of sectarianism in Lebanon date back to the Ottomans and their application of the mullah system, by which the Ottoman Sultan considered himself a Muslim Khalifa and removed non-Muslim groups from the circle of favor, leaving them to manage their personal and religious affairs. European countries began to use these non-Muslim sects and minorities as their base to oppose Ottoman rule and to penetrate the region, especially during the mid-nineteenth century when the Ottoman Empire began to weaken and collapse. Maronite France, Greek Orthodox Russia, Roman Catholic Austria, and Druze Britain branched out, while the Sunni and Shiite communities remained under the rule of the Ottoman authority. Sectarianism in Lebanon increased with the start of the French Mandate and the declaration of the state of Greater Lebanon in 1920, plus the declaration of the Lebanese Republic and the establishment of the Lebanese Constitution in 1926. Muslims objected to joining a state in which they would be a minority, because they had been under a Muslim majority in the days of Ottoman rule. Also, the representative councils at that time were distributed according to sectarian affiliation and not according to functional or scientific competence. From that time onwards, a quota system was adopted for all important administrative and political posts based on the percentage of the population belonging to each sect, particularly the main ones (Maronite, Orthodox, Druze, Sunni, Druze, Roman Catholic). This was enshrined after the end of the French Mandate and after the oral understanding at the time between the Maronite president of the republic, Bechara El Khoury, and the Sunni prime minister, Riad El Solh, known as the National Pact or the Charter of 1943, and after the Taif Agreement of 1989. These factors and the unbalanced historical development of the sects in Lebanon have deepened sectarianism in Lebanon and made it a direct trigger for igniting conflict and civil wars. Repeated attacks and the disruption of government work, combined with the absence of a concept of the state and its institutions, have created the feeling in every sect of being a weak minority that must rely on a superpower to secure its stability, permanence, and authority. See Abou Jaoude, "Salvation of the Lebanese," para. 1; Traboulsi, *History of Modern Lebanon* [Arabic: الحديث لبنان تاريخ ,طرابلسي ،1 الفقرة ،"اللبنانيين خلاص" ,جوده أبو ص ص], 185–88.

At the start of the twenty-first century, Lebanese society witnessed great transformations in construction, means of transportation, and communication,[21] while remaining open to acquiring more customs from the East and the West.[22] On the other hand, it remained rooted in the concepts of belonging and identity, in which loyalty to the community and external parties remained stronger than loyalty to the homeland and the state.[23] Every region continued to be stamped with the characteristics of the religious doctrine that constituted its demographic majority, while differences between sectors and classes of society remained.

Sectarianism and external links emerged from the societal and political reality that defined Lebanon between 2000 and 2021. This period was characterized by a series of crises, followed by international efforts to restore cohesion between two coalitions, one of which was pro-resistance, in other words, to Syria, Iran, and Hezbollah, and the opposing coalition loyal to Western and Arab countries.[24]

This rift has been evident since 2000, when Lebanese society, politicians, and citizens either called for the lifting of Syrian tutelage from Lebanon, including many Sunnis, Druze, and Christians; or on the other side, for remaining part of the Shiites, including small numbers of Sunnis, Druze, and Christians.[25] Facing international and popular pressure, especially at the

21. A study conducted in 2014 showed that 65 percent of Lebanese like to spend money on a life of luxury, travel, nightlife, and the acquisition of the latest electronic devices (Daher, "Austerity Has Become Necessary" [Arabic: ضاهر، «التقشف بات ضرورياً في حياة اللبناني»، الفقرة], para. 1).

22. Lebanese society is a typical case of globalization. Since ancient times, Lebanon has been open to both the East and the West due to its location on the Mediterranean at the meeting point of three continents: Asia, Africa, and Europe (Saadeh, *Philosophy of the Baasin* [Arabic: سعاده، فلسفة، ص ص], 334–35, 375–76).

23. Freiha, *Continuous Controversy* [Arabic: فريحة، الخلاف المستمر، ص], 158.

24. The "axis of resistance" is a name given to those countries (by themselves) that oppose US policy in the Arab world and support Arab national liberation movements. This axis is made up of Syria, Iran, and the Shiite Hezbollah in Lebanon, and Iraqi Shiite forces and the Houthi movement in Yemen. This Iran-led alliance aims to oppose the interests of the US and Israel in the region. As a result, an Islamic division has emerged in the Arab world between the Shiites who mainly support the Syrian-Iranian line, and the Sunnis, such as Saudi Arabia, that support the American line.

Hezbollah was founded and became renowned in the aftermath of Israel's occupation of southern Lebanon in 1982. It is an armed Shiite Islamic party headquartered in Lebanon and supported by Iran. Its intellectual roots go back to what is known as the Islamic Shiite Awakening that appeared in Lebanon in the 1960s and 70s. This was marked by religious and social activity, and the emergence of distinct religious references, such as Imam Moussa al-Sader and others. For more information on this party, refer to Norton, *Hezbollah*; Avon, *Hezbollah*.

25. Among the Christian parties calling for the Syrian army to remain in Lebanon

time of the assault on former Prime Minister Rafic Hariri and accusations directed at Syria, the Syrian army withdrew in April 2005.

In the parliamentary elections of summer 2005, Hezbollah won thirty-five seats and entered the government for the first time. Hezbollah also provoked the July 2006 war with Israel, which had withdrawn from the south in 2000, and reescalated the situation, especially after the understanding of 2006 between Hezbollah and the Free Patriotic Movement which represented a wide range of Christians. The country entered a phase of political stalemate, and the civil peace almost turned into a war between Sunnis and Shiites in May 2008, but for Qatar and some Arab countries concluding the Doha Agreement to end the dispute between the two parties, elect a president, form a government, and draft an electoral law that could satisfy everyone.[26]

While the Lebanese were enjoying the settlement of the Doha Agreement, war erupted in Syria and affected the Lebanese arena as a result of Hezbollah's participation in this conflict. There was a rise in sectarian tension between Sunnis and Shiites, a series of bombings in their regions, and disruption of the election of a president to the republic.[27] After two and a half years of a vacant presidency, a political settlement took place that led to the election of a president and the formation of a new government in 2016, and another in 2018. A surprise came on the night of October 17, 2019, when demonstrations swept across the country, followed by the collapse of the government a few days later as a result of public pressure. A new government was promptly assigned but soon resigned after the infamous Beirut port explosion. The appointment of another government was a form of "mission impossible" until September 2021, when it was barely put together. From 2019 onwards, the country has remained in a state of total chaos and collapse, aggravated by the COVID-19 pandemic, the devaluation of the Lebanese lira against exceptional rises in the American dollar, rocketing prices, the lack of imported medicines and withdrawal of subsidies on

---

at that time was the Marada Movement, headed by former minister Sleiman Franjieh whose family had traditionally led the organization since its founding in 1968.

26. Refer to Tay, "اتفاق الدوحة، محمد، طي."

27. The Syrian crisis began in 2011 within the framework of the Arab Spring. It was a multisided internal armed conflict, with the participation of international parties, between the Syrian government, led by President Bashar al-Assad, and Islamist groups and extremist fundamentalist organizations. The fear was that this war would extend to Lebanon and destabilize its political and security situation. The Lebanese government's policy of "self-distancing" and international desire to neutralize the conflict meant that Lebanon avoided involvement in the Syrian conflict (Salem, "Lebanon and Syrian Crisis," lines 113–14). For more information on the Syrian crisis, see, for example, Dam, *Destroying a Nation.*

medicines, and the interruption of fuel supplies as prices spiraled out of control as a result of the withdrawal of subsidies.

The collapse of the government and country is due to many reasons. Beyond the nonexistence of investment and absence of international or Gulf aid as a result of the political rift between supporters and opponents of Hezbollah and its dominance of state facilities, there is an increase in arbitrary employment within the public sector, faulty monetary policy, currency collapse, and the unplanned approval of ranks and salary scales in 2017 that did not take into account the exact cost. The war in Syria has also had a negative impact since 2011. Crossings have been closed, while more than two million Syrians were forcibly displaced and the majority sought refuge in Lebanon. Sufficient aid to assist with this problem was not provided, and the Lebanese government had to sustain the burden of the living needs of this group and smuggling to Syria to avoid the Caesar Act.[28] In addition, corruption has been widespread in the public sector for many years; the adoption of the Quarter Economic System damaged both agricultural and industrial sectors; and the reforms promised by the Lebanese governments during international donor conferences or after receiving Gulf aid never materialized, especially between the years 2000 and 2010.[29]

28. Economist and visiting professor at Cardiff Met University and ISM (International School of Management) Dr. Rock-Antoine Mehanna, in an interview conducted on Mar. 2, 2021. He stated that the ranks and salaries format had cost the treasury three times more than expected, and that the war in Syria had had a detrimental effect on the Lebanese economy, for example, by the closure of the Nassib border crossing between Syria and Jordan, through which Lebanon exports about 85 percent of its agricultural and industrial products. In addition, the economic waste and unemployment crisis worsened as a result of the massive influx of displaced people into Lebanon, their consumption of subsidized foodstuffs and energy, and their employment in low-income jobs.

The Caesar Syria Civilian Protection Act, known as the Caesar Act, is a law passed by the US Senate in mid-Dec. 2019 and signed a few days later by then-US President Donald Trump. The act aimed originally to punish Syrian President Bashar al-Assad for crimes against humanity in poisoning his own people and depriving them of any chance of military victory, which he achieved on the ground for political capital, so that he could stay in government until an unknown period. It also aimed to increase the financial, social, and political isolation of Assad, and to punish his allies and oblige him to accept a political solution to the Syrian crisis as per Resolution 2254 of the UN Security Council.

29. In his interview, Dr. Mehanna cited the international donor conferences that took place thanks to Prime Minister Rafic Hariri's international relations, especially with France, as well as Gulf donations: the Paris 1 conference in 2001 provided Lebanon with 500 million euros; and the Paris 2 conference in 2002 with 4 billion and 200 million euros. After the July 2006 war, Saudi Arabia provided financial support worth 1 billion dollars, Kuwait provided 500 million dollars, and Qatar and the rest of the Gulf countries rushed to provide financial aid to Lebanon to recover from its economic plight as a result of the war. A third (Paris 3) conference was held in 2007, which

All these issues exacerbated the deficit and prevented the state from paying its debts. Billions of dollars were smuggled abroad, and the money of depositors in banks was subject to seizure because banks had lent all their money to the state.[30] Thus, living conditions have become extremely difficult. Christians in Lebanon awaiting the dawn of a better tomorrow found themselves falling back into a cycle of frustration and concerns about the fate of their homeland, themselves, and their demographic and geographic status.

CHRISTIANS IN LEBANON BETWEEN DEMOGRAPHY AND GEOGRAPHY

In a country like Lebanon governed by religious communities, demography is at the head of the problems and is an implicit factor in social, political, and economic conflict. This is especially the case in light of the geographic changes undergone in the country around a hundred years ago in which the population shifted under the influence of sectarian politics with religious and intertwined factors. Lebanon became a country governed by eighteen sects according to the first and only census that took place in 1932 during the French mandate of Lebanon. Until then, an accurate population census had not been conducted in Lebanon because the Lebanese feared the potential impact of statistical figures on the size of each religious community in power. As the political system in Lebanon is based on the principle of sectarian quotas, it would not be appropriate for Christians to be greater numerically than Muslims, nor for there to be more Sunnis than the Shiites.

More recent local and international studies show that the percentage of Christians of the total number of indigenous people between 2000 and 2020 was 4 to 4.5 million.[31]

The 1932 census showed that Christians made up 51.2 percent of the total population of 785,543 at that time.[32] A CIA website indicated that the number of Christians in Lebanon in 2001 was 39 percent, compared with 59.7 percent for Muslims. These figures had changed by 2020, according

---

provided loans and grants amounting to 7 billion and 600 million dollars. As a result of the Doha Agreement sponsored by the Arab countries in 2008, Lebanon enjoyed a golden economic phase between 2008 and 2010, interspersed with a reduction in the budget deficit and an increase in economic growth thanks to increased Gulf investments and an influx of foreign and Arab tourists.

30. The smuggled money refers to prominent political figures and bank owners who are predominantly politicians.

31. See US Department of State, *Lebanon 2017*, para. 1; Courbage and Todd, *Rendezvous des civilizations*, 164.

32. Attieh, *Population in Lebanon* [Arabic: عطية، السكّان، ص], 46.

to the same website, to 33.7 percent for Christians and 61.1 percent for Muslims.[33] This result is roughly the same as in the study published by the International Information Company in 2018, which showed that Christians made up 30 percent and Muslims 70 percent.[34]

Another study issued by the Lebanese Information Center in 2013 and published in the international scientific journal *Yearbook of International Religious Demography 2018* indicated that the percentage of Christians in Lebanon in 2011 was 34.45 percent (38.22 percent, if relying on the bylaws of the electoral system for calculating the population) and will become 37.55 percent (40.18 percent) in 2030, increasing by 2045 to 39.03 percent (41.12 percent) of the total population.[35] These are strange and unreliable figures given that, in reality, Christian numbers are decreasing and fertility rates among Muslim women are higher; in 2004, birth rates were 1.53 newborns per Christian woman and 1.82 newborns per Muslim woman.[36]

Despite high and low rates published in studies, reality shows that the number of Christians is declining. Add to that high levels of emigration among Christians, especially as the catastrophic situation in Lebanon shows no hope for change or justice following the Beirut blast, the facts of which are still hidden by the government.

Maronites are widespread in the governorates of Mount Lebanon (to the north of the capital), of the North, of the Bekaa Valley, and of the South.[37] The Greek Orthodox are distributed in the city of Beirut, in the North, in the Aley district in Mount Lebanon, in the South, and in the Bekaa. Greek Catholics are spread across Beirut, Zahleh in the Bekaa, in the Chouf district in Mount Lebanon, and in the South, especially in the city and district of Sidon. The remaining Christian denominations are distributed between Beirut, Mount Lebanon, the Bekaa, and the South.

---

33. Dib, *This Ancient Bridge* [Arabic: ص، هذا الجسر العتيق، ديب], 330; Fleyfel, *Géopolitique des Chrétiens d'Orient*, 73.

34. If this aforementioned study is correct, then the number of Christians in Lebanon is 1,686,975, divided between residents and nonresidents as follows: Maronites (934,704), Greek Orthodox (329,865), Greek Catholics (213,193), Armenian Orthodox (94,780), Armenian Catholics (22,344), Syriac Orthodox (21,447), Syriac Catholics (13,105), Protestants (20,668), Chaldeans and Assyrians (3,594), and Christian minorities (33,275). According to the study, the number of Muslims is 3,821,717, divided between residents and nonresidents as follows: Sunnis (1,721,853), Shiites (1,743,718), Druze monotheists (295,664), Alawites. (55,677). The number of Jews is put at 4,805. See "Lebanese Are 5.5 Million" [Arabic: "اللبنانيون 5.5 مليون نسمة"،], para. 8.

35. Grim et al., *Yearbook*, 130.

36. Attieh, *Demography of the Mashreq* [Arabic: ص، ديموغرافيا المشرق، عطيه], 266.

37. Refer to the map on p. 25.

While Christians lived in 70 percent of the area of Lebanon up to 1975, by 2008 they lived in less than 30 percent, according to some estimates.[38] The reasons include emigration and the timid return of Christians to their villages after the displacement caused by the Mountain War and also after the Mountain Reconciliation.[39] They preferred to live in the Mount Lebanon governorate, especially the districts of Baabda, al-Matn, Kesrouan, and Jbeil, due to the proximity of these areas to the capital, and because they were originally Christian areas where the Christian concentration, especially of the Maronites, is highest. The Lebanese in general, and Christians in particular, think about the best way to ensure psychological stability, and they find this only by living with those who share sectarian and religious similarities.[40]

Christians residing in Beirut or Mount Lebanon have remained connected to their native villages and towns in north and south Lebanon and in the Bekaa. They still relocate to these areas for holidays, to celebrate religious feasts, and to bury their dead, especially if these areas have a permanent, strong, or acceptable Christian presence.[41]

38. Dib, *This Ancient Bridge*, 349.

39. The Mountain War was a series of violent clashes that took place during the Lebanese Civil War, especially between the years 1982 and 1984. This war pitted the Lebanese Army and the Lebanese Forces Party against a coalition of leftist and Islamist groups opposed to the government at the time, led by the Progressive Socialist Party with the support of the Palestine Liberation Organization and Syria. The conflict began when the Lebanese Army and the Lebanese Forces entered the Druze-majority Chouf region, southeast of the capital Beirut, to bring it back under government control, but came under stiff resistance from the Druze militias and their allies. During the war, many massacres of civilians were committed, especially after the withdrawal of the Israeli army, which was in this area led by Druze officers. These massacres caused the destruction of dozens of villages in the area and the displacement of Christian residents to Beirut and the districts of Metn, Kesrouan, and Jbeil. These conflicts were preceded by the displacement of about twenty thousand Christians from the Chouf district between 1977 and 1978, from the day after the Druze leader Kamal Jumblatt was killed and Christians were accused of killing him.

On Aug. 3, 2001, Patriarch Sfeir (1986–2011), in cooperation with Druze leader Walid Jumblatt, sponsored the historic Mountain Reconciliation that ended fighting between Christians and Druze, especially during the Mountain War in 1983.

40. Attieh, *Population in Lebanon*, 118. On the Christian preference to live in Christian areas, a seventy-five-year-old woman, Antoinette Habib, stated in an interview in 2021 that after the end of the war in Lebanon, she did not live with her family in the Christian areas of Beirut and also near to Jezzine, her original village in the south. She preferred to live in Kesrouan where the Maronite patriarch resides, as this provides her and her family with protection. She stated that whatever befalls him would befall her.

41. In a phone call, Dr. Chawki Attieh, professor of pemography at the Social Sciences Institute of the Lebanese University, clarified that it is not possible to know the number of Christians residing in the outer regions of Lebanon or in the capital and

Within this demographic and geographic reality, Christians in Lebanon tried as much as possible between 2000 and 2021 to maintain their presence and the heritage and traditions of their ancestors in preserving the land and attachment to their church, which constitutes the safety valve for the Christian presence in Lebanon.

CHRISTIANS IN LEBANON BETWEEN RELIGION AND STATE

The church in Lebanon is distinguished by the fact that its existence dates from prior to the state. This is due to the historical relationship between the Maronites and Lebanon from the seventh century AD onwards, and the fundamental role played by the Maronites in the formation of the Lebanese entity, especially between the seventeenth and twentieth centuries.[42] As a result, the Maronite patriarch became the Christian and national moral authority in Lebanon. Any discussion about the church in Lebanon now includes the Maronite Church and all the Christian churches, and the situation of the Maronites often reflects that of all Christians in Lebanon and the East.[43]

---

suburbs because statistics related to religious communities are almost absent. Mary Samarra stated in an interview in 2021 that for twenty years her town of Jdeidet Marjehyoun in the south had around 15,000 inhabitants (98 percent Christian). However, due to the area's remoteness from the capital and the frequent wars, 9,000 people remained in the town on the election lists, and there were about 2,000 permanent residents. The rest had migrated to Europe, America, and Canada, or left to work in the Arab countries or to Beirut. Those who had left to work in the Arab countries or migrated to Beirut generally retained links with their town, renovated their homes there, and went to the village for holidays or elections. Margueritte Salloum, in an interview in 2021, spoke about her town of Khirbet Kanafar in the western Bekaa. The number of residents is about 3,000 people (97 percent Christian), and about 1,000 people live in it. The rest are dispersed in Beirut and its suburbs. They generally return to the town on weekends or on holidays and religious occasions.

42. In the annual Lenten message to the faithful in 1990, Patriarch Sfeir said: "There is a historical fact that cannot be denied, which is that our Maronite Church—and we say it simply—had a great role in the formation of Lebanon, and its characteristics and the uniqueness of its features. Its clerics assumed temporal power alongside spiritual authority at different periods of time when Maronites camped in their mountains in the face of all invaders and conquerors, preserving for them their freedoms, religious beliefs and inherited customs, without creating hostility in their surroundings. And they knew how to deal with flexibility mixed with strictness, and they preserved with it the dignity, independence of opinion, and attitude they espoused" (Sfeir, في الكنيسة والسياسة, 10).

43. The Lebanese writer Fouad Ephrem al-Boustany recalled that at an international cultural conference in Iran in 1956, he met with the patriarch of the Nestorians (Christians who acknowledge two ecumenical councils: Nicaea in AD 325 and Constantinople

The church's relationship with the state centers on defending the concept of the homeland, freedom, and the sublime values stemming from it such as independence, justice, and human rights. In particular, the pluralistic reality in Lebanon prompts followers of sects to resort to religious references whenever the state is unable to address an issue that affects the essence of their being. This relationship between an official ecclesiastical institution, on the one hand, and the state or political authority, on the other, has often succeeded in ensuring the good of society and the nation. On other occasions it has failed for reasons that include the control of personal, factional, and minority interests in this relationship; lack of political experience by clerics; the absence of church planning, guidance, and studies for the future; the division of Christians and Christian parties into political, regional, and international affiliations; the church's failure to be neutral and to reconcile these parties and unite Christian ranks; and attempts by Christian leaders to exploit ecclesiastical authority to serve their political work. For example, the head of the Marada Movement, Suleiman Franjieh, attacked Patriarch Sfeir repeatedly and vehemently about Sfeir's calls for Syrian withdrawal. Sfeir had a sudden change of stance prior to the 2009 parliamentary elections and retracted his support for the 1960 electoral law, which is an ambition for Christians. Accordingly, Franjiyeh requested to adopt the law of the year 2000. Despite failures, a series of ecclesiastical achievements and stances emerged between 2000 and 2020. Perhaps the most prominent was the launch of the Council of Maronite Bishops headed by Patriarch Mar Nasrallah Boutros Sfeir (1986–2011) and the famous call on September 9, 2000, for the Syrian army to withdraw permanently from Lebanon.[44] The patriarch also made efforts between 2000 and 2005 to expel the Syrian army from Lebanon and lift Syrian guardianship through his tours in the United States of America and Canada, and in his refusal to amend the constitution to extend the term of the outgoing president of the republic in 2004.

---

in AD 381). Al-Boustany asked the patriarch about the situation of Christians in that country. The patriarch replied: "Oh dear, our situation is related to that of Bkerke. As long as Bkerke is fine, we are fine!" Bkerke is the area where the Maronite patriarch resides and the location of the patriarchal monastery. Refer to Boustani, *Saint Maron's Foundation* (Arabic: ص ،مارون مار مؤسسة ،البستاني), 88–89.

44. The statement said: "After Israel left, is it not time for the Syrian army to reconsider its deployment in preparation for its final withdrawal, pursuant to the Taif Agreement? Is it necessary for it to remain stationed near the Republican Palace, a symbol of national dignity, the Ministry of Defense, and everything else?" It is a sensitive place where the Lebanese feel greatly embarrassed by its presence, not to say a derogation from their sovereignty and national dignity." See Assembly of Maronite Bishops, Bkerké, "Call of Maronite Bishops," para. 3.

The church in Lebanon also launched the Political Conduct Charter in March 2009. This was based on the recommendations of the Maronite Patriarchal Synod (2003–2006) and the joint session of the Catholic, Orthodox, and evangelical churches held in March 2008. The charter was a collective endeavor to educate the conscience so political practice would not deviate from its objectives and role in serving the community, especially in the context of existing political practices in Lebanon.[45]

When the office of the president became vacant between 2014 and 2016, Patriarch Mor Bechara Boutros al-Rahi made repeated calls in his sermons and on his foreign trips for the void to be filled at the top of the state structure, especially as this post is reserved for Maronites and its vacancy creates a threat to the Christian presence.

Later, the patriarch referenced the intensified dispute over the role and presence of Hezbollah and attempts to plunge the country into regional conflicts. In summer 2020, he announced a memorandum on Lebanon and Active Neutrality, which he communicated to the United Nations and which proposed the internationalization of Lebanon.[46]

Throughout the past twenty years, the church in Lebanon with its patriarchs and bishops has not hesitated to convey to officials the distress of citizens when social crises intensify or when one sect or another is excluded from government appointments. According to Catholicos Aram I, the church cannot remain indifferent to these problems that relate to dignity and the rights of society. Accordingly, its prophetic vocation "forces it to take firm stances stemming from evangelical principles."[47]

---

45. The Political Conduct Charter summarized education by the church about the political community, its concept, goals, biblical and theological foundations, ethical exercise of political authority, relationship of the latter with the church and the areas of cooperation and interconnection between them, the independence of each of them in terms of powers, tasks and means, and the association of political action with the dignity of the human person, human rights, and the general good. See Maronite Center for Documentation and Research, *Charter of Political Action.*

46. First, the memorandum is based on Lebanon not entering into alliances, axes, political conflicts, or wars, regionally and internationally; and on any regional or international state refraining from interfering in its affairs, dominating, invading, occupying, or using its lands for military purposes. Second, the memorandum calls for Lebanese sympathy with issues of human rights and the freedom of peoples, especially Arab ones, on which their countries and the United Nations are unanimous. Third, the principle of active neutrality is based on strengthening the Lebanese state to be strong through its army, institutions, law, justice, internal unity, and creativity to guarantee both internal security and defense against any aggression. See the full contents of the memorandum in Al-Rahi, "Lebanon and Active Neutrality."

47. From a speech by Catholicos Aram I Kishishian entitled "Beyond Recession and Uncertainty" at the conference held at the Monastery of Our Lady of the

The Greek Orthodox archbishop of Beirut, Elias Awdeh, repeatedly raised the alarm and informed officials when they neglected their political practices or the rights of the Greek Orthodox in the functions of the state. Likewise, the bishop of the Maronite Archdiocese of Beirut, Paul Abdel Sater, was outspoken in his annual sermon and at the Mass for the feast of Maron, especially in his call for officials to resign.

This is how the relationship between the church and the state unfolded between 2000 and 2020. It is not a relationship of mutual hostility but is based on constructive criticism and on trying to preserve the rights and freedoms of Christians in society. This is especially important since the essence of the problem in Lebanon lies in the ongoing struggle of religious sects over power and influence, and the transformation of the sects in this struggle into sociopolitical blocs.[48] This is what prompted many, including the demonstrators in the October 17 revolution, to reject religious influence over the political system and to demand a civil society based on citizenship.

CHRISTIANS IN LEBANON BETWEEN SOCIETAL FREEDOM AND HIDDEN DISCRIMINATION

Christians in Lebanon are distinguished from other Christians in the Arab Mashreq in that they live in a society that enjoys freedoms, and especially religious freedom, thanks to the pluralistic status of Lebanon.[49] Lebanon's constitution stipulates freedom of belief and of education in its ninth and tenth articles, provided that the dignity of a religion or religious denomination is not violated.[50] In this regard, an observer of the status of Christians in

---

Mountain—Fatqa, on the "Christian Presence in Lebanon," Mar. 11–14, 2008. Aram I is the head of the Catholicosate of the Great House of Cilicia of the Armenian Apostolic Church in Lebanon Syria, Cyprus, the Persian Gulf, Iran, the United States of America, and others.

48. Monnan, "Church and Politics" (Arabic: مونان، "الكنيسة والسياسة"، ص).

49. Lebanon is considered a pioneer in religious dialogue. In 1954 the first Islamic-Christian conference in the world was held at the initiative of American Friends of the Middle East, and in 2019 Lebanon was designated by the United Nations as an official international center for dialogue between cultures and religions. The first joint Islamic-Christian festival was dedicated in Lebanon. In 2010, the Lebanese Council of Ministers approved a request submitted by the National Committee for Islamic-Christian Dialogue to convert the Christian Annunciation Day of the Virgin Mary, which falls on Mar. 25, into a joint national, Islamic-Christian holiday, with the aim of uniting Lebanese Muslims and Christians around a religious holiday to be celebrated together. The Virgin Mary has a special place in Islam, and an incident of her preaching is mentioned in the Holy Qur'an.

50. Article 9 of the Lebanese Constitution stipulates the following: "There shall be

Lebanon between the years 2000 and 2020 would note that Christians still enjoy religious freedom, whether in managing the affairs of their churches and spiritual courts that rule on issues of marriage and divorce; or in their rituals, worship, and feasts; or in their daily lives.[51] However, this freedom does not extend beyond the religious sphere and remains captive to the sectarian regime in the country. Procedures for marriage and divorce remain entrusted to religious courts only. The government recognizes civil marriage ceremonies performed outside the country, but mixed marriages are still rejected in many societies. Members of unrecognized Protestant sects were forced to register themselves as belonging to recognized religious groups in government records to ensure that their marriage contracts and other personal status documents were legally valid.[52]

This atmosphere of freedom and dialogue did not prevent the expansion of Sunni fundamentalist movements and terrorist groups, especially in the city of Tripoli in northern Lebanon. These groups conducted terrorist operations under the guise of religion to target the morale of the state and the army, and to execute external political plans linked to the growing Sunni-Shiite conflict in the region, including the war in Syria and the role of Hezbollah and its weapons. Although not often directed against Christians, the operations had purely political aims and led to deaths, especially among members of the army. Examples are the events of Donniyeh in 2000, Nahr al-Bared in 2007, and Arsal and Saida between 2013 and 2017, when the army planned to confront these terrorist cells and groups rapidly, dismantle them, and thwart their plans.[53] Terror attacks that directly targeted

absolute freedom of conscience. The state in rendering homage to the God Almighty shall respect all religions and creeds and shall guarantees, under its protection the free exercise of all religious rites provided that public order is not disturbed. It shall also guarantees [sic] that the personal status and religious interests of the population, to whatever religious sect they belong, shall be respected." Article 10 states: "Education shall be free insofar as it is not contrary to public order and morals and does not affect the dignity of any of the religions or sects. There shall be no violation of the right of religious communities to have their own schools provided they follow the general rules issued by the state regulating public instruction." See https://www.presidency.gov.lb/English/LebaneseSystem/Documents/Lebanese%20Constitution.pdf.

51. Unlike the Muslim communities in Lebanon, where some sheikhs receive their salaries from the government, Christian communities in Lebanon are independent but benefit from many allocations and exemptions from some taxes and fees. The budget for the Christian religious courts is deducted annually from the Ministry of Justice (about 4 billion and 100 million Lebanese pounds).

52. See US Department of State, *Lebanon 2017*.

53. Since the middle of the twentieth century, the city of Tripoli has been seen as a stronghold of radical Sunni Islamist groups. There are several reasons for this, including extreme poverty and class differences among its residents, which has allowed the spread

Christian civilians took place on February 5, 2006, in Beirut; in the town of al-Qaa on June 27, 2016; and in the town of Kaftoun on August 21, 2020.[54]

The Shiite Hezbollah, which is classified by the US as a foreign terrorist organization, continues to impose its authority over basic state facilities such as the airport, the port of Beirut, and in areas inhabited by a Shiite majority in the southern neighborhoods of Beirut and the south of the country. In these areas, it provides basic services like health insurance, education, and food aid. From time to time, Hezbollah controls entry into neighborhoods and areas under its control, as it did on May 7, 2008, in addition to its involvement in the war in Syria, and the smuggling of US dollars and fuel from Lebanon to Syria to avoid the Caesar Act.

Such events, although relatively numerous between 2000 and 2020, remained under control and did not affect the lives of the Lebanese in general or of Christians, who continued to enjoy communal and religious freedom and coexistence. Some Christians did flee to Israel upon its withdrawal from

---

of fundamentalist groups for religious and political purposes linked to external plans. At the beginning of 2000, violent confrontations took place between the army and Sunni militants from Tripoli who belonged to an extremist Islamic movement linked to al-Qaeda. This group was located in the northern hills in an attempt to overthrow the Lebanese regime and impose a fundamentalist Islamic system. Among the Christians, 5 army members and 2 civilians were martyred. In 2007, 171 martyrs were killed by the army, including 37 Christians, during a confrontation that lasted for 105 days with the extremist Fatah al-Islam organization, which was hiding in a Palestinian camp near Tripoli and had members that included Lebanese and Palestinians. Between 2013 and 2014 during the war in Syria, the army lost about 25 martyrs, including 10 Christians, in the army's response to ISIS. A large number of its affiliates infiltrated the Lebanese town of Arsal, adjacent to the Syrian border, with the aim of confronting Hezbollah, which participated in the war in Syria, or during the arrest of the Salafi Sheikh Ahmed al-Assir, who was supporting ISIS in Syria and inciting against Hezbollah.

54. Terrorist incidents that directly targeted civilian Christians included, on Feb. 5, 2006, a large number of demonstrators entering the Christian Ashrafieh area and attempting to attack property during a demonstration organized by an Islamic group to protest against the caricatures of Prophet Muhammad in a Danish newspaper. At the time, it was said that infiltrators entered the demonstration for political purposes. On June 27, 2016, suicide bombers from the ISIS organization from Syria entered the Christian town of al-Qaa, located on the Syrian border in the northern Bekaa. One of them, riding a motorcycle, threw a grenade at a gathering of citizens in front of the town's church, then blew himself up with an explosive belt. That was followed by three suicide bombers who blew themselves up, successively, after failing to implement their plan to kill a number of citizens and blow up an army station. This incident resulted in the killing of five Christian citizens. On the night of Aug. 21, 2020, three young Christians from the municipality police were killed in the town of Kaftoun in the north after they examined an unknown parked car and its passengers. The four passengers shot the young men and killed them immediately. It became clear later that the passengers were Syrians and Lebanese affiliated to an ISIS terrorist cell and planning a terrorist act, the objectives of which are still unknown.

southern Lebanon.[55] However, observers have noted societal discrimination of another kind and a hidden and systematic attack via the exclusion of Christians from state jobs or attempts to buy Christian homes after the Beirut blast.

A study published in 2018 showed the extent of sectarian disparity in public administrations and institutions. Christians made up 37 percent of salaried employees, and 23 percent of contractual and daily workers (casual labor), bringing the total of all Christians to just 29 percent of employees. Muslims made up 63 percent of salaried employees, and 77 percent of contractual and daily workers, bringing the total of all Muslims to 71 percent of employees. The study showed that the percentage of Muslims was divided equally between Sunnis and Shiites. A significant change was noted in public bodies. For example, in the departments and courts of Baabda, which was the center of the Chehab emirate, the judges were all Maronite, but the majority are now Muslims. The same is true in the Public Security Department, which was previously reserved for Roman Catholics but is now shared with the Islamic communities.

Following the explosion in Beirut's port, which affected mostly Christian areas, the remarkable thing was that foreign and Lebanese brokers made direct approaches to buy the demolished houses. Following the explosion in Beirut's port, which affected mostly Christian areas, the remarkable thing was that foreign and Lebanese brokers made direct approaches to buy the demolished houses. This issue was tackled by the Greek Orthodox archbishop of Beirut, Elias Awdeh, in one of his sermons: "Sin destroyed Beirut too many times. However, this city rose and it will always rise. Though, it will not rise again if we abandon it and sell our homes to strangers who are still hovering their money around the poor,

55. In the aftermath of the Israeli army's withdrawal from the south on May 25, 2000, any Lebanese who had dealt with Israel or the South Lebanon Army feared reprisals against them by Hezbollah or of being accused of conspiracy by the Lebanese state. At that time, their number was about 8,000 people (individuals with their families), including 6,000 Christians, especially Maronites, and 2,000 Shiites and Druze. After nearly a month, only about 2,500 Christians returned to sanctions applied on the accused (trials and imprisonment between a month and two years). Of the remaining Christians, about 900 of them went to Sweden, and the others were distributed in France, Germany, Denmark, Canada, America, and Australia. Some of them remained in Israel or in occupied Palestine. The Maronite Church still engages with those resident in Israel and tries to communicate with them and help them through the bishop of Haifa and the Holy Land, waiting for their cases to be resolved legally and allowing those who wish to return to Lebanon to do so. Many of these people refuse to return and have integrated into other societies where they have secured their livelihoods. Information and figures from the bishop of the Maronite Diocese of Tyr, Charbel Abdallah, and the priest of the parish of Rmeish Najib al-Amil on Apr. 17, 2021.

who see in its destruction nothing but a golden opportunity for exploitation, appropriation and displacement."[56]

Christians have lived in Lebanon for the first twenty years of this century within such a societal context, struggling to preserve their freedoms and to develop their country socially and culturally despite attempts to exclude them.

CHRISTIANS IN LEBANON BETWEEN SOCIAL AND CULTURAL INFLUENCES

The Christian presence in Lebanon has always had an influence on the image of the country on both social and cultural levels. Christians contributed to the Arab renaissance movement (al-Nahda) during the nineteenth and twentieth centuries, and in other accomplishments.[57] Their pioneering role continued in the early twenty-first century as they sought, as individuals or groups, to achieve a better society by developing and modernizing in industrial, agricultural, tourism, and economic aspects. Christians emerged in industry, trade, construction and public works, banking, modern agricultural activities, and the wine industry. They were also pioneers in activities such as skiing, tourism sectors such as restaurants and hotels, and the reviving of international festivals. Christians working in the Gulf and African countries also contributed to the flow of dollars into the country, especially during the recent financial crisis.

On the cultural level, Christians have excelled in literature, arts and humanities, printing and publishing, journalism and media, and the creation and development of media institutions. The field of literature, for example, saw the rise of Amin Maalouf, Alexander Najjar, and others. Human sciences witnessed the rise of Father Salim Daccache, president of Saint Joseph University of Beirut (USJ); Father Georges Hobeika, honorary president of the Holy Spirit University of Kaslik (USEK); and Minister Ghassan Salameh, head of the United Nations Mission in Libya. The singer Fayrouz

---

56 Boswall, "After Explosion."

57. The Arab renaissance (al-Nahda) is a state of mind that prevailed in Egypt, Lebanon, and other Arab capitals in the nineteenth century. Its most prominent manifestations are the spread of editing, the emergence of the press and publishing houses, the establishment of schools and universities, the revival of Arab heritage, arts and theater, the recovery of the Arabic language from its decline during the Ottoman era, and the demand for the establishment of modern European-style states. Prominent Lebanese Christians who pioneered the Arab renaissance include Ibrahim al-Yaziji, Nasif al-Yazji, Boutros al-Boustany, Gibran Khalil Gibran, Mikhail Naima, May Ziadeh, and Amin al-Rihani. For more information on the Arab Renaissance, see Hourani, *Arabic Thought.*

remains a symbol of Lebanon, and French President Emmanuel Macron requested to meet her on his visit to Beirut in the summer of 2020.

Although Christians, both residents and expatriates,[58] left their benevolent traces on society during 2000 to 2020, the role of the church in Lebanon cannot be overlooked, whether in its direct influence on society through its institutions or through the decisions of the Maronite Patriarchal Synod. From the previous century, the church had become aware of the government's negligence in the social sphere and sought to establish hospitals, schools, and universities to provide medical care, disseminate science and culture, and ensure job opportunities and housing for youth who wished to marry. By the early twenty-first century, these institutions were advanced and sophisticated, and served Muslims and Christians, Lebanese and non-Lebanese. This was referred to in the final statement of the joint session of churches in the Christian Presence in Lebanon conference of 2008: "Lebanese society in general owes these institutions without favor as Christians consider them part of their testimony and their message in the world."[59] However, these institutions face serious financial issues related to poor management and a lack of planning, in addition to the suffocating economic and monetary crisis in the country, the COVID-19 pandemic, and cuts to external aid from foreign institutions.

Texts and recommendations issued by the Maronite Patriarchal Synod between 2003 and 2006 formed a new constitution for Maronites that reevaluated the identity and mission of the Maronite Church in today's world.[60] The constitution has a pioneering role in spreading education, higher education and culture, and in engaging with public affairs and a variety of institutions inside the church. This abundance represents the nerve of Lebanese society, specifically of Christians.

CHRISTIANS IN LEBANON BETWEEN THEIR ECCLESIASTICAL AND MONASTIC INSTITUTIONS

Church institutions in Lebanon are affiliated with the Catholic, Orthodox, or evangelical churches. Institutions linked to the Catholic Church comprise

---

58. Lebanese Christians who have excelled in expatriate countries include businessmen Carlos Ghosn and Carlos Slim; Jacques Saada, founder of CGA CGM, the fourth largest container and transport company in the world; and Charlie Khoury, cofounder and CEO of NAR.

59. "Christian Presence in Lebanon," 46.

60. For the texts and recommendations of the synod, see Assembly of Maronite Bishops, Bkerké, *Maronite Patriarchal Synod 2003–2006* (Arabic: المجمع البطريركي الماروني).

those affiliated with patriarchates or archdioceses, and those affiliated with monastic orders or missions.[61] Institutions are governed by the bishop directly in the Orthodox Churches, or by the National Evangelical Synod in Syria and Lebanon for the evangelical churches.

In total there are nineteen hospitals providing healthcare and distributed as follows: Hotel Dieu (the property of the French state and administered by Saint Joseph University of Beirut); Saint George Hospital University Medical Center (for the Beirut Archdiocese of the Greek Orthodox); Lebanese Hospital Geitaoui—UMC (for the Maronite Sisters of the Holy Family); Notre Dame de Secours—Jbeil Hospital (for the Lebanese Order); Saint Joseph Hospital and the Psychiatric Hospital of the Cross (for the Sisters of the Cross); Heart of Jesus Hospital and the Hospital of Bhannes Hospitality Center (for the Charity Sisters); the Rosary Sisters' Hospital, Saint Charles Hospital, and Mgr Cortbawi Institute and Rehabilitation Hospital (for the Sisters of the Sacred Heart); Saint Therese, Saint Louis, and Saint Georges Hospitals (for the Maronite Sisters of Saint Theresa); Our Lady of Peace Hospital and Dar al-Rahma Hospital (for the Antonine Sisters); al-Mahabba Hospital (for the Maronite Bishopric of Deir al-Ahmar); and Hamlin Nursing Home and Hospital (for Evangelicals). The American University of Beirut Hospital is not affiliated with a specific religious community as desired by the founder, but the credit for its establishment and growth is due to the Evangelical Mission, specifically the Reverend Daniel Bliss (1823–1916).

61. These monastic groups are divided between the monastic orders that developed historically and originated in Lebanon from the seventeenth century and foreign monastic orders that carry out their Christian mission in this country. In the Maronite Church there are five male religious orders: the Lebanese Maronite Order, the Mariamite Maronite Order, the Antonine Maronite Order, the Lebanese Maronite Missionaries Association, and the Maronite Monastic Community—Mission de Vie (mixed). There are eight religious orders for females in the Maronite Church as follows: Nuns of the Lebanese Order, the Antonine Maronite Nuns, the Sisters of Saint Theresa of the Child Jesus, the Nuns of the Visitation, the Congregation of the Maronite Sisters of the Holy Family, the Maronite Missionaries of the Eucharist, the Maronite Sisters of our Lady of the Prairies, the Maronite Sisters of Saint John the Baptist, and Nuns of the Abandoned Christ. In the Melkite Catholic Church there are nine monastic orders, of which four are for males: the Basilian Chouerite Order, the Basilian Salvatorian Order, the Aleppo Basilian Order, and the Association of the Pauline Fathers. Five are dedicated for females, namely: the Basilian Choueirite Sisters, the Basilian Aleppian Sisters, the Basilian Salvatorian Sisters, Missionary Sisters of Our Lady of Perpetual Help, and the Sisters of Our Lady of Good Service. In addition, there are some fifty foreign monastic orders run by missionaries. Some of them have a historical presence in Lebanon, such as the Jesuits, the Capuchins, the Lazarians, and the Franciscans. This is in addition to the twenty-five Orthodox monasteries, which include monks and nuns who follow the local bishop, unlike the Catholics where each monastic order has its own independent structure and authority.

For higher education, there are eleven universities distributed as follows: Saint Joseph University of Beirut—USJ (Jesuits); the Holy Spirit University of Kaslik—USEK (Lebanese Maronite Order); University of Balamand (Greek Orthodox); Notre Dame University—NDU (Mariamite Order); the Antonine University (Antonine Order); La Sagesse University (Maronite Archdiocese of Beirut); the Holy Family (Nuns of the Holy Family); Haigazian University (Armenian Evangelicals); the Middle East University—MEU (Adventist Church); in addition to the American University of Beirut—AUB and the Lebanese American University—LAU established by the Evangelists.

In addition to these institutions of higher education, there are faculties and institutes that teach theology, liturgy,[62] religious sciences, and Islamic-Christian dialogue to prepare the priests of tomorrow and to nurture believers who desire deeper studies in religious, cultural, and pastoral aspects of postgraduate studies. These institutions include the Pontifical Faculty of Theology and the Institute of Liturgy at the Holy Spirit University of Kaslik; the Faculty of Religious Sciences, the Higher Institute of Religious Sciences and the Institute of Islamic and Christian Studies at Saint Joseph University-Beirut;[63] the Faculty of Theological Sciences and Pastoral Studies at the Antonine University—Baabda; the Faculty of Religious and Theological Sciences, the Institute of the Family, and the Institute of Religious Education at Sagesse University—Beirut; the Saint Paul Institute for Philosophy and Theology—Harissa; St. John of Damascus Institute of Theology at the University of Balamand—Koura; and the Near East School of Theology (NEST)—Beirut. There are also numerous pastoral centers to inform believers about the principles of the Christian faith and Christian education. These centers are affiliated with dioceses, parishes, or religious orders.

There are 368 schools distributed as follows: 307 schools for Catholic denominations (united under the banner of the General Secretariat of Catholic Schools in Lebanon); 20 Greek Orthodox schools (affiliated with metropolitans); 35 schools for evangelical denominations (part of the Evangelical Schools Association); 3 schools for the Armenian Orthodox; and 3 schools for Syriac Orthodox. In the academic year 2019–2020, Catholic

---

62. "Liturgy" is a word of Greek origin meaning the work of the people or community. It is used to denote Christian rituals, the most important of which is the Mass or the Eucharist.

63. The Institute of Islamic and Christian Studies is the first institute established in 1977 in Lebanon and the East for training on Islamic-Christian dialogue and on Islamic-Christian relations in a solid academic, scientific, and practical spirit.

schools had 185,137 students and 16,287 teachers, whereas evangelical schools had about 20,000 students.[64]

Other institutions include the Middle East Council of Churches and the committees and organizations emanating from the Council of Catholic Patriarchs and Bishops in Lebanon, which was established in 1967 for mutual work, organization, and cooperation among Catholic churches.[65] These organizations are the following: Caritas Lebanon, the Lebanese Center for Pontifical Apostolic Actions, the Scouts Association of Lebanon, the Association of Fraternities in Lebanon, the General Chaplaincy of Prisons in Lebanon, University Pastoral Work, Tele Lumière Television, and Radio Voice of Charity and Charity TV.[66]

Church institutions or societies concerned with social and cultural affairs include the Maronite Social Foundation (the Maronite Fund) to secure homes for people with limited income or those wishing to marry; the Mutual Health Fund for assistance in medicine and hospitalization; the Maronite Center for Research and Documentation; the Apostolic Association of Churches for the Promotion of Christian Presence in Lebanon and the

64. Statistical information from the secretary general of Catholic schools, Father Boutros Azar the Antonine, and the secretary general of evangelical schools, Dr. Nabil Osta.

65. The Middle East Council of Churches, based in Beirut, is a religious body comprising the four ecclesiastical families in the Middle East, i.e., Orthodox, Eastern Orthodox, evangelical, and Catholic. It has other offices in Cairo, Limassol, Amman, Jerusalem, and Tehran. The council's goal is to work to promote the spirit of Christian unity among the different churches in the region by providing means of dialogue and by conducting joint studies and research that explain the traditions of the member churches. It also establishes common prayers, especially a week of prayer for the unity of Christian churches; this is in addition to the defense of human rights and advocating for justice and equality in citizenship in the countries of the Middle East.

The seventeen episcopal committees from the Council of Catholic Patriarchs and Bishops are: the Theological and Biblical Committee, the Committee for the Mission of the Laity, the Media Committee, the Ecumenical Relations Committee, the Lebanese Expatriate Committee, the Culture and Cultural Property Committee, the Committee for Catholic Schools in Lebanon, the Higher and University Education Committee, the Christian Education Committee in Lebanon, the Committee of Christian-Islamic Dialogue, the Justice and Peace Committee, the Family and Life Affairs Committee in Lebanon, the Pastoral Committee for Health Services in Lebanon, the Legal Affairs Committee and Spiritual Courts, the Inter-Church Missionary Cooperation Committee, the Pontifical Theological College Committee, and the Charity Services Committee.

66. Scout movements related to churches include the Cedar Scouts associated with the Lebanese Maronite Order, the Maronite Scouts associated with the Maronite Church, the Orthodox National Scouts associated with the Greek Orthodox Church, the Christian Scouts associated with the Greek Catholic Church, and the Syriac Scouts.

Fraternities are organizations in Catholic parishes concerned with pastoral work, including prayers and spiritual activities.

East; the Maronite League; the Maronite Foundation for Expansion to urge the Lebanese community to adhere to its Lebanese heritage; the Patriarchal Foundation for Development; the Maronites Gathering for Lebanon; the Solidarity Network for Aid;[67] the Supreme Council for the Greek Catholic Community, which engages in social, political, and economic issues that affect members of the Catholic community; the Society of Saint Vincent de Paul; and other movements and associations within parishes, in addition to a large number of orphanages and elderly care centers or infirmaries that are mainly run by female monastic associations, along with publishing houses and Christian libraries.

From 2000 to 2021, these institutions contributed to encouraging the church's role in supporting Christians in Lebanon and enabling Christians to follow the example of Jesus "in wisdom and stature, and in favour with God and man" (Luke 2:52 KJV), and to remain steadfast in their homeland and on their land despite the difficulties and challenges they may face.

CHRISTIANS IN LEBANON BETWEEN DIFFICULTIES AND CHALLENGES

Lebanon and its Christian population in particular are at a crossroads and face grave challenges as follows:

1. The implementation of the Taif Agreement faced a series of difficulties and challenges that prevent the establishment of a citizenship state, most notably:

    *   The loss of presidential powers that enabled the holder to act as an arbitrator on controversial issues. The country became ruled by more than one head, and this consolidated the policy of quotas, which strengthens loyalty to the religious community in lieu of the loyalty of a citizen to the homeland. Selective implementation of the Taif Agreement may have deepened the challenges faced by Christians, especially in treating them fairly and not degrading them.

    *   The difficulty of holding parliamentary elections outside of sectarian restrictions and based on the governorates or Lebanon as

67. The Solidarity Project was launched in spring 2020 as a partnership project between the Lebanese Maronite Order, the Maronite Foundation for the Diaspora, and the Gilbert and Rose-Marie Chagoury Foundation, with the blessings of Patriarch al-Rahi. It aims to support Lebanese families, especially Christians, who are suffering from the economic situation in Lebanon due to the economic crisis and the coronavirus pandemic.

a single electoral district. Sectarian divisions have reached unprecedented levels, and Muslims are dominant demographically. Christians see a civil state with not only the abolition of political sectarianism but an end to all manifestations of sectarianism, starting with the unification of personal status laws and voluntary civil marriage legislation.

- Lack of agreement on a unified defense strategy to disarm Hezbollah or to place it under the command of the Lebanese army, especially as Christian groups were disarmed immediately after the Taif Agreement. Other non-Christian groups still possess arms, such as the Shiite Amal Movement, led by Nabih Berri, and the Progressive Socialist Party, led by Druze leader Walid Jumblatt.

2. The growing Sunni-Shiite conflict in the region since the 1990s feeds divisions between Christians, especially between the Lebanese forces that oppose both Hezbollah and the Free Patriotic Movement.[68] Christians' own vision of the future is becoming more and more divided between a view of the Sunni majority in the region as a threat to the Christian existence, and therefore seeking to join with religious communities and states that would contain the potential Sunni resurgence; and a view that considers resistance and confrontation, especially in mobilization backed by Iran, as the source of an existential danger. Add to this the absence of the church's role in Lebanon and its failure to conduct Christian-Christian reconciliation and strategic planning to strengthen the situation of Christians in the future.

3. The absence of consensus on financial and economic reform to exit the tunnel of bankruptcy and debt faced by Lebanon.

4. It is believed that there are huge quantities of oil and gas to the north and south of the Lebanese coast. Thus, Lebanon will fall prey to internal conflicts and external conspiracies in attempts to gain control of the country's assets and political powers in the absence of an internationally recognized demarcation of the maritime borders.

5. Psychological frustration among Christian youth related to their loyalty to their homeland and the strong urge to emigrate. Statistics have shown that more than 60 percent of young Christians want to emigrate, according to Father Tony Khadra, head of the Labora Foundation that sources job opportunities for Christian youth. Patriarch

68. The Sunni-Shiite conflict in the region is a struggle for economic and religious influence, manifested in war-political conflicts such as those in Yemen, Saudi Arabia, Iraq, Syria, and Lebanon. For more information on this topic see Agha and Mali, "Real Divide."

al-Rahi has also warned of emigration by young educated Christians, including doctors, university professors, and lawyers.[69] Migration increased dramatically after the explosion in the port in August 2020 and during the severe deterioration in economic conditions throughout 2021. Lebanon lost about one thousand doctors and nurses, plus a large number of university and school academics whose earnings were reduced drastically by the surge in the US dollar. This is in addition to the departure of a large number of school and university students to schools in Cyprus or universities in Europe and America.

6. The absence of a strategic vision of Lebanon's regional and international role. The country lost its leadership in the last two decades, especially in the service sectors, and its renowned coexistence of religions and cultures has diminished due to internal conflicts and divisions. In the midst of this confusion and uncertainty, Christians face great challenges and the loss of their superiority in fields such as education and culture. However, the biggest challenge is for Lebanon to emerge from this period of decline and rise to the ranks of leadership again in new roles that keep pace with the crowded competition for preeminence among the countries of the region.

CHRISTIANS IN LEBANON BETWEEN PROSPECTS AND FUTURE ASPIRATIONS

It is difficult for Christians in Lebanon to look to the future to determine their horizons or define their aspirations, as the existing situation deprives them of that opportunity. According to the theologian and one of the fathers of the church, Saint Augustine: "How can a man who faces the challenges and storms of life inform us about everything, how it will be, and how would the conditions affect him?"[70] However, there is space for Christian hope adorned with Jesus's saying: "I have told you these things, so that

69. On immigration, the final statement from the Christian Presence in Lebanon Conference held in 2008 was the following: "It is a bleeding that increases day after day for Christians from the region, especially from Lebanon, as this country loses energies, talents, and multiple capabilities whose absence constitutes a threat to its future. Infection in various segments of this society. Migration may be beneficial to individuals, but harmful in most cases to the family, the church and society, and if it continues, it will alter the demographic reality of the homeland, exposing its message and presence to loss. This matter must be addressed to find out the causes that led to it, and to find effective solutions to reassure people of their future on their land and the homeland of their fathers and grandfathers."

70. O'Donnell at al., "St. Augustine."

in me you may have peace. In this world you will have trouble. But take heart! I have overcome the world" (John 16:33). A state of turmoil, challenge, and anxiety has emerged recently among Christians in light of the difficult internal and external developments. Several important discussions have been launched among Christian groups about the future of Christians in Lebanon and their role.

One of the most prominent discussions appeared in the document *We Choose Abundant Life* launched in Beirut in September 2021 by a number of Christian theologians and thinkers.[71] The document reviewed the reality and conditions of Christians in the Middle East and presented practical ideas and suggestions to confront challenges and chart the future prospects for Christians in Lebanon and in other countries of the Middle East. The key points in this document to face the challenges are continuing ecumenical unity between churches, approaching the issues of the region and its people on the basis of a national and regional contextual theology; renewing ecclesiastical and theological discourse that suits existing conditions; adopting new democratic policies for Christians in the Middle East away from repressive authorities; strengthening the relationship with youth; developing Islamic-Christian dialogue with a new vision; strengthening the presence of Christians in state institutions; addressing public affairs issues; establishing civil laws for personal status and achieving equality among citizens; adopting state neutrality towards religions and commitment to citizenship; and aligning with issues of freedoms, human rights, democracy, and the peaceful transfer of power.

Bishop Samir Mazloum, the former patriarchal vicar-general and director of the Maronite Center for Research and Documentation,[72] links the future of Christians in Lebanon with the future of Christians in general in the Middle East. Lebanon has a different status from other countries as it is not only for Christians or Muslims but is characterized by pluralism, diversity, freedom, dialogue, equality, and coexistence. The uniqueness of Lebanon, according to Mazloum, lies in its unique constitution and civil and nonreligious laws that are fair to all, unlike other countries of the East and the Arab world. While Lebanon is known for the plurality of its religious

71. Pastor Prof. Mitri Raheb from Palestine (founder and president of Dar al-Kalima University), Mrs. Soraya Bechealany from Lebanon (former general secretary of the Middle East Council of Churches), Parch Rouphael Zgheib (Lebanon), Parch Khalil Chalfoun (Lebanon), researcher Ziad El Sayegh (Lebanon), Sister Emilie Tannous (Lebanon), Rev. Georges Jabra al-Kopti (Jordan), Rev. Najla Kassab (Lebanon), Mr. Asaad Elias Kattan (from Lebanon and resides in Germany), Mr. Michel Nassir (from Lebanon and resides in Switzerland), and Father Gabriel Alfred Hachem (Lebanon). See Bechealany et al., *We Choose Abundant Life*.

72. Following an interview at the Maronite Patriarchate in Bkerke on Apr. 23, 2021.

communities, this plurality exists within a balanced legal framework between the Christian and Islamic religions. The logic of national belonging prevails over the logic of religious affiliation, and the rights of all Lebanese are fully secured without discrimination.

Thus, according to Mazloum, the fate of Christians is linked to the fate of Lebanon, or to the ability of the Lebanese to preserve this ideal image. If the forces that want to change the human, cultural, and civilizational face of Lebanon prevail, then the Christian presence will be in danger. The Lebanese entity would also be in danger, as Lebanon is meaningless with only one religious community. If the Lebanese people as a whole want to set up a new regime for the country, then they must, according to Mazloum, take into account the existing system or the current formula, which time has proven to be vital and which has many benefits in terms of freedom, pluralistic acceptance, and coexistence. Any imbalances in practice and defects in existing implementation must also be considered. The proposal of partition as a fair solution for Christians and Muslims would not be possible, because historical experiences have shown that the small size of Lebanon does not allow this in terms of habitation or economic and agricultural production.

In conclusion, the only solution to chart new horizons and future aspirations for Christians in Lebanon and to enable an exit from the recent crisis, according to Mazloum, remains the return of the Lebanese to a Christian-Christian dialogue, and then to a Christian-Islamic one to spread the language of awareness, understanding, and love. This could improve imbalances in the Lebanese system with the aim of advancing the Lebanese state on the political, social, and economic levels.

Even if the bishop's words seem full of logic, positivity, and hope, he is mistaken because he holds the Lebanese alone responsible for the future of their country. In fact, Lebanon's future prospects are clouded by worrying concerns about the fate of Christians who are in a worsening and continuing existential crisis today. The problem lies in the fact that the Lebanese identity is not the same for all components. Only Christians cling to a Lebanese entity that gives them this unique space of freedom and political action. Muslims reluctantly accepted the state of Greater Lebanon, but their affiliations are still not Lebanese.

In light of this difference, conflict of all kinds in Lebanon can be understood, whether within the same sect or within different groups. The call for positive neutrality is, in fact, the ideal solution to a long-running complication, but is there anyone who agrees with it nationally, regionally, and internationally? What is the role of the Maronite patriarchate in bringing Christians together? Why has it not yet moved in this direction, and we find the patriarch sometimes in one direction and sometimes in another? Why does he not lead the way, even if his role is religious and not political?

CONCLUSION

On the creation of civilizations, the philosopher and historian Arnold Toynbee said: "Civilizations, I believe, come to birth and proceed to grow by successfully responding to successive challenges. They break down and go to pieces if and when a challenge confronts them which they fail to meet."[73]

All the groups of Lebanese today defy this existence. Their condition is like a ship at sea torn apart by storms from all sides; they are drowning day after day in internal and external crises, especially as Lebanon has not been a topic of global political debate for some time. The current focus is on preserving Israel's security and the disarmament of Hezbollah that threatens it, in addition to the US-Iranian negotiations and the repercussions of these on the region, and on Lebanon in particular.

It is true that what Christians are undergoing now is not new to them because their history in this country was a continuous tidal movement written in the blood of martyrs. However, their reality today is extremely dangerous because they are increasingly divided in a real struggle "between those who believe in the original responsible and existential personal freedom, and between those who are raised under this freedom with the intention of using it for other purposes."[74]

Twenty years into the third millennium, will Christians in Lebanon listen to the wisdom of Hegel and imitate the sailor who must rely on his own intelligence and mobility to control the fluctuating waves of the sea, and live their time in the best way? Or will they surrender to reality and go into a deep sleep, reassured by the quote of Jesuit Father Tom Sikking that Christians of the East have no fear of extinction because Christianity is not a number but a message?[75] Subsequently, would they become part of the choir waiting for a funeral that has not yet arrived and join their brothers in Syria, Iraq, Palestine, and the Occupied Territories?

Every time Lebanon is mentioned, the crisis of minorities everywhere and the crisis of values, alongside the absence of honor in politics, come to the fore in a world dominated by authoritarianism and self-worship. Accordingly, shall our contemporary world be devoid of the victory of right over wrong?

73. Toynbee, *Civilization on Trial*, 56.

74. Malek, "Lebanon, an Entity" (Arabic: ص «لبنان، كِيَانٌ» ،مالك), 28.

75. Dagher, *Bring Down the Walls*, 67.

BIBLIOGRAPHY

Abdel Samad, Nada. *Wadi Abu Jamil: Stories about the Jews of Beirut.* [In Arabic.] Beirut: Dar An-Nahar, 2009.

Abou Jaoude, Salah. "The Salvation of the Lebanese Is in Their Hands." [In Arabic.] *An-Nahar*, Mar. 25, 2021. https://salahaboujaoude.com/2021/03/25/.

Agha, Hussein, and Robert Mali. "The Real Divide in the Middle East." [In Arabic.] *Al-Akhbar*, Mar. 13, 2019. https://al-akhbar.com/Opinion/267652.

Al-Hourani, Youssef. *Lebanon in the Values of Its History: A Study in the Philosophy of the History of Lebanon—The Phoenician Era.* [In Arabic.] Beirut: Dar al-Mashriq, 1972.

Al-Rahi, Bechara. "Lebanon and Active Neutrality." [In Arabic.] Lebanon Debate, Aug. 17, 2020. www.lebanondebate.com/news/494068.

Al Salibi, Kamal. *The Modern History of Lebanon.* New York: Caravan, 1993.

Assembly of Maronite Bishops, Bkerké. "The Call of the Maronite Bishops in the Year 2000." [In Arabic.] Lebanese Forces, 2000. https://www.lebanese-forces.com/2014/09/20/bkerke-call-2000/.

———. *The Maronite Patriarchal Synod 2003–2006: Texts and Recommendations.* [In Arabic.] Bkerké, Leb.: N.p., 2006.

Attieh, Shawky. *Demography of the Mashreq.* [In Arabic.] Jounieh, Leb.: Al-Mashreq Center for Research and Studies, 2019.

———. *Population in Lebanon: From Political Reality to Economic and Social Change.* [In Arabic.] Beirut: Dar Nelson, 2014.

Avon, Dominique. *Hezbollah: A History of the "Party of God."* Cambridge, MA: Harvard University Press, 2012.

Bechealany, Souraya, et al. *We Choose Abundant Life: Christians in the Middle East; Towards Renewed Theological, Social, and Political Choices.* Beirut: We Choose Abundant Life Group, 2021. online.anyflip.com/mijbx/mawd/mobile/index.html.

Boswall, Jacob. "After Explosion, Lebanese Say 'Beirut Is Not for Sale' to Corrupt Developers." *Alarabiya*, Aug. 23, 2020. https://english.alarabiya.net/features/2020/08/23/After-explosion-Lebanese-say-Beirut-is-not-for-sale-to-corrupt-developers.

Boustani, Fouad Ephrem. *Saint Maron's Foundation: The Maronite Nation—The Maronite Patriarchate.* [In Arabic.] Beirut: Circuit, 1985.

"The Christian Presence in Lebanon." Joint proceedings of a conference of the Catholic, Orthodox, and Evangelical Churches, Our Lady of the Mountain Monastery, Fatqa, Lebanon, Mar. 11–14, 2008. Further bibliographic information unavailable.

Courbage, Youssef, and Emmanuel Todd. *Le rendez-vous des civilizations.* Paris: Seuil, 2007.

Dagher, Carole. *Bring Down the Walls: Lebanon's Post-War Challenge.* Basingstoke, UK: Palgrave, 2001.

Daher, Karen Elian. "Austerity Has Become Necessary in the Life of the Lebanese." [In Arabic.] *Independent Arabia*, Jan. 9, 2020. https://www.independentarabia.com/node/85421/.

Dam, Nikolaos Van. *Destroying a Nation: The Civil War in Syria.* New York: Tauris, 2017.

Dib, Kamal. *This Ancient Bridge: The Fall of Christians in Lebanon, 1920–2020.* [In Arabic.] 3rd ed. Beirut: Dar An-Nahar, 2013.

El-Hajj, Kamal Youssef. *Christ and Lebanon*. [In Arabic.] Beirut: Armenian Evangelical Central High School Press, 1970.

El-Helou, Christian. *Church History in Brief*. Beirut: La Sagesse University Press, 2009.

Fleyfel, Antoine. *Géopolitique des Chrétiens d'Orient: Défis et avenir des chrétiens arabes*. Paris: Harmattan, 2013.

Freiha, Nemer. *The Continuous Controversy over Identity and Destiny (1860–2020)*. [In Arabic.] Centennial Series for Greater Lebanon 1. Beirut: Saer al-Mashriq, 2020.

Grim, Brian, et al. *Yearbook of International Religious Demography 2018*. Yearbook of International Religious Demography 5. Leiden, Neth.: Brill, 2018.

Hayek, Michel. *Writings on the History and Spirituality of the Maronite Church*. [In Arabic.] Edited and translated by Daniel Zogheib. Liturgical Heritage Series 1. Jounieh, Leb.: St. Paul Library, 2009.

Hendler, Sefi. "Beirut's Last Jews." *Ynet News*, Aug. 19, 2006. https://www.ynetnews.com/articles/0,7340,L-3292543,00.html.

Hiro, Dilip. *Lebanon Fire and Embers: A History of the Lebanese Civil War*. New York: St. Martin's, 1992.

Hitti, Philip. *History of Lebanon: From the Earliest Historical Era to the Present Era*. [In Arabic.] Translated by Anis Freiha. Beirut: Culture, n.d.

Hourani, Albert Habib. *Arabic Thought in the Liberal Age, 1798–1939*. Cambridge: Cambridge University Press, 1983.

Khalaf, Samir. *Lebanon in the Middle of Violence: A Reading in the Internationalization of Classical Conflicts*. [In Arabic.] Translated by Shukri Rhayem. Beirut: Dar An-Nahar, 2002.

Khazen, Farid. *The Breakdown of the State in Lebanon (1967–1976)*. Cambridge, MA: Harvard University Press, 2000.

Khuri, Fuad I. *Being a Druze*. London: Druze Heritage Foundation, 2004.

Malek, Charles. "Lebanon, an Entity and a Destiny." [In Arabic.] In *Lebanon Concept and Challenges*, edtied by Jad al-Kosseifi, 11–35. Kaslik, Leb.: Holy Spirit University Press, 2011.

Maronite Center for Documentation and Research. *The Charter of Political Action in Light of the Teaching of the Church and the Specificity of Lebanon*. Zouk Mosbeh, Leb.: Maronite Center for Documentation and Research, 2008.

Monnan, Pascal. "The Church and Politics in Lebanon: Constants of the Past for the Future." [In Arabic.] *As-Safir*, Oct. 25, 2007.

Norton, Augustus R. *Hezbollah: A Short History*. Princeton, NJ: Princeton University Press, 2014.

O'Donnell, James, et al. "St. Augustine: Christian Bishop and Theologian." *Britannica*, July 20, 1998; last updated Jan. 4, 2023. https://www.britannica.com/biography/Saint-Augustine.

Paliki, George. "Two Speeches: Before and After the Visit to Lebanon." [In Arabic.] *Al-Masarrah* 83 (July–Oct. 1997) 716–20.

Saadeh, Youhanna Salim. *The Philosophy of the Basin of the Mediterranean and the Lebanese Commitment (in the Writings of Dr. René Habchi)*. [In Arabic.] Kaslik, Leb.: Holy Spirit University Press, 1993.

Salem, Paul. "Lebanon and the Syrian Crisis: Implications and Dangers." Carnegie Middle East Center, Dec. 11, 2012. https://carnegie-mec.org/2012/12/11/can-lebanon-survive-syrian-crisis-pub-50298.

Sfeir, Mar Nasrallah Boutros. في الكنيسة والسياسة [On church and politics]. Bkerké, Leb.: N.p., 1990.

US Department of State. *Lebanon 2017 International Religious Freedom Report*. US Department of State, Jan. 2019. https://www.state.gov/wp-content/uploads/2019/01/Lebanon-2.pdf.

Tay, Mohammed. "طي، محمد، اتفاق الدوحة: ميثاق أم عُرْف أم تسوية مؤقتة" [The Doha agreement, custom, or a temporary settlement]. Dirasat, Mar. 29, 2010. http://dirasat.net/uploads/item_mak_m/2260195.pdf.

Toynbee, Arnold J. *Civilization on Trial*. New York: Oxford University Press, 1948.

Traboulsi, Fawaz. *History of Modern Lebanon: From the Emirate to the Taif Agreement*. [In Arabic.] 4th ed. Beirut: Riad al-Rayyes, 2013.

Tueini, Ghassan. *Une guerre pour les autres*. Preface by Dominique Chevalier. Rev. ed. Beirut: Dar An-Nahar, 2004.

Christians in Palestine

Bernard Sabella

THE SOCIOPOLITICAL AND ECONOMIC CONTEXT OF PALESTINE

PALESTINE IS A UNIQUE country that continues to suffer and survive daily under a belligerent occupation and an unfinished question of war and peace. The Israeli occupation, which has become more entrenched since the Oslo Accords signed in 1993 by the Palestine Liberation Organization (PLO) and the state of Israel, imposes a variety of rules, laws, measures, and restrictions that render Palestinians and the Occupied Palestinian Territory captive to Israeli political, economic, and security considerations.

Indicators on health, education, and social services point to a country that rates with middle-level income countries thanks to low mortality rates, high life expectancy, moderate income, gross domestic product per capita, and almost universal education. Yet in other aspects, Palestine ranks with less advantaged countries of the world due to one of the highest fertility rates per woman, and a high population rate in which almost 40 percent of the population are below the age of fifteen. One of the highest global population densities per square kilometer is in the Gaza Strip.[1] The continuous Israeli siege of the Gaza Strip adds to the woes and frustrations of Palestinians, in addition to the political division between Fatah (Ramallah) and Hamas (Gaza).

Palestinian Christians, particularly in East Jerusalem and the West Bank, appear to have accommodated themselves, like their fellow Palestinians, to

1. See United Nations Relief and Works Agency, "Where We Work." In particular, the eight Palestinian refugee camps in the Gaza Strip have some of the highest population densities in the world: 5,046/km² (13,069.1/mi²).

the current situation despite it not being conducive to stability and a strong rule of law. The dire situation in the Gaza Strip since 2007 has led to further shrinking of the local Christian community as young members elect to remain in foreign lands when they travel to pursue their higher education or seek employment. There is a general feeling of despondency across the population; the *World Happiness Report* for 2018–2020 ranks Palestine 125th on the a list of 149 countries, with Lebanon at 123rd, Jordan at 127th, and Egypt 132nd. For comparative purposes, Israel was ranked 12th, with Bahrain and UAE ranking 22nd and 25th respectively.[2]

Despite the constraints placed on the Palestinian economy by the Israeli occupation, Palestinians have developed survival strategies. The social and political situation adds pressures on the population, Christians included. One salvaging factor for Palestinian youth is the access to dozens or so of universities and junior colleges that offer hundreds of thousands of students the opportunity to learn skills and have hope for a better future. Over 60 percent of students enrolled in higher education in Palestine are women, a fact that reflects a major transformation in the position of women in society. Christian educational and medical organizations, and those offering a variety of social, legal, and human rights services, are an important part of a vibrant Palestinian civil society.[3]

Palestinians Rate Themselves as Middle Class

An interesting note that reflects socioeconomic transformations during the first three decades of Israeli occupation is that two-thirds of Palestinians from a large representative sample described themselves as belonging to the middle class.[4] The trend towards a middle class among Palestinians started in the cities and towns that were dominated from the nineteenth century by urban "notable" families, particularly in Jerusalem, but spread from the hilly region from Hebron in the south to Nablus in the north, and the coastal towns of Jaffa and Haifa. One would expect that the development of the middle class would spark a parallel identification across society aside from that of the political nationalist one. However, sociologists studying the voting behavior of Palestinians under the Palestinian Authority (PA)

2. See Helliwell et al., "World Happiness." There are six categories: gross domestic product per capita; social support; healthy life expectancy; freedom to make your own life choices; generosity of the general population; and perceptions of internal and external corruption levels.

3. Akroush, *Mapping of Christian Organizations*.

4. Hanf and Sabella, *Date with Democracy*, 67.

in 1996 and 2006 noted that Palestinians voted for candidates from their own localities rather than for those with a national platform. This points to the predominance of a local perspective rather than a broader national one. This "ethno-localism" is important to identity formation and, accordingly, has an influence on social relations. Local identification among Palestinians appears parallel to broader national identity, if not stronger. This may shed light on why in certain localities, such as Bethlehem or Ramallah, confessional identification has become linked with local identification and has enabled an openness in relations across religions that is not necessarily experienced in other localities.[5]

The Oslo Accords changed the status of the PLO cadres from the revolutionaries of the sixties and seventies, with a liberation nationalist objective and raison d'être, to paid public functionaries and employees following the relocation of the PLO to the Occupied Palestinian Territories and the establishment of the Palestinian Authority in 1993. The zeal, pride, and sense of purpose that characterized the rise of the PLO have since been transformed into more practical and mundane considerations, particularly by middle-class Palestinians seeking good education for their children, quality healthcare and housing, and other essential services. Christian Palestinians, most of them describing themselves as middle or upper middle class, opt for long-term gratification of health, education, housing, and other essential life services that will secure the future for themselves and their children.

Higher Education Institutions and the Consolidation of Middle-Class Values

The flourishing of higher education institutions in the early seventies created the nucleus for an intellectual or academic elite who were co-opted, as seen in Birzeit University, into ministerial positions or were elected to the Palestinian Legislative Council on the platforms of political factions. These universities and technical colleges helped to create a new cadre of educated and skilled Palestinians who became a significant component of the white-collar labor force, including in public services. This cadre also competed for jobs and opportunities in the private sector, and in the networks of civil society, international organizations, and foreign cooperation foundations, further enhancing the middle-class predisposition within society. University graduates who were activists in PLO-affiliated student and other mass-based organizations on and off campus ended up working in the different civil and security agencies of the Palestinian Authority. The spread of higher

5. Legrain, "Autonomie palestinienne."

education across the Occupied Palestinian Territories became a source for upward mobility for young people. Palestinians have come to see education, and specifically higher education, as an asset for personal and family advancement that cannot be eradicated by the vicissitudes and difficulties of life under a prolonged occupation.

Israel Hegemonic Control of Palestinians and the Palestinian Territories

The Oslo Accords stipulated that the Palestinians would have their own state by 1999. Instead, the reality on the ground saw the establishment of the Palestinian Authority alongside the division of the West Bank, comprising 2,183 square miles, into different areas: A (20 percent) representing sole Palestinian control; B (20 percent) joint Palestinian-Israeli control; and C (60 percent) sole Israeli jurisdiction. This was supposed to be a transitional stage but has become permanent. The divisive arrangement affects the socioeconomic, cultural, political, and legal realities of Palestinians. Endlessly drawn out negotiations between Israel and the PLO to reach a permanent solution have failed to resolve outstanding issues of Jerusalem, Palestinian refugees, Israeli settlements, or natural resources and borders.[6]

Amid the derailment of the peace process and the inability to reach mutual understandings on the political status of Palestinians, two intifadas broke out in the Occupied Territories: the Intifada of the Stones, 1987–1993, and al-Aqsa Intifada, 2000–2003.[7]

Following the first intifada and the establishment of the Palestinian Authority, the manifestations of an ongoing occupation became further entrenched as settlement activities, the indiscriminate killing of Palestinians by Israeli soldiers and settlers, the Judaization of Jerusalem, and the overall lack of progress in the political process combined to ensure the hegemonic control of Israeli occupation. The failure of US-led efforts to bring the two sides to an agreement on these and other issues led to al-Aqsa Intifada, which was triggered by the visit of the late Ariel Sharon to al-Haram al-Sharif, the Noble Sanctuary where al-Aqsa Mosque is located, in 2000. Al-Aqsa Intifada was violent and characterized by a vicious cycle of violence with Israeli "overkill" tactics, plus the takeover by the Israeli military of

---

6. See Editors, "Oslo Accords."

7. For the Intifada of the Stones that transpired between Dec. 9, 1987, and Jan. 19, 1993, see Stork, "Significance of Stones"; for al-Aqsa Intifada that transpired between Sept. 28, 2000, and Jan. 25, 2006, see Interactive Encyclopedia of the Palestinian Question, "I. Ottoman Rule."

Palestinian cities and towns. Israeli tanks entered Bethlehem in April 2002, and the infamous siege followed on the Church of Nativity.[8]

Using the pretext of stopping suicide bombings, the Israeli government and military decided to construct a 700 km Separation Wall between Israel and the Occupied Palestinian Territories. The wall has swallowed around 9 percent of Palestinian land. Designed initially as an annexation wall, it has become a wall of apartheid to control the movement of Palestinians and has had dire socioeconomic and overall humanitarian costs that violate the basic human rights of Palestinians. East Jerusalem was made an enclave by the construction of the wall, which separated the city hermetically from the rest of the West Bank and from Bethlehem. The violence and the construction of the wall contributed to a wave of emigration by Christian youth, especially from the Bethlehem area, as they saw their economic and social prospects disappear. The historic twinning of Jerusalem and Bethlehem as the two holiest cities of Christendom was severed by the Separation Wall that encircled Bethlehem and made access to Jerusalem impossible without special permits and authorizations.[9]

Mounting violence and confrontations led the religious leadership in the Holy Land, Palestine, and Israel to meet in 2002 in Alexandria and to issue the First Alexandria Declaration of the Religious Leaders of the Holy Land.[10] One of the results of this initial gathering was the establishment of the Council of Religious Institutions in the Holy Land (CRIHL) to encourage religious leaders of all three persuasions to become models for seeking peace, ending violence, and working towards resolution of the conflict between Israelis and Palestinians. These efforts, regardless of questions of efficacy, remain witness to the intricacies that weave religion into political questions of the land, its ownership, and religious significance.[11]

Recurring Confrontations in Gaza

Since July 2007 when Hamas, the Islamic Resistance Movement, wrested the Gaza Strip from the Palestinian Authority, four major military confrontations/wars on Gaza have taken place. The August 2014 war stands out for the large number of 2,100 Palestinians killed, the extent of the damage and

---

8. See Weaver, Review of *Bethlehem Besieged*.

9. On the separation wall or barrier, see B'Tselem, "Separation Barrier."

10. See Tantawi et al., "Alexandria Declaration 2002."

11. For the specific five objectives of the council, see Peace Insight, "Council of Religious Institutions."

devastation wrought by Israeli military action, and the long-term socioeconomic and humanitarian effects on life in the Gaza Strip.[12]

In May 9–20, 2021, the war on Gaza caused considerable destruction of residential and commercial buildings. Around 260 Palestinians were killed, and the core physical and service infrastructure of the Gaza Strip was badly hit.[13]

These two military confrontations between Hamas and Israel tell the story of the Gaza Strip. Israel insists on a hermetic siege of the strip, imposed since 2007, while Hamas political and military platforms call for armed struggle to end Israeli occupation. The religious-based movement promotes a public sphere impregnated with religious fervor and compliance. The Hamas founding charter, written in 1988, states that Hamas "adheres to the permissibility of Islam with regards to followers of other religions. It is not hostile towards them, except those who fight it." According to Hamas, followers of Islam, Christianity, and Judaism coexist in security and safety.[14] Hamas officials strive to respect the rights of Christians to their rites and rituals within church compounds, and seek to redress complaints by Christians and their institutions whenever these occur. Hamas has competitors with more fundamentalist views such as Daesh, ISIS, and some Salafi groups, but these remain under surveillance by Hamas as it strives to demonstrate openness. Some Hamas representatives undertake occasional ceremonial visits to the Christian community and its leaders. Nonetheless, the overall situation in the Gaza Strip affects all the population adversely. Innumerable suicides among young Gazans, risky attempts at illegal migration to Europe, and the dwindling of the Christian population are facts of life under the difficult living conditions that leave no one untouched. Christian elders in the Gaza Strip predict that within a few years, all that will remain of the long Palestinian Christian heritage in the Gaza Strip will be the church buildings, a couple of schools, and the Christian-run hospital and clinics.

12. See World Bank, "World Bank."

13. See World Bank Group, *Gaza Rapid Damage.*

14. See Amer, "Hamas Has Positive Legacy." Hamas believes in and manages its Palestinian relations based on pluralism, democracy, national partnership, acceptance of the other, and adoption of dialogue. The aim is to bolster the unity of ranks and joint action for the purpose of accomplishing national goals and fulfilling the aspirations of the Palestinian people. See *Middle East Eye* Staff, "Hamas in 2017." The modified charter does acknowledge the Christian dimension of Palestinianism. It must be noted that even those Hamas-affiliated personalities, usually religious clerics, who undertake to visit Christian leaders in Gaza to congratulate them on their holy feasts and to stress the unity of all Palestinians, are themselves highly critical of Christianity and its beliefs, particularly the Trinity, the crucifixion, and the resurrection of Jesus Christ, and they disseminate such messages in public on occasion.

Dependence on International Aid

The Palestinian economy is not independent but is reliant on Israel and strangled by numerous control mechanisms, whether those stipulated or not in the Oslo Accords and the Paris Protocol on Economic Relations between the PLO and Israel. Economic and financial dependency is a chronic feature, not merely international aid but also the export of relatively cheap labor to the Israeli labor market.[15] Since the creation of the Palestinian Authority in 1993, international aid amounting to billions of US dollars has covered the ongoing expenses of the PA and financed various programs in the West Bank and Gaza Strip, especially in areas where investment in the physical and social infrastructure is an imperative.[16] Yet, accusations of corruption and the current political stalemate, combined with the dire economic effects of the COVID-19 pandemic, have led to a decline in international aid and increased financial pressure on the PA to comply with peacemaking deals that are perceived by Palestinians as a humiliating surrender of their rights and historical roots on the land.

Amid this pessimistic outlook, there are some rays of hope. Enterprising young Palestinians, Christians included, have ventured into the IT market and other business endeavors that secure some sort of financial and economic stability and long-term inducement. This optimism is linked to individual efforts at economic improvement; the overall economic and financial environment remains adversarial to the long-term prospects of an independent Palestinian economy.

DEMOGRAPHIC FIGURES ON RELIGIOUS AND DENOMINATIONAL COMPOSITION—PALESTINIAN CHRISTIAN POPULATION TRENDS

The dynamics of the Palestinian population put a heavy burden on the working age population (fourteen to sixty-five years) responsible for feeding and nurturing a younger generation that comprises 40 percent of the total population. Population growth in the West Bank and Gaza in 2020

---

15. For the Paris Protocol, see Shohat and Ala, "Gaza-Jericho Agreeement." The preamble of the Paris Protocol spells out the need for economic and financial cooperation as a basis for the purpose of achieving a just, lasting, and comprehensive peace. For Palestinian labor force in Israel, see Palestinian Central Bureau of Statistics, *Labour Force Survey*.

16. See World Bank, "World Bank."

translates into an annual birth rate of close to 127,636 babies: 68,640 in the West Bank and 58,996 in the Gaza Strip.[17]

By 2050, the number of Palestinians in the Occupied Territories is expected to number close to eleven million people. Young people may be inclined to emigrate due to the lack of employment opportunities; the continuing political impasse; Israel's hegemonic control; expansionist settlement activity; and rising political, religious, and social extremism. Worst-case scenarios may see public anarchy in the ongoing relationship of occupation, confrontation, and conflict.

Palestinian Christians are small in number and make up fifty thousand of the population of five million in the Palestinian Territories. Christianity has links dating from the early church and to the geography, history, and culture of this area. Among the older communities that make up the church in Palestine, there are remnants of Christians who speak Aramaic, the language spoken by Christ himself. Armenians have made pilgrimages to the Holy Land since the fourth century when Armenia adopted Christianity as its religion, and they continue to live in the Armenian Quarter as the center of the Armenian Patriarchate, albeit with a population of less than a thousand today. The Copts and Ethiopians recount how their ancestors accompanied Saint Helena, the mother of Emperor Constantine, early in the fourth century as she discovered the true cross, which heralded the conversion of her son and the beginning of the Byzantine era in Palestine; and like the Armenians, they have venerated the holy places in pilgrimages ever since.

Palestinian Christians have always been part of their social and national Arab context. The growing identification of Christians in Palestine, including those of a different national or ethnic origin such as the Armenians, with a national Palestinian and Arab identity was not simply a reaction to their status as a separate religious community but also an affirmation of a shared history. The complexity of historical attachment by local Christians to the land of roots makes up a kaleidoscopic picture that intertwines the national, ethnic, religious, and linguistic differences within Palestinian society.

The Greek Orthodox Church, mostly of Arab congregation and Hellenic clergy, counts some 24,000 faithful or close to 51 percent of the Christian population in the Palestinian Territories.[18] It was the Council of Chalcedon convoked by Emperor Marcian in 451 that divided Christianity into the

17. For these and other statistics on the Palestinian population in 2020, see Palestinian Central Bureau of Statistics.

18. For the Byzantine period and the impact of the Council of Chalcedon on the split of churches between Chalcedonian and non-Chalcedonian, see Pace, "Jerusalem in the Time."

Chalcedonian versus the non-Chalcedonian churches. The Chalcedonian churches followed the decision made by the council on the two natures of Christ as supported by the emperor. The non-Chalcedonian churches stuck to their position on the one nature of Christ. Both the Greek Orthodox and the Greek Melkite Churches claim a hereditary affiliation to the patriarchate of Antioch under royal Byzantine patronage, which was instrumental in the decision of the Chalcedonian Council on the two natures of Christ.

The thirteen officially recognized churches in Palestine are divided into Chalcedonian and non-Chalcedonian churches. The Chalcedonian churches are those pertaining to the Greek Orthodox Church family and the Roman Catholic Church family, comprising the Latin, Greek Catholic Melkite, Syriac Catholic, Armenian Catholic, and the Maronite Church. The Franciscans under the Custody of the Holy Land make up an important part of the Catholic Church family. The non-Chalcedonian churches include the Syriac, Armenian, Coptic, and Ethiopian Eastern Orthodox Churches. The Protestant churches—the Episcopal Anglican Church and the Lutheran Church—are more modern and date from the nineteenth century.[19]

For Christians in Palestine and worldwide, Jerusalem, Bethlehem, and Nazareth are clearly the location of their roots, ever living and nourishing, as stated in a November 1994 memorandum by the thirteen heads of churches in the Holy City.[20] In 2017, the Palestinian Central Bureau of Statistics conducted a census in the Palestinian Territories of the West Bank and Gaza Strip. Christian Palestinians numbered 46,850: 45,712 in the West Bank and 1,338 in the Gaza Strip. The Christian population in the West Bank is concentrated in the central areas of Bethlehem with 23,165, followed by Ramallah with 10,255, and Jerusalem with 8,558, making up 92 percent of the entire West Bank Christian population. Christians comprise less than 2 percent of the population of the West Bank and East Jerusalem at 2.5 million Palestinians. In the Gaza Strip of over 2 million inhabitants, Christians make up less than 0.06 percent of the entire population. Gaza City was the first Christian city in the world, and a Gaza school of Christian theology developed there in the early era of Christianity.[21]

19. For a brief historical synopsis on each of the thirteen officially recognized churches, see Sabella, "Palestinian Christians Centennial."

20. For the text of the memorandum, see Greek Orthodox Patriarch of Jerusalem et al., "1994 Memorandum."

21. Palestinian Central Bureau of Statistics, "Population Survey." For the beginning and brief history of Christianity in the Gaza Strip up to modern times, see Lamport, *Encyclopedia of Christianity*.

Palestinian Christians: One Million Globally

Palestinian Christians are estimated to be close to one million worldwide today, including third and fourth generations of early immigrants, and make up close to 8 percent of the thirty-five million Palestinians worldwide. Palestinians in the West Bank and Gaza Strip make up 35 percent of the global Palestinian population, those in Israel around 14 percent, and those in Jordan 23 percent. The remaining 28 percent of Palestinians are scattered in different Middle Eastern countries, primarily Lebanon and Syria, as well as in the Americas, Australia, and Europe. In contrast, only 17 percent of all Palestinian Christians are found in historic Palestine: the West Bank, Gaza Strip, and Israel. The vast majority of the Palestinian Christian population shifted abroad during different waves of emigration. Palestinian Christian emigration from the Bethlehem and Ramallah areas started towards the end of the nineteenth and the early twentieth century. A major wave of Christian emigration was from the Bethlehem area to South and Central America when the Ottomans introduced a conscription law in 1909 obliging Christian or non-Muslim youth to join the Ottoman army. The famine that hit Palestine in the first couple of years of World War I, caused by the blockade of the Syrian coast by the allies, led to another wave of emigration, this time from the Ramallah area to the US. In 1948, close to sixty thousand Palestinian Christians became refugees during the first Arab-Israeli war, along with three-quarters of a million other Palestinians. Many of the Christian refugees eventually migrated to the Americas and some to Australia, where the Christian Palestinian community in Sydney that hails originally from Jerusalem is larger than the present Christian Palestinian community in Jerusalem itself.[22]

RELIGION, CHURCH AND STATE RELATIONS

The PA officially recognizes the thirteen Christian churches based on the status quo adhered to by both the governments of Jordan and Israel. The Palestinian amended Basic Law of 2003, article 4, states: "Islam is the official religion in Palestine. Respect for the sanctity of all other divine religions shall be maintained." While the law specifies that the Sharia "shall be a principal source of legislation," it also guarantees equality before the law and judiciary "without distinction based upon race, sex, color, religion, political views or disability." Article 18 specifies: "Freedom of belief, worship and the

22. For a centennial overview of the Palestinian Christian population between the 1920s and 2020s, see Sabella, "Palestinian Christians."

performance of religious functions are guaranteed, provided public order or public morals are not violated."[23]

The formalities of church-state relations extend to protocol and practical matters. The president of Palestine attends Christmas midnight Mass in Bethlehem, and Christmas has been declared a national holiday, a step that emphasizes the oneness of the Palestinian people. Church leaders often pay visits to the president and the prime minister to discuss matters of concern to their churches and communities. Whenever mention is made of Muslim holy sites in official and public pronouncements, particularly in government-run media outlets, Christian holy sites are also mentioned. This sensitivity to inclusion of the holy places of both Islam and Christianity is intended to emphasize that Palestinian religious heritage is a shared legacy of both Muslims and Christians. It is also a message to the international community that Palestinians, irrespective of religion, receive respect for their holy places and beliefs.

The spirit of legislation in promoting freedom of belief and equality before the law, as well as the inclusivity of official and public statements on Christian and Muslim holy shrines, is countered by rising religious sentiments and identifications. The adoption of a religiously tilted narrative and content in textbooks and in overall pedagogy, plus popular manifestations in the public sphere, optimizes the significance and place of the majority religion. The educational system and its curriculum in the public government schools is often discussed by Christian Palestinian spokespersons who draw the attention of educators and decision-makers to selective highlighting of the importance of the holy places and history of the majority religion to the detriment of Christianity and its long history and heritage. In a discussion about an unpublished study on the content of the Palestinian curriculum, the director of Sabeel in Jerusalem referred to the methodology by which the curriculum deals with Christianity. He stated that those in the Ministry of Education in charge of the curriculum are open to suggestions and do respond to ideas for improvement.[24] The religious curriculum needs to be developed in a professional manner that will lead to students being open to others and to avoid selective misinterpretations of religious texts and the beliefs of others. As a Muslim religious figure once opined on interfaith dialogue, it is important to share the same life experiences and to

23. See the Palestinian Basic Law (https://www.palestinianbasiclaw.org).

24. Sabeel's study of the Palestinian curriculum was completed in 2018. A phone conversation in Dec. 2021 with Omar Harami, the director of Sabeel in Jerusalem, confirmed the need for Christian educators to be strategic about the religious curriculum and to present their input to the Ministry of Education, which, from experience, is receptive to ideas and input to improve the curriculum.

compare notes on how we deal with them irrespective of our religions. He advised not to focus on theological or doctrinal matters but to emphasize the need to respect each other irrespective of religious beliefs and doctrinal instructions. His advice highlights the impossibility of finding a doctrinal or theological common ground for learning and openness to others and their different belief systems.

At an official level, the relationship between church and state in Palestine may be categorized as a legal, pragmatic, and ceremonial one. One development to consider when discussing these relations is the presidential decree in 2012 that set up the Higher Presidential Committee of Churches Affairs (HC) in Palestine.[25] The committee seeks to regulate and facilitate relations between churches and the PA. It is the first of its kind among neighboring countries; even in Israel there is no such body that deals with the church and Christian affairs in a unified manner. Ideally, all issues or problems related to churches would be covered by the committee, and it should be the one body to deal with all aspects of relations between the state and churches. The HC facilitates visits by the heads of churches of neighboring countries and gives small grants to renovate and maintain churches. Its members actively participate in preparations for the Christmas celebrations in Bethlehem in consultation with the different churches and their heads, mostly related to ceremonial aspects and the status quo. Some HC members took part in the planning and supervision of the renovation of the Nativity Church in Bethlehem that was arranged through negotiations among the churches by the PA. The committee inevitably gets involved in resolving land disputes and issues between churches and citizens, and also between individual citizens. Complaints about land violations are often on the agenda and consume much of the time of active HC members as they juggle legal decisions with family feuds over land. The committee is also the address for "unrecognized" churches and Christian religious communities, the "free churches" on civil matters, birth and marriage certificates, etc., for their members. A milestone on this matter was the presidential decree signed by President Mahmoud Abbas in 2019 that allows evangelical churches in Palestine to issue marriage licenses, open church bank accounts, and purchase land in the name of the church.[26]

The committee follows the directives of the Palestinian president to ensure the smooth organization of religious celebrations throughout the year, particularly those of Easter and Christmas. The committee regularly

25. On the presidential decree and the current composition of the committee, see the Higher Presidential Committee of Churches Affairs in Palestine (https://hcc.plo.ps/en/about-us).

26. See Casper, "Palestinian Evangelicals."

publishes messages of solidarity on TV or in the media to mark national events and religious occasions. They also comment whenever religious sites come under attack from extremist Jewish groups, as happens often in al-Aqsa Mosque with the almost daily incursions of groups of zealot Jews into the Haram al-Sharif compound.

Unifying the intricacies or complexities of relations between churches and the state under the umbrella of one body is a practical consideration to deal with thirteen different churches in Palestine that are officially recognized, as well as those that are not recognized. This is a positive aspect to the committee that brings all church affairs and relations with the government under one roof. However, the setting up of the committee, however worthwhile its purpose, remains part of a confessional system that relegates a special place to churches and Christian communities. Some may argue that its function as the intermediary of the PA on church affairs conflicts with the principle of equality of all before the law. The committee can mediate, intervene, and facilitate church and Christian affairs, yet it can be frustrating when the PA fails to enforce legal rulings and decisions of its courts, especially on complex land issues. There are instances of encroachment and trespass on the properties of Christians in Bethlehem and elsewhere. Although this also occurs among Muslims, it is resolved by the families, usually large, extended tribes. Christians do not have the same powerful, extended families and often fall prey to land and property trespassers without anyone to support them. The committee does not have powers to enforce the law or to stop the perpetrators of land and property theft when the PA appears unable to do so.

The HC works to extend relations with international faith-based organizations and churches, especially in the United States and Europe, where greater awareness is needed of the Palestinian issue and the place of Christian Palestinians as an integral part of Palestinian society and history. Often, these relationships and exchanges involve eloquent Christian Palestinian theologians and heads of churches who participate in conferences, seminars, and exchanges organized by the HC. Research on Christian communities is part of the HC mission, but no research has yet been published, even though a special research committee exists composed of respected academics and scholars. The HC seeks to ensure that the presence and contribution of Palestinian Christians are included in the overall Palestinian landscape. Accordingly, it produces documentaries and undertakes various activities to highlight this aspect.

The HC is a positive tool, but its functions and outreach need to be well defined on intra-church relations, interfaith, and national matters. Clearly, the existence of the status quo and the tradition of the millet system mean that churches in Palestine must be treated differently than how the PA treats the religious Muslim establishment.[27] The question is whether a secular government-appointed body such as the HC can be successful in managing the different complexities relevant to churches and their faithful. The attempt to provide leadership amid numerous variants of religious and secular leaderships, with an increasing feeling by the public of overall instability and loss of direction, puts the HC in a difficult position. The committee and its areas of competence and intervention need to be formalized to ensure sustainable outreach to local churches and their faithful. The committee also needs to be sensitive to the issue of inclusive citizenship and to gear its outreach to the Palestinian public on this basis away from confessional inferences. Outreach to international churches and faith groups requires greater systemic and strategic cooperation with Palestinians and their institutions long associated with such efforts.

FREEDOM OF RELIGION, SOCIETAL DISCRIMINATION, POTENTIAL HARASSMENT

Freedom of religion is narrowly defined as per article 18 of the Basic Law referred to above. Sharia is a principal source of legislation in Palestine, and Islam with its prescriptions and proscriptions remains paramount in the exercise of the individual right to freedom of religion and to civil matters regarding marriage, the family, and statutes. In contrast to societies where freedom of religion is a personal choice par excellence, in Palestine freedom of religion balances the right of Christians and non-Muslims to celebrate and to pray within their own compounds without interference from the overall public sphere that is predominantly Muslim.

Living side by side over centuries and passing through similar vicissitudes and experiences, Christians and Muslims have bonded. The political context with the mass dispersal of Palestinians in 1948 affected all Palestinians and has shaped a Palestinian national identity that crosses the boundaries of religion, geography, and political divisions.

---

27. The Ottoman millet system translates into autonomous religious, administrative, and judicial arrangements for non-Muslim communities. It was initiated by Imperial Decree Khatt-i-Sherif 1839, which is the first charter of liberties and guarantees to Muslims and non-Muslims, and assures "to our subjects a perfect security to life, honor and fortune." These same guarantees were confirmed in Khatt-i-Humaioun of 1865, which granted Christian "millets" or religiously autonomous communities some internal autonomy and judicial personality under a responsible head, the patriarch. See Issa, *Minorités Chrétiennes de Palestine*, 61.

Since the 1970s and 80s, the public sphere has felt the impact of religion and its recurring expressions moving away from inclusivity. The return to religion among Palestinians and elsewhere in the Arab world has multiple explanations. What is relevant here is how the increasing religious identification affects relations between Muslims and Christians. How do our personal and communal religious definitions and practices affect the pedagogy and psychology of communities as they nurture their offspring and draw the boundaries and parameters of their communities?

Examples of cross-religious sensitivities or stereotypes abound. Social discourse with others who are yet "to see the light," i.e., to be part of the "true" religion, is kept to a minimum. Property cannot be sold to or alienated from a nonbeliever, and intermarriage is frowned upon by both Christians and Muslims as an infraction of communal solidarity and family unity. Adoption of babies born out of wedlock or who were abandoned and in care, mostly of Christian religious orders, is not allowed by law for non-Muslims. In mixed marriages where the father is a Muslim, children are automatically registered in their identity cards as Muslims with no other option. Social occasions, particularly weddings, are becoming less of an open public celebration as they are restricted by some to religious affiliation. Preference for renting properties and choosing neighbors based on religious affiliation reflects prejudgments and stereotypes by both Christians and Muslims alike.

A particular manifestation of intercommunal tension lies with the handling of issues over land and real estate. Christians tend to see these disputes as discriminatory in nature. The taking over of land or property belonging to Christians, not only in the Bethlehem area where there has been no land registry since Ottoman times in contrast to the north of the country, is seen as a disturbing phenomenon in which the powerful and numerical majority usurps the rights of the numerical minority. Whenever property theft and infractions occur, Christians point to a mentality of victimhood and weakness. The inefficiency or inability of the PA to enforce court rulings adds to the mistrust, even though this type of dispute is not restricted to Muslims and Christians but extends across society irrespective of locality or religion. The selective perception by Christians of mistreatment can also be seen in other instances. A junior official of the Ministry of National Economy entrusted to enforce expiry dates on perishable food items stated that if expired goods are confiscated from a Christian merchant, the usual response is that the ministry would not do that to a Muslim merchant. On the other hand, if a Muslim merchant's goods are confiscated, his reaction is that this would not happen to a Christian, because he has the protection and influence of his church.

Gaza

The number of Christians in the Gaza Strip is dwindling, as described above. The religious environment together with the harsh Israeli siege makes life difficult and provides the push to seek a better life elsewhere. Estimates are that 40 percent of Palestinian Christians in Gaza have left since Hamas took over in 2007. There were also instances when Christians felt that their lives or property were under threat. In October 2007, Rami Ayyad, the director of the Bible Society in the Gaza Strip, was abducted and killed. Hamas condemned the attack and promised to bring the perpetrators to justice. The Bible Society bookstore had been bombed six months earlier and had ceased to operate as a result. Recently in August 2021, the Bianco seashore resort in the north of the Gaza Strip was attacked with an explosive device by a Salafi-Jihadist group inspired or associated with the Islamic State. Condemnation of the attack was expressed by all political groups, including Hamas. The pretext for the attack was that the resort planned to have a mixed-gender concert, which conflicts with the fundamental Islamic belief of strict separation by gender. When asked about the attack, some Gazans approved and others disapproved. This attack points to increasing religious extremism fueled by those who seek stricter application of Islamic laws and rules. Attacks by the Salafi-Jihadist group have not been restricted to Christian sites, as there is a history of conflict with Hamas and bombings and confrontations have occurred even within mosques.[28] In 2013 Hamas issued a law forbidding coeducation in schools. This caused difficultites for Christian and private coeducational schools. Nonetheless, Gaza's five Christian schools with 3,500 students continued to conduct classes on a coeducational basis without interference, as did the UNRWA schools that also have a policy of coeducation.[29] While Hamas sees the development of Salafi-Jihadist groups as a threat to its rule and control, it has been flexible on the issue of coeducation in schools despite the 2013 law. However, for Christians and others who seek to conduct their lives in a free environment, the future does not bode well.

28. For Hamas-Salafi friction with a history of bombings of Hamas targets and confrontations with the Salafists in Gaza mosques, see The Guardian, "Palestinian Salafist"; For the kidnapping and murder of Rami Ayyad, see Rizq, "The murder of Rami Ayyad"; For the Bianco Resort attack, see Abou Jalal, "Gaza resort attacked."

29. See *Albawaba News*, "Hamas Passes Law"; for Christian schools that continue with their coeducation classes, see Fides, "Holy Land."

SOCIOCULTURAL IMPACT OF
CHRISTIAN COMMUNITIES

The impact of education on young minds brought up in an environment of cultural openness, which characterizes many of the church schools and the three main universities, has broadened the perspectives and options of Palestinian youth. Often, this has resulted in the pursuit of higher education and a preference to go abroad to attain professional degrees, particularly by those with foreign language skills. Those who return home tend to join international organizations and diplomatic missions, or start their own enterprises, whether in IT, tourism, pharmaceutical, digital printing, ceramics, photography, and the other evolving professions of a digital age. Surveys show that Palestinian Christians are found in the liberal professions, and an impressive percentage of nongovernmental and human rights organizations have been established and are currently run by Christian Palestinians. Politically, Palestinian Christians are at ease with secular-leaning political factions, which tend to call for a society based on the equality of rights of all citizens. This inclusive perspective appeals to Christians. Together with other like-minded compatriots and political and social activists, Christians are weary of confessionalism and prefer the pan-Arab and Palestinian identity over narrow religious identification.

Questions of Identity

In his book *In The Name of Identity: Violence and the Need to Belong*, Amin Maalouf speaks of "patchwork identities" or what are currently referred to as "hybrid identities," an apt description of the status of indigenous Christians in Palestinian and Arab society. Identity is supposed to remain static under different conditions, as expressed by leaders of the Christian church in Palestine and elsewhere in the Arab world who call on Christians to remain rooted in their ancestral and faith identities, and to remain part of their society and its landscape irrespective of changing environments. Thus, Christians are to be loyal to their identities as Palestinians, Arabs, Syriacs, Armenians, etc., rooted in the ancestral traditions of the more than thirteen different churches to which they belong. They are also to be loyal to the language, culture, geography, and the Palestinian ecosphere with all its variations, flora, and fauna. These loyalties pertaining to layered identities are exactly what "patchwork identities" are all about.

Historically, most Palestinian Christians have opted for the identity of being a Palestinian and an Arab before being a Christian of a particular church.[30]

Given the reality of the changing religious environment from the late 1970s with the influence of the Iranian revolution, Palestinian Christians, like other Christians in the Middle East, have had to cope with identity issues and challenges.[31] The increased politicization of religion in the region and beyond has resulted in Christians withdrawing inwards, thus heightening their religious identity. The encompassing identity of one Arab nation, exemplified by a yearning for one Arab homeland with its attendant sociocultural manifestations of which Christian Arabs were major contributors, has been replaced by a religious identity that equates Arabism with Islam and vice versa, and subsequently excludes others not of the same religion. This increases the sense of marginalization among Arab and Palestinian Christians. At times when greetings were exchanged on Muslim religious holidays referring to the Arab and Muslim world, some non-Muslims felt that these were inclusive greetings. They were not, because those who included the Arab and Muslim world in their greetings were equating Arab with Muslim and did not mean the term "Arab" to include non-Muslims. No wonder then, that for some Muslim Palestinians and Arabs, Christians and other non-Muslim religious communities are not "Arab," because they are from a different religious persuasion. Although this point conflicts with a long shared history of Arab and Palestinian Christian involvement and commitment to political, developmental, and societal issues, starting with the Arab Awakening, it is included here to stimulate further discussion and exchange across Palestinian and Arab society. The pervasiveness and domination of the religious sphere over other spheres in society contributes to the feeling among some Christians of being excluded and not being members of the "in-group."

MAJOR INSTITUTIONS AND MOVEMENTS WITHIN CHURCHES

The institutions and movements within churches can be categorized under three broad categories: instrumental service-oriented; hierarchical and pastoral; theological and contextual reflection.

30. See Varsen, *Palestinian Armenian*. Varsen highlights in her book how her Armenian and Palestinian identities converge.

31. For books that touch on the question of identity, see Raheb, *Palestinian Christians*; Raheb, *Diaspora and Identity*; Raheb, *Shifting Identities*; and Raheb, *Palestinian Identity*.

Instrumental Service-Oriented

A 2021 study sponsored by CNEWA-Pontifical Mission and Dar al-Kalima University entitled *Mapping of Christian Organizations in Palestine: Social and Economic Impact* summarizes the extent of the activity and outreach of these organizations across Palestinian society. The 296 organizations include ninety-three schools, universities, and vocational centers; nineteen healthcare facilities; forty-seven social protection institutions; seventy-seven cultural and tourism centers; thirty-eight youth and scout centers; one environmental center; and twenty-one local and international development agencies that deliver a variety of services to hundreds of thousands of Palestinians. These organizations are the third largest employer in the Palestinian Territories after the PA and UNRWA with over nine thousand employees, and they invest over 400 million USD annually in the local economy. Of note are the four specialized hospitals in Jerusalem run by churches that serve a population of 330,000 patients. Services include pediatric kidney dialysis, pediatric cancer services, complicated cardiac operations, specialist maternal health, eye care, blood bank, and other sophisticated services for people with disabilities.[32]

Hierarchical and Pastoral

Churches have their parishes where they serve the spiritual and other needs of parishioners. Church websites enumerate the parishes and the pastors catering to each parish, although some of these websites are dated. Unlike churches elsewhere where parishioners themselves support their church hierarchies, churches in the Palestinian Territories are expected to provide a variety of services, including housing, educational scholarships, and financial or in-kind handouts to poorer parishioners. This is explained by the fact that the churches were historically more resourceful than their faithful and were responsible not only for the spiritual welfare of their parishioners but also their material and daily well-being. This dependence on the churches has been explained by the practice of the millet system under the Ottomans, vestiges of which still linger. Another factor of this dependency by the faithful on their churches is linked to the perceived wealth and resources of churches in overseeing the shrines and holy places associated with the life of Jesus and the birth of Christianity. Historically, the churches' wealth allowed them to acquire vast areas of land and other real estate properties in localities related to the life and mission of Jesus Christ and across Palestine. In

32. Akroush, *Mapping of Christian Organizations*, 10–11.

addition, the financial support received by some churches from their church partners and benefactors, particularly from Western countries, raised the expectations of the local faithful to be included in this generosity. Another source of income for churches before the pandemic was pilgrimages and the contributions that the pilgrims brought with them as they worshiped in the holy places. These pilgrimages generate jobs and employment opportunities for the local population, but some argue that the income generated by pilgrimages far outweighs the costs to the churches of running the holy shrines and their affairs.

The pastoral role of the church necessitates the establishment of seminaries, dissemination of catechismal literature, and upkeep of different services from church buildings to cemeteries. It also involves encouraging and guiding a variety of youth, women, and community movements and scout groups in activities and exchanges within the church and with the broader community. While churches contextualize the activities of these parish-related movements and groups in different ways, there remains strong identification by those parishioners and youth involved in their Palestinian context and its challenges.

The thirteen recognized churches listed previously adhere to the status quo system inherited from Ottoman times. The system continues to regulate relations among churches within the holy places, such as in Bethlehem and Jerusalem, and allows churches to run their own internal affairs and those of their parishioners in civil matters such as issuing marriage, divorce, and birth certificates; or in running their own schools, seminaries, and other educational and social service institutions. Churches have their own "religious courts" that examine issues related to the civil status of their parishioners, including authenticating wills and other documents and testimonies. The churches are entitled to print and disseminate material needed to run their services or to report on the activities of youth, women, scouts, and other movements and groups. The rulings of church courts on civil matters are recognized by the respective governments in Palestine, Jordan, and Israel. Where possible, the government undertakes to implement church court rulings with respect to divorce, alimony, and child custody. The relative "autonomy" in these matters gives the impression that churches are protected from the encroachment of the state. At the same time, this autonomy reflects the vestiges of a confessional system from Ottoman times in which the authorities wanted to defuse the strength of national identification by stressing religious identification.

Churches undertake, independently and in concert, to reach out in dialogue and exchange to other religious groups in society, especially the Muslim majority. Aside from the services and employment opportunities offered irrespective of religious background, the churches see that part of their Christian witness is to engage with others in examining ways and means to meet the challenges facing society. Some churches turn these exchanges into programs and activities such as teaching music to encourage the joint development of personal and communal skills.[33] Most churches would state that their outreach in schools, youth movements, hospitals, and clinics is offered to the general population on a basis of openness and acceptance of differences. There are some in the church hierarchies who insist that with the services rendered, the position of churches on controversial political and social issues should be in prayerful reflection rather than in issuing overt statements that take a stance with one side over another or advance one issue over other issues. According to those who take this position, the churches will always be here in witness to Jesus Christ and his salvation message. Others argue that prayers and thoughtful reflections are called for but should sit side by side with responses to the worries, woes, and challenges of the living stones—the parishioners—and the larger Palestinian community. These people argue, what good is it if churches adhere to their holy sites and prayers while most of the faithful abandon the land to find greener pastures elsewhere? Another persistent question is, how do the churches deal with the ongoing injustice caused by a prolonged Israeli occupation? Thus, while the salvation message of Christ's life and resurrection, and accordingly the continuity and sustainability of the churches with their hierarchical setups, may be the key preoccupation of church and spiritual leaders, the realities on the ground beg questions of involvement and relevance. Some of the faithful view the insistence by church leaders on Christ's salvation message and prayers as a reclusive policy intended to shield the heads of churches and Christian religious leaders from engaging directly with the serious political and social issues facing society and the region. Or is this insistence on the salvation message of the church at times of uncertainty a way to preserve the church and its continuity in the Holy Land?

Theological and Contextual Reflection

The development of a Palestinian contextual theology should be viewed as part of the indigenization of the local church that started in the 1970s. The installation of Palestinian Protestant bishops, and the eventual elevation of Father Michel Sabbah to the Latin patriarchal seat, heralded the way for the

---

33. See the extent of cultural and educational activities undertaken by the Franciscan Custody of the Holy Land (https://www.custodia.org/en/culture-and-education).

development of theological and contextual reflections and publications by Palestinian pastors, priests, and lay persons.[34]

Theological and contextual reflection in the Palestinian context cannot be understood without the individuals who motivated it and advanced it both at home and to a broader international audience. The June 1967 war in which Israeli occupied Palestinian lands and annexed East Jerusalem prompted Palestinian Christians to ask questions about their identity and role amid the traumatic changes affecting their lives as Palestinians: "Who are we? What is the meaning of our presence in the Holy Land? What is our identity? What is our vocation, mission, and witness? What does it mean to be an Arab Palestinian Christian here and now?"[35]

One of the first organizations that sought to find answers to these identity questions or to expose the injustices suffered by Palestinians was al-Liqa' Center founded by the late Geries Khoury in the early 1980s. The goal of al-Liqa' and its founder was to emphasize that both Christians and Muslims experienced occupation and life similarly. Hence the motto that Palestinians refused to be divided into two by sectarian identification was highlighted by al-Liqa' and repeatedly emphasized in its meetings and conferences. What united Palestinians was much stronger than elements of division, real or imagined. Articles and interventions from the two annual conferences published in *Al-Liqa' Journal* were intended to reach a wider audience, including university students, especially at Bethlehem University, and foster an attitudinal change for an inclusive society in which there would be religious openness and understanding of each other. Al-Liqa' preached to the converted, as the same people attended its annual conferences and the same arguments were presented over and over again. The circle never widened, although the contributions of the research and exchange by al-Liqa' sparked discussion on identity and relationship to other groups in society. This was important as neighboring Arab societies, Iraq and Syria, were witnessing painful transformations that affected their religious and national identities.[36]

34. See Diocese of Jerusalem, "Anglican Bishops in Jerusalem," on the appointment of Bishop Najib A. Cubain in 1958 as the first Arab bishop of the Episcopal Church in Jerusalem and the Middle East. Bishop Daoud Haddad was elected by the Synod of the Evangelical Lutheran Church as first Arab bishop in 1979; see Act Palestine Forum, "Evangelical Lutheran Church"; Latin Patriarchate of Jerusalem, "H. E. Michel Sabbah." Patriarch Michel Sabbah of the Latin Roman Catholic Church was the first Palestinian Arab in five centuries to be elevated in 1987 to the post of Latin patriarch.

35. See interview of Rafiq Khouri, Dec. 28, 2017, discussed in Marteijn, "Revival of Palestinian Christianity."

36. See al-Liqa' Center (http://www.al-liqacenter.org.ps/).

In the late 1970s and 80s, the Catholic Justice and Peace Commission was initiated by the Catholic Church in Jerusalem, but it remained a reflective commission that did not touch base with the grassroots. The statements it issued exposing the difficult conditions of life for Palestinians under Israeli occupation were shared with similar commissions in different countries and with the Catholic hierarchy in Rome and elsewhere.[37]

In 1989 Naim Ateek, an Anglican pastor in Jerusalem, published *Justice and Only Justice: A Palestinian Theology of Liberation.* The book countered the biblical arguments used mostly by Christian Zionism and highlighted calls for justice for the oppressed and disinherited Palestinians on biblical grounds and commandments. Soon after the publication of the book, Sabeel Ecumenical Liberation Theology was founded.[38] Sabeel organized yearly international conferences to raise awareness among Sabeel Friends, mostly in North America and Europe, of the realities of Israeli occupation and the injustices committed against Palestinians. One memorable conference was held at Bethlehem University in June 1998 on "The Challenge of Jubilee: What Does God Require?" in which the late Professor Edward Said and Dr. Hanan Ashrawi, among other prominent speakers, addressed the packed auditorium.[39] Sabeel gathered a group of local people as a base for its international outreach. This group remained limited in its recruitment efforts and in its overall impact on discussion and exchange with the larger society. To its credit, Sabeel continues to organize ecumenical prayer days in Jerusalem to mark events in Palestine and elsewhere, and facilitates meetings of pastors and clergy, youth, women, and others to discuss issues of relevance and to map ways forward.

Mitri Raheb is a contextual theologian with many publications in different languages and who officiated as pastor of the Lutheran Christmas Church in Bethlehem for many years. Raheb launched his rich publishing career, now comprising over sixteen books and scores of articles, in 1995 with *I Am a Palestinian Christian.*[40] He believes that theology by itself cannot provide the answers to the ills and challenges of society, and espouses the complementarity of public engagement with theology. In 1995 Raheb established Dar al-Nadwa in Bethlehem, transforming the buildings adjacent to one of the narrow streets in Bethlehem into a center for conferences,

---

37. For statements issued by the commission, see Latin Patriarchate of Jerusalem, "Justice and Peace Commission."

38. For the variety of activities undertaken by Sabeel, see https://sabeel.org/.

39. For a detailed description of the conference and its speakers, see Kelly, "Third International Sabeel Conference."

40. For an updated list of Mitri Raheb's publications, see https://www.mitriraheb.org/en/pdf-list/publications.

arts and crafts, film production and screenings, and a variety of cultural and social activities. In 2006, Raheb launched the establishment of Dar al-Kalima College, which was officially designated as a university in August 2021.[41] In 2011 Diyar Publishing was launched and has published scores of books on Palestinian Christianity, society, history, and cultural and artistic manifestations. In January 2014, Raheb published the impressive *Faith in the Face of Empire: The Bible through Palestinian Eyes*. He sought to show how the reality of empire impacts the context of the Bible as it relates to the experience of conflict between Israel and the Palestinians. Accordingly, he offers a different interpretation of the biblical text rooted in the Bible itself and the Palestinian context. This sheds light on an understanding of the ongoing conflict in the Holy Land from the perspective of the occupied and the oppressed. Raheb has expressed the pain experienced by Palestinians during the Israeli occupation of Bethlehem and the Church of Nativity siege between April and May 2002 with his emotive book published in 2004, *Bethlehem Besieged: Stories of Hope in Times of Trouble*, which was very well received. The media outreach and the global conferences and seminars in which Rev. Raheb participates or that he organizes attest to a commitment to justice for Palestinians and to inclusive societies in the Arab Middle East in which differences are a positive factor in meeting the challenges of citizenship. Recently, Raheb published *The Politics of Persecution: Middle Eastern Christians in an Age of Empire* and attended a series of book launchings in the United States, with outreach to audiences in Europe and worldwide.

Of note is Raheb's initiation of CAFCAW, the Christian Academic Forum for Citizenship in the Arab World, which brings together scholars, young graduates, and activists in civil society to share research, experiences, and insights. The focus is on Lebanon, Egypt, Jordan, and Palestine, as well as attention to developments in Syria and Iraq. In December 2014, CAFCAW was launched in Beirut with the document *From the Nile to the Euphrates: The Call of Faith and Citizenship*, which was elaborated by a group of Arab intellectuals, academics, and theologians in conference and seminar deliberations. The document highlights ten critical issues or topics for further exchange and discussion, among them just constitutions and the rule of law, the dignity and security of every individual, a healthy quality of life for all, gender justice, and a hopeful future for youth. Full citizenship is at the heart of the forum's agenda and is seen as an essential and necessary condition to create more peaceful, democratic, and prosperous societies in the Arab world.[42]

41. See Dar al-Kalima University (http://www.daralkalima.net/?Lang=1).

42. Diyar Consortium, *From the Nile*. For CAFCAW and related activities, see https://cafcaw.org.

In 2005 a spirited group of active religious and public figures came together under the leadership of Patriarch Emeritus Michel Sabbah and elaborated what would become the Kairos Palestine document, modeled after the 1985 Kairos South Africa document. Published in 2011, Kairos Palestine addressed the issue of continued Israeli occupation and reached out to Muslims, Jews, the Israeli occupation authorities, and global public opinion to sensitize them to the "sin of occupation" and the fact that the evil was occupation itself and not the people enforcing it. It was a message of nonviolence out of Palestinian Christian witness and compassion, and it spelled out the human and other costs of a continuing occupation to both the occupier and the occupied. Beside Patriarch Michel Sabbah, some of the other authors of Kairos Palestine are Rifat Kassis, the convener of the group; Archbishop Atallah Hanna; Reverends Mitri Raheb and Naim Ateek; and Yusef Daher, the director of the Jerusalem Inter-Church Center. Recently, in December 2021, the Kairos message was reemphasized in a national meeting of Bethlehem-area Christians headed by Patriarch Emeritus Michel Sabbah to discuss the affinities and shared lives of Palestinian Christians with the larger society.[43]

Both the YMCA and the YWCA are active organizations in the West Bank, and the YMCA in the Gaza Strip. They render important educational, social, and sporting opportunities for young men and women, including a rehabilitation center in Beit Sahour that was initially established to serve those rendered disabled during the second intifada. The Joint Advocacy Initiative of the YMCA and YWCA Palestine reaches out to different YMCAs and YWCAs, and to wider audiences, to bring to their attention the appalling conditions of life for Palestinians under occupation. Part of their advocacy activity involves the planting of olive trees, particularly in areas where settlers have uprooted ancient olive trees to deprive hundreds of Palestinian farmers of their earning potential. The YMCA East Jerusalem is part of the ACT Alliance Palestine Forum, together with the Evangelical Lutheran Church, the Department of Service to Palestinian Refugees of the Middle East Council of Churches, and several international church-related organizations that tend to Palestinians afflicted by the continuing conflict in Gaza and the dire economic and social conditions in the West Bank.[44]

Following the second intifada, the two Protestant bishops in Jerusalem called on the international community and churches in the West to witness

43. For the Kairos document and news of events and activities, see www.kairospalestine.ps.

44. For more details on their activities, see East Jerusalem YMCA (www.ej-ymca.org), Joint Advocacy Initiative (www.jai-pal.org/en), and YWCA Palestine (https://ywca.ps/home).

the injustice caused by continued Israeli occupation and the construction of the Separation Wall that started in 2002. As a result, different church partners across the world, but specifically in Western countries, cooperated to set up the Ecumenical Accompaniment Program in Palestine and Israel (EAPPI). This program brings volunteers from other nations to accompany Palestinians in areas of the West Bank most susceptible to violence and the negative effects of the Separation Wall, military checkpoints, and settler intimidation of Palestinian communities in Hebron. The COVID-19 pandemic brought the program to a halt, but plans are being made to resume it once the pandemic is over.[45]

In 2010 Bethlehem Bible College, which is associated with Palestinian evangelical Christians, launched its first biennial "Christ at the Checkpoint" conference attended by Evangelicals from the United States and the Holy Land. According to the conference website, "The mission of 'Christ at the Checkpoint' is to challenge Evangelicals to take responsibility to help resolve the conflicts in Israel/Palestine by engaging with the teaching of Jesus on the Kingdom of God." To achieve this, one of the conference four objectives is to "discuss the realities of the injustices in the Palestinian territories, and create awareness of the obstacles to reconciliation and peace," targeting Evangelicals whose biblical-based support for Israel is not sensitive to the injustices suffered by Palestinians constitutes outreach to a key group that has blindly supported Israel and its policies, settlement activities, and punitive measures against Palestinians.[46] Additional outreach efforts, sponsored in part by the Higher Committee, include a gathering in Atlanta of heads of churches in Jerusalem with their counterparts in the US and in the presence of former President Jimmy Carter.[47] Recently, in December 2021, the heads of Jerusalem churches issued a statement warning of the threats faced by Christians and churches from radical Jewish fringe groups. The statement also called for the protection of Jerusalem's distinct and historic quarters, and preservation of the cultural integrity of the Christian Quarter similar to the legal protection given to the Jewish Quarter in the Old City of Jerusalem.[48]

45. See EAPPI (https://eappi.us).
46. See Christ at the Checkpoint (https://bethbc.edu/christ-at-the-checkpoint/).
47. See Carter Center, "Atlanta Summit."
48. See Episcopal News Service, "Anglican Archbishop."

MAJOR CHALLENGES

Challenge of Palestinian and Arab Contexts

Palestine remains a country under occupation with all the ills that this brings. As we strive to end Israeli occupation, we are faced with a multitude of difficulties and challenges. First, how do you confront occupation? Our preference as Palestinian Christians, as illustrated in the movements and institutions of the church discussed above, is by nonviolence. This tactic is also espoused by Palestinian compatriots who practice popular nonviolent resistance in the face of Israeli settlers and soldiers in rural areas of the West Bank threatened with expropriation. Due to our faith and linguistic-educational connections, we also understand the challenge of reaching out to international audiences, mostly in the West, to raise awareness of the realities of injustice and to encourage them to engage with their politicians, churches, and societies. This challenge is not restricted to "reachable" groups, as there is an obligation, expressed in the writings of Palestinian theologians and eloquently brought out in the Kairos Palestine document, to reach out to Israelis who are unaware of the ills of occupation and who cannot acknowledge Palestinians and their rights as a people. The failure to connect with Israeli and Jewish groups emanates from fear of being accused of accommodating the occupation or, worse, of collaborating with the enemy. Moral and religious courage is needed in assessing the feasibility of exchanging with Jewish and Israeli groups to open them up to the Palestinian narrative. This is problematic at a time of more settlement building, Judaization of the Holy City, refusal by Israeli politicians of a Palestinian state, and complete denial of the rights to which Palestinians are entitled under international law and UN resolutions.

Another challenge relates to our dialogue with our Muslim compatriots. With all the activities, movements, and institutions that the churches operate for the benefit of all Palestinians, there is always the feeling that Christians have to be the initiators of dialogue and exchange. It is rare in conferences and seminars addressing Christian Palestinian positions on political, religious, and other issues to see many Muslim compatriots. Thus, Muslim compatriots are unaware of the investments made by Christian Palestinian clergy and laity in promoting justice and the end of Israeli occupation of Palestinian lands. The gulf in awareness stems from lack of knowledge, or sometimes unwillingness to learn about different others, but gives the impression that Christian Palestinians have their path and Muslim Palestinians their own path. Palestinians live in the one and same reality: what affects one part affects all parts.

The rise of religion in the public sphere, or "Islamization" as some refer to the phenomenon, poses a problem to Palestinian Christians who have always lived side by side with Muslims. In fact, the "dialogue of life" in which Muslims and Christians live side by side in public and private institutions, education, daily exchanges, neighborliness, or social and cultural life are placed into question by some. Localities inhabited by Christians, such as the Bethlehem and the Ramallah areas, have more convivial relationships across communities, as social and other bonds remain strong. But the perception of Christians and secular Palestinians is that the public sphere in general, and even everyday language and exchanges, is permeated or interpreted by a strictly religious approach. This approach can become reductionist in nature, explaining everything by religion, which necessarily blurs a more comprehensive appraisal of the lived situation and the realities that influence the lives of all Palestinians. As someone pointed out, faith and belief are of the heart and should remain so, but in explaining and interpreting facts we need to rely on causal and proven explanations.

One of the challenges perceived by Palestinian Christians is intermarriage. While the phenomenon has not been studied, the spread of higher education and the opening of the labor market to women, among other socioeconomic and cultural developments, creates greater opportunities for young men and women to meet. When these encounters end in marriage, families of both religions object. Often, Christian families have a stronger reaction to intermarriage because of social, religious, and family considerations. Perceptions and misperceptions abound on the subject, even though intermarriage remains relatively rare statistically.

Another growing challenge is the encroachment on private land, homes, and properties. This is not unique to Christians but is felt particularly harshly by them because they see themselves the weaker party when it comes to protecting their property rights. The inability of the PA to enforce court rulings, described above, leaves weaker groups in Palestinian society, not only Christians, at risk of falling prey to land and property trespass without recourse to the law and public enforcement. The increasing value of land and real estate for development purposes, especially given the limited space available for Palestinian building due to Israeli restrictions, has attracted organized groups and those looking for a quick fortune.

The Arab context has moved from the national aspirations that accompanied the Arab Awakening to those of religious and narrower ethnic and country-by-country identifications. Even within the same country, divisions along parameters have become the norm with Shi'a and Sunni Islam, Alawites, Christians, Yazidis, and Kurds as examples. The transformation in identities points to a failure experienced by all Arab states in the post-colonial period. The burgeoning middle and upper classes have failed, and instead the military and the militants, usually belonging to ethnic and religious groups, have taken over. The consequences and impact of "empire," as Raheb and other Arab intellectuals have pointed out, have touched all aspects of Arab life and have brought the dissection and tribalization of Arab societies to the fore. Palestine is not immune to these developments. The disquieting fact is that these developments, with continuing Israeli occupation and a political impasse, create a psychological environment in which Christians and secular individuals seek an exit. It is a push factor that prompts young people to think about leaving. Exploration of how Arab civil societies can evolve into citizenship societies remains limited and highlights the overall failure to move in this direction. One result of the disquieting developments is that religious and ethnic communities separate from society, sometimes physically as well as within their own geographic space.

Interchurch Relations and Those of the Faithful with Hierarchies

Some churches tend to concentrate on their own affairs and managerial problems as they face mounting financial and administrative challenges. Misunderstandings can arise with congregations who see church preoccupations as distant from their own concerns and problems. Other churches view their pastoral work as a collateral necessity to their presence in the Holy Land. They portray their missions as ministering to the locals while focusing on the preservation of holy sites associated with the life of Jesus Christ. Nonetheless, throughout centuries of association between the different hierarchies and the local Christian population, dependency by locals on the churches was the norm, whether through provision of employment, education, healthcare, housing, or other essentials. This dependence stood in the way of the development of local Christian communities parallel to and with their churches. Instead of the faithful supporting the churches, it was the other way around. This situation gave more power to the church hierarchies and a feeling of marginalization of the indigenous Christian population.

With today's socioeconomic and social developments, many younger educated Christians are distancing themselves from their churches and going their own way. The outreach of churches, especially during the COVID-19 pandemic, has been minimal despite some efforts here and there, and this has added to the woes of a troubled relationship between the church hierarchies and locals.

Given the realities of the different churches, their scopes of operation and their missions, it is unlikely that they will ever come together to reach out to their constituencies. The fragmented nature of the churches will continue, with each catering to its own flock and its narrow preoccupations, despite the calls and ceremonious coming together in the Week of Prayers for Christian Unity and other interchurch gatherings.

Amid these realities, the lay faithful are not of the same mind when it comes to dealing with their estrangement from their churches. Some opt to attend the church services regularly without expectation of any material return. Others view the church as an exclusive club for families who are friendly with the parish priest and pastor. Some remain uninterested in activities run by churches exclusively for their adherents, as they see their context in a broader perspective. Issues related to church hierarchical relations with the faithful include that of nationality and the call to "Arabize" the hierarchies of local churches. The Greek Orthodox Patriarchate has been at the center of this call for decades. Even in the Latin or Roman Catholic Church that has the precedent of having two Arab patriarchs, there are some who want future patriarchs to be of Arab descent. Other issues are the perception or misperception of decisions made by the heads of churches, as in the Syriac and Armenian Churches, regarding real estate and other identification with broader social and political contexts.

How can the churches come closer to the faithful? What does it take for churches to reach out to young, educated Palestinians to draw them in? Is the future set for the demise of local communities as more members cease to attend church services and churches focus on mundane, administrative, and clerical matters or the management of properties and holy places? Is there a way to bring the hierarchies down from their ivory towers to become closer to their constituents and their concerns and interests? Difficult questions indeed, which require answers for the survival and sustainability of the church in Palestine.

Palestinian Christian Diaspora?

An important challenge for churches and their relationship with their local faithful is that of Palestinian Christian diasporas worldwide. Apart from special events in which members of diaspora communities visit or interact with their original towns and villages, especially during difficult periods when military confrontations and major developments make headlines, there is no system in place to maintain contact between these communities and the local Christian population. Much work needs to be done on this aspect. A group of local lay people and clergy from different churches could join with members of the diaspora to draw up a joint road map for relations between diaspora communities and the home country. Sustained contacts and support from diaspora communities is required. Aside from emotive identification and financial contributions, the rich experience of the Palestinian diaspora communities in business, finance, industry, entrepreneurship, academia, and other areas of expertise could help to support local communities to remain in their towns and cities. We should not expect the diaspora communities to initiate, although at times of crisis they do, but we should seize the initiative ourselves and start a process of strategic outreach to these diaspora communities.

Palestinian Christian faithful highlight the challenges of the past two or three decades as emigration, economic conditions, Islamization, issues of identity, and intermarriage, in that order. They are also weary of the challenges facing their churches and interchurch relations. The ongoing Israeli occupation, the Separation Wall, measures undertaken by the Israeli occupation forces in the Palestinian Territories, and the absence of peace also weigh heavily on the minds of Palestinian Christians. Without conditions that would allow for a just and lasting peace, with the end of Israeli occupation and the exercise of the inalienable right to a state, Palestinian Christians fear that emigration and the hemorrhaging of their own people will continue.[49]

Emigration has always been perceived as the greatest challenge to the continued existence of Palestinian Christians. The fact that over eight out of ten Palestinian Christians are abroad provides an additional pull factor for remaining members of families to join the other members already overseas.

Economic conditions depend on the political vicissitudes experienced in the country and region. At times of political turbulence and confrontation in Palestine, and the absence of pilgrims and tourists on which Bethlehem and Jerusalem rely for their economies, youth are particularly susceptible to emigration and joining family members abroad. Without lasting peace, emigration will continue to rise sporadically among Christians and Muslims alike.

FUTURE PROSPECTS

The heritage that our parents, grandparents, and great-grandparents left us is that this land of Palestine is ours. Throughout history, the connections

49. See Sabella, "Palestinian Christians"; Raheb, *Emigration, Displacement and Diaspora*.

and links that crosscut Christian, Muslim, Jewish, and other religious and ethnic communities in Palestine were more varied than simply the religious element or the politicized identity of more recent times. As indigenous Palestinian Christians, we cannot ignore the challenges facing our society, whether political, with the objective of ending the Israeli occupation; social, with the shaping of a society that responds to the needs and requirements of all of its citizens in an age of electronics and pandemics; cultural, by maintaining the traditions that strengthen our common identity as a people rooted in the land and its history and heritage; or economic, in strengthening the possibilities and opportunities open to young people, irrespective of their religious, political, or personal preferences. Without linking and opening to others we cannot survive either as Christian believers or as devoted Palestinians. The future is guaranteed by reaffirming the best of our Palestinian past and present, by celebrating our humanity, and overcoming the prejudices that come with narrow identities, those identities that Amin Maalouf cautioned could lead to violence and the exclusion of others. It is only fitting to end with the optimistic and assertive reflection of Latin Patriarch Emeritus Michel Sabbah who reaffirmed, in an exchange with young people, that as Palestinian Christians we have no option but to stay put on our land, to look fear in the eyes, and to rely on ourselves and on our fellow Palestinians to overcome the challenges facing our beloved land.[50] Optimism still requires that Palestinian Christians and their churches embark on a strategic assessment of the Christian presence in the Holy Land and the prospects for Christians in this land. As this chapter points out, there are various sources of strength and serious reflection on developments, political and other, affecting society and all its people. These strengths with the intellectual richness exhibited should be brought together to reflect strategically on the future. This may be one of the foremost challenges facing Christians and their presence in the land of roots.

BIBLIOGRAPHY

Abou Jalal, Rasha. "Gaza Resort Attacked for Holding Mixed-Gender Concert." Al-Monitor, Aug. 12, 2021. https://www.al-monitor.com/originals/2021/08/gaza-resort-attacked-holding-mixed-gender-concert.

Act Palestine Forum. "Evangelical Lutheran Church in Palestine & the Holy Land." Act Palestine Forum, n.d. http://actpalestineforum.org/about/members/evangelical-lutheran-church-in-jordan-the-holy-land/.

50. From personal notes of exchange held at Notre Dame Center in Jerusalem, Sept. 2022. See also Sabbah, "Eighth Pastoral Letter," which carries Sabbah's insistent call on Palestinian Christians to be part of the land and the people who live on it.

Akroush, George. *Mapping of Christian Organizations in Palestine: Social and Economic Impact*. Bethlehem: Diyar, 2021. https://www.daralkalima.edu.ps/uploads/files/Mapping%20of%20Christian%20Organizations%204Final.pdf.

Albawaba News. "Hamas Passes Law against Co-Ed Education, Leaving Christian Schools in Gaza to Fear Closure." *Albawaba News*, June 21, 2013. https://www.albawaba.com/news/hamas-passes-law-against-co-ed-education-leaving-christian-schools-gaza-fear-closure-501019.

Amer, Adnan Amu. "Hamas Has a Positive Legacy with Christians but It Faces a Serious Test." *Middle East Monitor*, Jan. 7, 2019. https://www.middleeastmonitor.com/20190107-hamas-has-a-positive-legacy-with-christians-but-it-faces-a-serious-test/.

Ateek, S. Naim. *Justice and Only Justice: A Palestinian Theology of Liberation*. Foreword by Rosemary Radford Ruether. Maryknoll, NY: Orbis, 1989.

B'Tselem. "The Separation Barrier." B'Tselem, Nov. 11, 2017. https://www.btselem.org/topic/separation_barrier.

Carter Center. "Atlanta Summit of Churches in the USA and the Holy Land, April 19, 2106." United States Conference of Catholic Bishops, 2016. https://www.usccb.org/resources/atlanta-summit-churches-usa-and-holy-land-april-19-2016.

Casper, Jayson. "Palestinian Evangelicals Gain Official Recognition." *Christianity Today*, Nov. 27, 2019. https://www.christianitytoday.com/news/2019/november/palestinian-evangelicals-gain-official-recognition.html.

Diocese of Jerusalem. "Anglican Bishops in Jerusalem." Diocese of Jerusalem, n.d. https://j-diocese.org/wordpress/anglican-bishops/.

Diyar Consortium. *From the Nile to the Euphrates: The Call of Faith and Citizenship; A Statement of the Christian Academic Forum for Citizenship in the Arab World*. Bethlehem: Diyar, 2015.

Editors, History.com. "Oslo Accords." History, Feb. 16, 2018; updated Aug. 21, 2018. https://www.history.com/topics/middle-east/oslo-accords.

Episcopal News Service. "Anglican Archbishop, Other Heads of Churches and Patriarchs Issue Statement on the Current Threat Holy Land Christians Face." ENS, Dec. 14, 2021. https://www.episcopalnewsservice.org/2021/12/14/anglican-archbishop-other-heads-of-churches-and-patriarchs-issue-statement-on-the-current-threat-holy-land-christians-face/.

Fides. "Holy Land: Christian schools in Gaza Reopen without Problem." *ICN*, Sept. 29, 2013. https://www.indcatholicnews.com/news/23313.

Greek Orthodox Patriarch of Jerusalem, et al. "1994 Memorandum of Their Beatitudes the Patriarchs and of the Heads of Christian Communities in Jerusalem." World Council of Churches, Nov. 14, 1994. https://www.oikoumene.org/resources/documents/1994-memorandum-of-their-beatitudes-the-patriarchs-and-of-the-heads-of-christian-communities-in-jerusalem.

Guardian. "Palestinian Salafists Pose Dangerous New Problem for Hamas." *Guardian*, June 10, 2015. https://www.theguardian.com/world/2015/jun/10/gaza-salafists-problem-hamas-islamic-state-isis.

Hanf, Theodor, and Bernard Sabella. *A Date with Democracy: Palestinians on Society and Politics, an Empirical Survey*. Translated by John Richardson. Freiburg: Arnold Bergstraesser Institut, 1996.

Helliwell, John F., et al. "World Happiness, Trust and Deaths under COVID-19." In *World Happiness Report 2021*, 15–56. https://happiness-report.s3.amazonaws.com/2021/WHR+21_Ch2.pdf.

Interactive Encyclopedia of the Palestinian Question. "I. Ottoman Rule: 1 January 1516 to 2 November 1917." Interactive Encyclopedia of the Palestinian Question, n.d. https://www.palquest.org/en/overallchronology?sideid=6526.

Issa, Anton. *Les Minorités Chrétiennes de Palestine à travers les Siècles*. Jerusalem: Franciscan, 1976.

Kairos Palestine. "A Moment of Truth: A Word of Faith, Hope and Love from the Heart of Palestinian Suffering." Kairos Palestine, nd. https://www.kairospalestine.ps/index.php?view=category&id=11.

Kelly, Ellaine. "Third International Sabeel Conference in Bethlehem Attracts Record Number of Participants." *Washington Report on Middle East Affairs*, Apr. 5, 1998. https://www.wrmea.org/1998-april/third-international-sabeel-conference-in-bethlehem-attracts-record-number-of-participants.html.

Lamport, Mark A., ed. *Encyclopedia of Christianity in the Global South*. London: Rowman and Littlefield, 2018.

Latin Patriarchate of Jerusalem. "H. E. Michel Sabbah." Latin Patriarchate of Jerusalem, n.d. https://www.lpj.org/curia/patriarch-michel-sabbah.html.

———. "Justice and Peace Commission." Latin Patriarchate of Jerusalem, n.d. https://www.lpj.org/posts/statements-of-justice-and-peace-commission.

Legrain, Jean-François. "Autonomie palestinienne: la politique des néo-notables." *Revue du monde musulman et de la Méditerranée* 81–82 (1996) 153–206. https://doi.org/10.3406/remmm.1996.1761.

Maalouf, Amin. *In the Name of Identity: Violence and the Need to Belong*. New York: Arcade, 2012.

Marteijn, Elizabeth S. "The Revival of Palestinian Christianity Developments in Palestinian Theology." *Exchange* 49 (2020) 257–77. https://doi.org/10.1163/1572543X-12341569.

Middle East Eye Staff. "Hamas in 2017: The Document in Full." *Middle East Eye*, May 2, 2017. https://www.middleeasteye.net/news/hamas-2017-document-full.

Pace, Carl. "Jerusalem in the Time of Emperor Justinian (527–565 CE)." SlidePlayer, Jan. 2008. https://slideplayer.com/slide/17007012/.

Palestinian Central Bureau of Statistics. "Indicators." PCBS, n.d. https://www.pcbs.gov.ps/site/881/default.aspx.

———. *Labour Force Survey: (October–December 2020) Round (Q4/2020)*. Ramallah, Pal.: PCBS, 2021. https://www.pcbs.gov.ps/portals/_pcbs/PressRelease/Press_En_15-2-2021-LF-en.pdf.

———. "Population Survey." [In Arabic.] PCBS, 2017. https://www.pcbs.gov.ps/Downloads/book2364.pdf.

Peace Insight. "Council of Religious Institutions of the Holy Land." Peace Insight, last updated Dec. 2013. https://www.peaceinsight.org/en/organisations/crihl/?location=israel-palestine&theme.

Raheb, Mitri. *Bethlehem Besieged: Stories of Hope in Times of Trouble*. Minneapolis: Fortress, 2004.

———, ed. *Diaspora and Identity: The Case of Palestine*. Bethlehem: Diyar, 2017.

———. *Faith in the Face of Empire: The Bible through Palestinian Eyes*. Maryknoll, NY: Orbis, 2014.

————. *Palestinian Christians: Emigration, Displacement and Diaspora.* Bethlehem: Diyar, 2017.

————. *Palestinian Identity in Relation to Time and Space.* Bethlehem: Diyar, 2014.

————. *The Politics of Persecution: Middle Eastern Christians in an Age of Empire.* Waco, TX: Baylor University Press, 2021.

————. *Shifting Identities: Changes in the Social, Political, and Religious Structures in the Arab World.* Bethlehem: Diyar, 2016.

Rizq, Philip. "The Murder of Rami Ayyad." MidEastWeb, Oct. 15, 2007. http://mideastweb.org/Rami_Ayyad_Murder.htm.

Sabbah, Michel. "Eighth Pastoral Letter of Patriarch Sabbah." Latin Patriarchate of Jerusalem, Mar. 2008. https://www.lpj.org/archives/eighth-pastoral-letter-patriarch-sabbah-march-2008.html.

Sabella, Bernard. "Palestinian and Arab Christians: The Challenges Ahead." [In Arabic.] Unpublished paper delivered on Sept. 22, 2004, at al-Multaqa al-Fikri al-ʿArabi, Amman, Jordan.

————. "Palestinian Christians Centennial Historical & Demographic Developments." *Journal of South Asian and Middle Eastern Studies* (forthcoming).

————. *Palestinian Christians: Historical Demographic Developments, Current Politics and Attitudes towards Church, Society and Human Rights; The Sabeel Survey on Palestinian Christians in the West Bank and Israel—Summer 2006.* Friends of Sabeel North America, 2007. https://catalog.ihsn.org/citations/45539.

Shohat, Avraham, and Abu Ala (Ahmed Korei). "Gaza-Jericho Agreement." Apr. 29, 1994. https://unctad.org/system/files/information-document/ParisProtocol_en.pdf.

Stork, Joe. "The Significance of Stones." *Middle East Report* 154 (Sept./Oct. 1988). https://merip.org/1988/09/the-significance-of-stones/.

Tantawi, Mohammed Sayed, et al. "The Alexandria Declaration 2002." United States Institute of Peace, Jan. 21, 2002. https://www.usip.org/programs/alexandria-declaration.

United Nations Relief and Works Agency for Palestine Refugees in the Middle East. "Where We Work." UNRWA, May 2021. https://www.unrwa.org/where-we-work/gaza-strip.

Varsen, Aghabekian. *A Palestinian Armenian: The Intertwine between the Social and the Political.* Bethlehem: Dar al-Kalima University Press, 2021.

Weaver, Dorothy, Jean. Review of *Bethlehem Besieged: Stories of Hope in Times of Trouble,* by Mitri Raheb. *HTS Theological Studies* 64 (Jul./Sept. 2008). http://www.scielo.org.za/scielo.php?script=sci_arttext&pid=S0259-94222008000300028.

World Bank. "The World Bank in West Bank and Gaza." World Bank, n.d. http://www.worldbank.org/en/country/westbankandgaza.

World Bank Group, et al. *Gaza Rapid Damage and Needs Assessment.* Washington, DC: World Bank, 2021. https://unsco.unmissions.org/sites/default/files/gaza_rapid_damage_and_needs_assessment_july_2021_1.pdf.

Epilogue

Middle Eastern Christian Thought in the Twenty-First Century

Mitri Raheb

THE FINAL DECADE OF the twentieth century was one infused with hope. Global and regional optimism was high following the fall of the Berlin Wall in 1989, the release of Nelson Mandela from prison in 1990 and the end of the South African apartheid regime, the dissolution of the Soviet Union in 1991, the Arab-Israeli Madrid Peace Conference in 1991, the Oslo Accords between Israel and the PLO in 1993, and the peace treaty between Jordan and Israel in 1994. Peace movements ecstatically celebrated the dawn of a new era in which states could beat their swords into ploughshares (Isa 2:4).

Churches were enthusiastic about these events and engaged in many of the processes. Polish Pope John Paul II, together with Ronald Reagan and Mikhail Gorbachev, was instrumental in the dissolution of the Soviet Union and the ending of the Cold War; Bishop Desmond Tutu joined Nelson Mandela and F. W. de Klerk in becoming the icons who dismantled apartheid; and Palestinian Christians Hanan Ashrawi and Albert Aghazerian were the spokespeople for the Palestinian delegation at the Madrid Peace Conference. Churches, Christian clergy, and lay individuals in the Middle East engaged in these processes and reflected on them intellectually. Christians are not mere spectators in the Middle East and have proved to be active players and engaged citizens who care about their societies and who work for a better future. Theological documents are an important resource to trace the evolvement of Christian thought during the first two decades of the twenty-first century.

In this concluding chapter, we will look briefly at four important documents that reflect Christian theological thinking and societal engagement. These reflect the status of churches and Christians, and represent a form of public theology for the Middle Eastern context. The first two statements were issued in Palestine and the latter two are regional statements. This provides both a local and a regional perspective.

THE HEADS OF CHURCHES IN JERUSALEM

The signing of the Oslo Accords between Israel and the PLO in 1993, and between Israel and Jordan in 1994, prompted the thirteen heads of the Christian churches in the Holy Land to communicate their vision of peace for the city of Jerusalem. The Oslo Accords did not cover the issue of Jerusalem, as this was postponed, along with other so-called final status issues, for discussion within five years in the hopes of achieving a peace treaty by 1998. The first memorandum of the heads of the Christian communities was issued on November 14, 1994, six months after the signing of the Gaza-Jericho Agreement of May 4, 1994. The memorandum included a list of points with these emphases:[1]

1. Jerusalem is a Holy City for the people of the three monotheistic religions. Its unique nature of sanctity endows it with a special vocation of calling for reconciliation and harmony, and not for conflict and disharmony.

2. The Arab-Israeli peace process is on its way towards reaching a resolution to the conflict, and yet, Jerusalem has been sidestepped in the process. It is crucial to reflect on the core issues in order to resolve the conflict.

3. The positions of both the Israeli and Palestinian sides are divergent and conflicting.

4. History teaches us that Jerusalem "cannot belong exclusively to one people or to one religion. Jerusalem should be open to all, shared by all. Those who govern the city should make it 'the capital of humankind.'"[2] Hence, Jerusalem has a universal and inclusive vocation.

5. The memorandum considered the vision of Jerusalem in both the Old and New Testaments and acknowledged its foundation for all liturgical traditions and pilgrimages.

1. For the following, see Raheb, "Jerusalem," 44–45.
2. Raheb, "Jerusalem," 44.

6. Jerusalem has been home for Christians over the course of two thousand years, and the local church with its faithful has always been actively present in the city. This continuing presence of a living Christian community is inseparable from the historical sites. It is through the "living stones" that the holy archaeological sites take on "life."

7. Jerusalem has two dimensions. On the one hand, it is a Holy City due to its link with the history of salvation. On the other hand, it is a Holy City due to its local community of Christians, alongside the local Muslim and Jewish communities who were born and live in the city.

8. The memorandum hereby presents the legitimate demands of Christians in Jerusalem in this respect:

> The right to full freedom of access to the holy places, freedom of worship, and rights of property ownership, custody, and worship that churches have acquired through "firmans" and that are protected in the status quo; the right to come on pilgrimage to Jerusalem; the human right of freedom of worship and of conscience, both as individuals and as communities; civil and historical rights that allow Christians to carry out religious, educational, medical, and other duties of charity; the right to have their own institutions such as hospices, institutes, and study centers. The memorandum highlights that these rights are not to be granted to Christians simply because they are Christians but because they are nationals who deserve their basic social, cultural, political, and national rights on an equal footing with the other monotheistic religions in the city.

9. The memorandum notes that it is necessary to accord Jerusalem "a special judicial and political statute which reflects the universal importance and significance of the City."[3] The memorandum hereby demands:

- That the association of the "representatives from the three monotheistic religions, in addition to local political powers, ought to be associated in the elaboration and application of such a special statute" for Jerusalem.[4]

- For the international community to find ways to be engaged in and guarantee the stability and permanence of this statute.

---

3. Raheb, "Jerusalem," 45.
4. Raheb, "Jerusalem," 45.

During the Camp David summit, the Greek Orthodox, Latin, and Armenian Orthodox patriarchs sent a letter on July 17, 2000, addressing President Bill Clinton, Prime Minister Ehud Barak, and President Yasser Arafat.[5] The letter summarized what was in the memorandum of 1994 with the following additions: the patriarchs appealed "to ensure that the Christian communities within the walls of the Old City are not separated from each other" (in response to the suggestion that the Armenian Quarter be joined to the Jewish Quarter). The letter noted that: "We regard the Christian and Armenian Quarters of the Old City as inseparable and contiguous entities that are firmly united by the same faith."[6] The letter also suggested having representatives from the three patriarchates and the Custody of the Holy Land at the Camp David summit meeting where the future of Jerusalem was to be discussed in order to safeguard the presence and maintain the rights of the collective churches. We can sense the optimism of the heads of churches in these two statements. They believed that peace was on the horizon. For them, peace starts in Jerusalem, an open city with an inclusive character, a city for two people and three religions with international guarantees and status.

Twenty years later, this optimism has faded. In 2021–2022 the heads of churches released four statements related to Jerusalem. The first came in the wake of the events at al-Aqsa Mosque and Sheikh Jarrah in May 2021: "We, the Patriarchs and heads of churches of Jerusalem, are profoundly disheartened and concerned about the recent violent events in East Jerusalem. These concerning developments, whether at al-Aqsa Mosque or in Sheikh Jarrah, violate the sanctity of the people of Jerusalem and of Jerusalem as the City of Peace. The actions undermining the safety of worshipers and the dignity of the Palestinians who are subject to eviction are unacceptable. The special character of Jerusalem and the status quo that exists compels all parties to preserve the already sensitive situation in the Holy City of Jerusalem. Growing tension, backed mainly by right-wing radical groups, endangers the fragile reality in and around Jerusalem. We call upon the international community and all people of goodwill to intervene in order to put an end to these provocative actions, as well as to continue to pray for the peace of Jerusalem."[7]

A second statement was issued in April 2022 in response to the occupation by Jewish settler groups of the Petra Hotel, a Greek Orthodox property in the Old City of Jerusalem. "The seizure of the Little Petra Hotel by the

5. Raheb, "Jerusalem," 45.

6. Raheb, "Jerusalem," 45.

7. Latin Patriarchate of Jerusalem, "Patriarchs and Heads."

radical extremist group Ateret Cohanim is a threat to the continued existence of a Christian Quarter in Jerusalem, and ultimately to peaceful coexistence of the communities of this city. The heads of churches have repeatedly
warned of the illegitimate actions of extremists who have pursued a pattern
of intimidation and violence. In occupying the Greek Orthodox Church's
property, the Little Petra Hotel, Ateret Cohanim has committed criminal
acts of break-in and trespass. They act as if they are above the law, with no
fear of consequences. This issue is not about individual properties but about
the whole character of Jerusalem, including the Christian Quarter. The
Little Petra Hotel stands on the pilgrim route for the millions of Christians
who visit Jerusalem each year. It represents Christian heritage and speaks of
our very existence in this place. Israeli radical extremist groups like Ateret
Cohanim are already targeting and hijacking our beloved Old City of Jerusalem, and imposing their illegitimate and dangerous agenda on all sides.
We refuse this and we say that this will lead to instability and tension at
a time when all are trying to de-escalate and build trust to work towards
justice and peace. Acts of coercion and violence cannot lead to peace."[8]

The latest statement on Jerusalem was issued in May 2022 following the
attack on Shireen Abu Aqleh's funeral. "The police stormed into a Christian
health institute, disrespecting the Church, disrespecting the health institute,
disrespecting the memory of the deceased, and forcing the pallbearers almost to drop the coffin. The Israeli police's invasion and disproportionate
use of force, attacking mourners, striking them with batons, using smoke
grenades, shooting rubber bullets, and frightening the hospital patients,
is a severe violation of international norms and regulations, including the
fundamental human right of freedom of religion, which must be observed
also in a public space."[9]

During the visit of President Biden to the Church of the Nativity on
July 15, the Greek Orthodox patriarch told the US leader that there are "unprecedented attacks by Israeli radical groups" to drive Christians out of the
Holy City through vandalism, including attacks on churches, insults against
clergy, attempts to block the faithful from places of worship, and attempts
to seize Christian real estate.[10] In December 2021, Fr. Francesco Patton, the
Catholic Church's custos of the Holy Land and guardian of the Christian
holy places in the Holy Land, wrote in an opinion piece published by the
UK's *Daily Telegraph* that the Christian "presence is precarious and our future is at risk." Patton described how the lives of many Christians have been

---

8. Latin Patriarchate of Jerusalem, "Statement by the Patriarchs."
9. Latin Patriarchate of Jerusalem, "Statement Concerning the Violence."
10. *TOI* Staff, "Meeting Biden."

made "unbearable by radical local groups with extremist ideologies" and added: "It seems that their aim is to free the Old City of Jerusalem from its Christian presence, even the Christian Quarter."[11]

Britain's archbishop of Canterbury, Justin Welby, in a joint article written with the Anglican archbishop of Jerusalem, Hosam Naoum, warned of a "concerted attempt to intimidate and drive away" Palestinian Christians.[12] These documents show that the vision of Jerusalem as an open city with an inclusive character for two people and three religions, articulated by the heads of churches at the end of the second millennium, has been replaced in the twenty-first century by the realization that Israel is moving ahead with a process of Judaization of Jerusalem that allows Jewish settler groups the right to occupy Christian properties and the plaza of al-Aqsa Mosque. Thus, the character of the city is being changed to a city for one people only, Israelis, and for one religion, exclusively Jewish.

KAIROS PALESTINE

In December 2009, a group of Palestinian Christian leaders, both clergy and lay individuals, launched the Kairos Palestine document in Bethlehem.[13] The Greek name of Kairos was chosen, meaning an opportune and special moment in history. It was intended to create a connection to the South African Kairos document written by South African theologians and lay individuals in 1985 at the height of the apartheid regime there. This South African document was an important Christian reflection and an urgent call for a "prophetic theology" that would confront both the "state theology" that supported apartheid and the "church theology" that failed to take the systemic oppression seriously. There is no doubt that this document was key in dismantling apartheid in South Africa.[14]

By 2009 it was clear that the so-called "peace process" was not leading anywhere: there was no peace and not even a process. The Palestinian armed struggle did not create the results intended. Everything seemed to have come to a standstill, and the world appeared to have accommodated an ongoing Israeli occupation and settler-colonial practices. In sympathy with Palestinian suffering, the authors of Kairos Palestine wanted to offer words of faith, hope, and love, first and foremost to the Christian community in

11. Patton, "Holy Land Christians."

12. Welby and Naoum, "Let Us Pray."

13. For background information on Kairos Palestine, see https://www.kairospalestine.ps/.

14. The Kairos document appears at Kairos Palestine, "Moment of Truth."

Palestine, to the churches in the *oikumene*, as well as to Muslim and Jewish people of goodwill. In the section on faith, the authors presented their Christian faith in the triune God who created every person with dignity; and in Jesus, the incarnated word of God; and in the Holy Spirit who enables us to understand the written word of God. The document moves on to critique Western theologians who weaponize the Bible in support of Israeli settler colonialism against the indigenous people of the land, making the "good news" "bad news" for Palestinian displacement and dispossession.[15] In this context, the document calls the occupation of Palestinian land a sin against God and humanity.[16]

In the second section on hope, the authors state clearly that there is no hope on the horizon for an end to occupation and freedom for the Palestinian people. The question posed is how to maintain hope when there is nothing to hope for. The document highlights the importance of Christian hope as a means to remain steadfast on the land, resilient in this context, and active in changing the situation.[17] The document lists several signs of hope: the social, educational, and theological institutions run by the church in Palestine; interfaith initiatives launched by the church with Jews and Muslims; the resilience of the Christian community against all odds; the groups advocating justice for Palestinians in churches abroad and also within Jewish peace movements.[18] The document warns about theologies that bestow theological qualities on Israel or any other state.

In part 3, about love, the authors struggle with the meaning of Christian love, including love of the enemy in the context of occupation. The document makes clear that love of the enemy does not imply acceptance of injustices but to resist the system of oppression creatively without demonizing individuals or an entire people.[19] The document expresses support for the BDS (boycott, divestment, and sanctions) movement espoused by Palestinian and international NGOs.[20] The document stresses the importance of resistance via a culture of life rather than of death, which implies a critique of suicide bombing.[21]

The document ends with a call for the Palestinian Christian community to remain steadfast on the land and to work on building a just society.

15. Kairos Palestine, "Moment of Truth," §2.3.3.
16. Kairos Palestine, "Moment of Truth," §2.5.
17. Kairos Palestine, "Moment of Truth," §3.2.
18. Kairos Palestine, "Moment of Truth," §3.3.
19. Kairos Palestine, "Moment of Truth," §4.2.1.
20. Kairos Palestine, "Moment of Truth," §4.2.6.
21. Kairos Palestine, "Moment of Truth," §4.2.5.

This appeal reaches out to the Muslim community with a message of love and coexistence, and calls on them to reject all forms of religious fundamentalism. It reaches out to the Jewish community in calling for an end to animosity and occupation, and to grasp the opportunity for coexistence based on justice. The document thanks churches worldwide who support the Palestinian struggle for freedom and invites Christians from the *oikumene* to come and witness for themselves. The document condemns all form of racism, including antisemitism and Islamophobia. It rejects the idea of a religious state, Jewish or Muslim, because this does not respect equality or diversity.[22] Finally, the document calls for a just solution in Jerusalem based on a vision and international legitimacy as a city for two people and three religions.[23] This Kairos document was translated into over thirty languages, and global Kairos groups advocating for Palestinian rights were established in almost twenty countries.

In July 2020, members of Kairos Palestine and Global Kairos for Justice issued a joint statement under the title "Cry for Hope: A Call to Decisive Action; We Cannot Serve God and the Oppression of the Palestinians." By 2020 it was clear to Palestinians that the peace process no longer existed and that the situation had become much more critical.

> We have arrived at a critical point in the struggle to end the oppression of the Palestinian people. The state of Israel's adoption of the Nation-State Law in 2018 legalized institutional discrimination in Israel and the Palestinian territories, officially depriving Palestinians of their rights to life, livelihood, and a future in their homeland. Recent acts of the US administration have supported Israel's ongoing project of land-taking and attaining control over the entire territory of Palestine. These include the 2018 move of the US embassy to Jerusalem, the announcement in 2019 that the US government no longer deems West Bank settlements to be "inconsistent with international law," and the 2020 "Peace to Prosperity" plan. Fueled by US support and emboldened by the ineffectual response of the international community, Israel's newly formed coalition government has cleared the way for outright annexation of around one-third of the occupied West Bank, including the Jordan Valley. These developments make it transparent that we have come to the end of the illusion that Israel and the world powers intend to honor and defend the rights of the Palestinian people to dignity, self-determination, and the fundamental human rights guaranteed

22. Kairos Palestine, "Moment of Truth," §9.4.
23. Kairos Palestine, "Moment of Truth," §9.5.

under international law, including the right of return for Palestinian refugees. In light of these events, it is time for the international community to recognize Israel as an apartheid state in
international law.[24]

Palestinian Christians and their global partners used this document
to emphasize that a moment of truth has arrived and decisive action is
urgently needed. In this context, the authors recall important junctures
in modern church history where the church had to declare "status confes-
sionis," meaning that what is at stake is the credibility of the Gospel and
nothing less. They recall the engagement of the German theologian Dietrich
Bonhoefer against Nazi Germany and the designation by the World Council
of Churches of apartheid as racism. The declaration of Israel as an apartheid
state was prophetic, as some months later, three human rights organizations
declared Israel to be an apartheid state.

The Kairos Palestine movement is a clear example of how a group of
Palestinian Christian clergy and lay individuals, with support from their
international partners, dared to speak truth to power; name injustice; and
engage in the struggle of their people for justice, dignity, and freedom. At
the same time, this document can be seen as a desperate cry for justice. The
Palestinian Christian community realized that most of the official church
bodies in the global North do not dare to confront the state of Israel. As a
result, they feel abandoned by the global North, and at the mercy of Israel
and its settler-colonial groups.

FROM THE NILE TO THE EUPHRATES: THE
CALL OF FAITH AND CITIZENSHIP

In December 2014, a group of academics from six Middle Eastern countries
gathered in Beirut upon the invitation of Diyar Consortium/Dar al-Kalima
University College in Bethlehem to launch the Christian Academic Forum
for Citizenship in the Arab World, with its founding document *From the
Nile to the Euphrates: The Call of Faith and Citizenship*. Although the forum
was meant to gather Christian academics from the region (mainly Egypt,
Lebanon, Jordan, Palestine, Syria, and Iraq), the members were eager to
include Muslim academics. The title of the document prompted many questions, as it could be misunderstood as an echo of a biblical code hijacked by
the Zionist movement. Rather than using an imperial term like the "Middle
East," the authors chose to use the two main sources of life and the cradle

24. Kairos Palestine and Global Kairos for Justice, "Cry for Hope."

of civilization to underline the unity of this region as an "entity that cannot soar high and freely like a bird without the power of both its wings, the Nile and the Euphrates, with Palestine as its beating heart."[25] Without any doubt, this document was one of the first Middle Eastern documents of "public theology" and a manifestation of a theology of citizenship. As a document of contextual theology, the authors began by analyzing the current context and identifying the main challenges facing the region as a whole, not merely the Christian community.

The document identifies in the second part ten major challenges facing the region that influence the present and future status of Middle Eastern Christians. This is the first Middle Eastern theological document to adopt the macro level as a starting point. Three of the challenges identified stem from an unhealthy relationship between religion and the state. In consecutive studies, the region ranks lowest in terms of the separation between religion and the state. In fact, religion, particularly Islam, is weaponized by those in power to retain control, and by their opponents to win power. Israel declares itself to be a Jewish state, and both Christians and other communities are marginalized. Another challenge is the weak or absent rule of law in individual countries, which makes life difficult for vulnerable groups and minorities. They feel themselves to be at the mercy of political dictators or under threat from religious fundamentalist groups. In the absence of the rule of law, human rights abuses and inequalities become the norm. A third problem referred to in the document is the emphasis on "state security" versus "human security." The Arab Spring exposed the flaws of this approach that fails to provide security for the state or for citizens.

In conjunction with these three challenges are four challenges related to the mismanagement of natural and human resources. "In the absence of competent management skills, prosperity turns to deprivation, people continue to suffer political repression and, amid growing divisions among clashing identities, the area's energies are wasted, its resources pillaged, its archaeological heritage plundered, and its brainpower estranged or drained. Daily existence is often a bitter endurance test and people become aliens at home, caught up in ethnic, religious or political factions, or are marginalized as refugees victimized by wars, ethnic cleansing, genocidal campaigns or religious persecution."[26] Those most affected by these developments are the women of the region who continue to be marginalized and suffer under a systemic gender gap based on the absence of civic personal status law, male-dominated societies, and conservative religious traditions and

25. Diyar Consortium, *From the Nile*, §1.3.2.
26. Diyar Consortium, *From the Nile*, §2.4.3.

cultural biases. Youth make up more than half of the region's population and face high unemployment and poor education. With globalization and the information revolution, young people find themselves caught between a virtual reality they tap into through their devices and the real life they experience in their respective countries. This drives young people either to emigrate in search of better opportunities or to turn to religious fundamentalism in an attempt to escape reality. As a result of these multiple problems, the authors conclude that there is a lack of human dignity and a deteriorated quality of life.

The last three challenges identified by the document are cultural and theological in nature. The authors feel that while religious groups are mushrooming in the region, deep human spirituality is lacking. Many of the religious manifestations are based on superstition and irrationality that do not support a unifying vision of equal citizenship. Thus, the subtitle of the document is the call of faith and citizenship. It is not enough for secular forces in society to engage in civil society. People of faith need more than ever to engage in building a different society based on diversity and equality.

The authors articulate this commitment in section 3: "In light of the preceding, we deem it most fitting to focus on our Christian, human, and national roles in addressing these urgent challenges confronting our societies. We want to mobilize active Christian participation in the process of the awakening that our region needs today. We want to do this in ways that are relevant to our times." The authors realize that "the future of the Christians of the Middle East is tied closely to the future of the Middle East itself. We do not claim that there is a solution for Christians alone or that there is a magic recipe for the region as whole. Certainly, we do not presume that Christianity is the answer, just as we do not consider Islam to be the answer. In fact, we do not believe that there is a religious solution to the crisis that this region suffers. We believe, however, that religion holds lofty human values that can constitute an essential element for the progress and development of our societies. It is here that we exist and are rooted. Our homelands have demands on us. We are committed to this calling. And we are loathe to ignore or run away from our duty."[27]

The document ends with a form of recontextualized Christian creed that spells out the commitments as Christians to an active faith and as citizens through active participation in their individual societies. It is interesting to note that the Christian Academic Forum for Citizenship in the Arab World continues to be active in analyzing the challenges facing the region and in proposing ways to make a positive contribution to a better future.

27. Diyar Consortium, *From the Nile*, §3.1.

What makes this document special is that does not take the status of Middle Eastern Christians as the starting point but as a sociopolitical macro lens to view the context as a whole. The authors consider the major challenges facing the region as a whole and formulate their commitment as Christians to staying in the region and engaging in bringing the desired change for all.

WE CHOOSE ABUNDANT LIFE: CHRISTIANS IN THE MIDDLE EAST; TOWARDS RENEWED THEOLOGICAL, SOCIAL, AND POLITICAL CHOICES

This last major Christian document was launched in Beirut in September 2021 by a group of religious and lay individuals from the region and constitutes another example of a theology for the public space. As a document in contextual theology, it starts with the realities. It sees a decisive moment in the present context: "Today, once again, we find ourselves confronted with the choice between blessing and curse, life and death. We are called to opt for life in spite of all that this may entail in commitment, sacrifice, and perseverance. We are required to use all our capacity to serve the wellbeing of our fellow humans, to work towards the renewal of our churches and institutions, and to strengthen our witness and active presence among our brothers and sisters of all religions and diverse intellectual and cultural perspectives. Today, as we ask God for forgiveness for our weaknesses and mistakes throughout history, we draw from the mercy of God and his forgiveness strength and steadfastness to reject the culture of death and choose life."[28]

The authors are aware that the "geopolitical situation in the Middle East today is extremely complex. Amid the many events taking place in this region, Christians face all kinds of fragmentation, from demographic decline to the gradual fading of our presence and witness. This makes it imperative to embark on an in-depth examination of our situation, drawing on a calm critical reading based on an informed theological vision and rigorous scientific approaches."[29]

The document starts with a description of the context in which Christians in the Middle East are living. Second, it sets out the challenges they face. Finally, it proposes choices and policies for adoption. The document describes how the region has been marked by a rich religious and ethnic culture and politics throughout human history. This diversity constitutes the

---

28. Bechealany et al., *We Choose Abundant Life*, §1.

29. Bechealany et al., *We Choose Abundant Life*, §2.

strength of the region, although it was often a source of conflict and wars. How to deal with and manage this diversity therefore becomes a major issue.

Historically speaking, the document rejects three approaches: Pan-Arabism as a radical secular ideology to dilute differences, the designation of social groups as majority and minority, and the "alliance of minorities" to face the majority. All these models failed because they are not based on equal citizenship. The document then highlights another historic contribution in which Middle Eastern Christians were involved, that is, the Arab renaissance in the late nineteenth century with the emphasis on reason. "The point here is that reason represents what is general and common among human beings. The state cannot be built on particularities such as religion, race, or color, but on what humanity has in common. This principle is the backbone of the modern democratic state and the foundation of the idea of citizenship."[30] The authors are aware that Middle Eastern societies did not embrace the "project of modernity expressed by the renaissance" and were overrun by globalization, which enhanced transnational religious movements, a culture of consumerism, and a tendency to cling on to particularity and narrow identities. Besides the renaissance and globalization, the authors describe the Arab Spring as another decisive moment in the history of the region. "Citizenship, both as a concept and as a value, spearheaded the Arab Spring uprisings in Tunisia, Egypt, Syria, and, later on, in Iraq and Lebanon."[31] Although the Arab Spring did not bring about the intended change, it was nevertheless "the starting point for new ways of looking at the relationship between citizenship and other elements of identity such as religion, confession, race, and color, based on citizenship as an umbrella that acknowledges, embraces, and respects differences. . . . Within this framework, meaningful terms were evoked such as 'unity in diversity' (Egypt) or 'management of diversity' (Lebanon)."[32] A last and current challenge facing the region and the globe is COVID-19 as a result of an entanglement of globalized capitalism and eco-colonialism that damaged fragile states with volatile medical, educational, and environmental structures in the Middle East.

From the larger context, the document moves to describe the ecclesiastical and theological context. Five main features are highlighted. First, the diversity of the churches and religions as a special feature of the region from the outset, later expanded by the arrival of the Catholic and Protestant churches. This diversity sometimes led to cross-fertilization, and at other

---

30. Bechealany et al., *We Choose Abundant Life*, §12.

31. Bechealany et al., *We Choose Abundant Life*, §21.

32. Bechealany et al., *We Choose Abundant Life*, §23.

times to competition. Second, the document highlights the necessity of democratic structures based on togetherness of lay people and clergy in synodal structures. The authors are bold in critiquing their churches: "Unfortunately, in our churches today we often see the people of God—especially women and youth—marginalized in major decisions. We often see the growth of an authoritarian spirit which obliterates shared responsibility, balanced governance, and a spirit of accountability between people and their pastors. It is not uncommon to see forms of corruption eroding church institutions, especially in the health and education sectors, which inevitably leads to the decline of their role in spreading the spirit of the Gospel and Christian values."[33] After highlighting the role of theological and spiritual formation, the document tackles the issue of declining numbers, the role of Christians, and the phenomenon of emigration. Finally, the document sheds light on the role of the church in society. It underlines the fact that churches have a structure and a language that are outdated and unsuitable for people today. In addition, the document states: "It appears today that the Christian role is declining due to their decreasing numbers, in addition to the ability of others, notably Muslims, to get by without 'their services.' This decline is often accompanied by exaggerated speech about the importance of the Christian role. By dwelling on the roles they played in the past, some Christians seem to fall into the trap of not constructively shaping their present and future."[34]

The second part of the document is entitled Challenges of the Present and Stakes of the Future." It starts with the observation that the "old Middle East" has failed, but the new "has not been shaped." This gives Christians the possibility of engaging in the shaping of a new social contract where "the Christians of the Middle East are required, along with our Muslim brothers and sisters, and our other partners, to delve deep into building a civil state where citizenship can be applied without discrimination or exception,"[35] while "reinventing Arabism as a cultural space and an inclusive cultural concept."[36] The second challenge is related to synodality and the need to move from sectarianism to the concept of church with a role for women and youth in the church leadership. The third challenge is the culture of human brother/sisterhood. The document refers to the document signed by Pope Francis and the grand imam of al-Azhar in Abi Dhabi in February of 2019 as a new chapter in interfaith relations. The final challenge is a theological

---

33. Bechealany et al., *We Choose Abundant Life*, §34.

34. Bechealany et al., *We Choose Abundant Life*, §52.

35. Bechealany et al., *We Choose Abundant Life*, §59.

36. Bechealany et al., *We Choose Abundant Life*, §62.

one requiring the development of contextual theology for the Middle East that takes the "social, economic and political developments seriously and uses them as a starting-point for pondering on what God wants from us here and now."[37]

The third and final part of the document is entitled "Choices and Policies." "I have set before you life and death . . . choose life" (Deut 30:19b). The social, political, and theological realities in the Middle East today, with all the challenges they pose, place before Christians crucial choices that require a profound change of mindset. This change requires us to move from an obsession with existence and survival to taking the risk of presence and witness. It means building durable policies based on biblical principles and enshrined in the prophetic role we need to play, the significance of our witness to the resurrected Christ, and our engagement in our societies with their different geopolitical contexts."[38] The document ends by listing the main choices and policies needed today.

CONCLUSION

The twenty-first century has been marked by immense challenges in which Christians in the Middle East have found themselves in the eye of the storm. What these documents clearly demonstrate is that the twenty-first century has seen the rise of contextual theologies, first in Palestine and later in the region, with Christian leaders who care for their societies and churches, analyze the changing contexts, and are committed to engaging in the shaping of the future of the region. It is up to the people of the Middle East, whether Christian, Muslim, Jew, or atheist, to shape the future they want. This is not an easy task at all. The odds are immense and should not be underestimated. Nevertheless, the answer is to engage in building a different future for all. These documents show that there is no future for the Christians of the Middle East without a society based on equal citizenship, systems of good governance, a fair social contract, and sustainable economic development: these are all vital ingredients for peace. There is no future for Christians without a future for all. Conversely, a continuous Christian presence in the Middle East is crucial to maintain the pluralistic character of the region. Without a Christian presence, the Middle East will become mono-religious, monocultural, and thus poorer in every aspect.

Many Middle Eastern Christians throughout history have understood that they have no option but to get involved in the national and regional

37. Bechealany et al., *We Choose Abundant Life*, §74.
38. Bechealany et al., *We Choose Abundant Life*, §80.

struggle for social and political transformation. Over a period of two millennia, Middle Eastern Christianity survived one empire after the other by developing great elasticity in adjusting to changing contexts. It is obvious that the visibility and vitality of Middle Eastern Christianity in the twenty-first century have waned. Numbers have dwindled to a historic low of 2 to 3 percent today. Nevertheless, this has not deterred Christians from contributing to their communities and advocating for neighborly relationships; equal citizenship; and open, tolerant, and pluralistic societies. Even when Middle Eastern Christians find themselves in the eye of the storm, they do not give up easily. Based on their faith in their Lord who stills the storm, they stay alert, engaged, and faithful to their call. This is another story of resilience to celebrate.

BIBLIOGRAPHY

Bechealany, Souraya, et al. *We Choose Abundant Life: Christians in the Middle East; Towards Renewed Theological, Social, and Political Choices.* Beirut: We Choose Abundant Life Group, 2021. online.anyflip.com/mijbx/mawd/mobile/index.html.

Brown, Brian J. *Apartheid South Africa! Apartheid Israel! Ticking the Boxes of Occupation and Dispossession.* N.p.: N.p., 2022.

Diyar Consortium. *From the Nile to the Euphrates: The Call of Faith and Citizenship; A Statement of the Christian Academic Forum for Citizenship in the Arab World.* Bethlehem: Diyar, 2015.

Kairos Palestine. "A Moment of Truth: A Word of Faith, Hope and Love from the Heart of Palestinian Suffering." Kairos Palestine, n.d. https://www.kairospalestine.ps/index.php?view=category&id=11.

Kairos Palestine, and Global Kairos for Justice. "Cry for Hope." Cry for Hope, n.d. https://cryforhope.org/.

Latin Patriarchate of Jerusalem. "Patriarchs and Heads of Jerusalem Churches Concerned about al-Aqsa Mosque Worshippers and Sheikh Jarrah Families." LPJ, May 10, 2021. https://www.lpj.org/archives/patriarchs-and-heads-of-jerusalem-churches-concerned-about-alaqsa-mosque-worshippers-and-sheikh-jarrah-families.html.

———. "Statement by the Patriarchs and Heads of Local Churches of Jerusalem on the Illegal Seizure of the Little Petra Hotel." LPJ, Apr. 4, 2022. https://www.lpj.org/archives/statement-by-the-patriarchs-and-heads-of-local-churches-of-jerusalem-on-the-illegal-seizure-of-the-little-petra-hotel.html.

———. "Statement Concerning the Violence at St Joseph Hospital during Shireen Abu Aqleh's Funeral." LPJ, May 16, 2022. https://www.lpj.org/posts/statement-concerning-the-violence-at-st-joseph-hospital-during-shireen-abu-aqleh-s-funeral.html.

MennoPIN, ed. *Kairos Palestine: A Moment of Truth.* N.p.: MennoMedia, 2016.

Patton, Francesco. "Holy Land Christians Are at Threat of Extinction." *Telegraph*, Dec. 18, 2021. https://www.telegraph.co.uk/news/2021/12/18/holy-land-christians-threat-extinction/.

Raheb, Mitri. "Christianity in the Middle East, 1917–2017." In *History of Global Christianity*, edited by Jens Holger Schjørring et al., 3:375–95. Boston: Brill Academic, 2018.

———. "Israel, Palestine and Jordan." In *The Rowman & Littlefield Handbook of Christianity in the Middle East*, edited by Mitri Raheb and Mark A. Lamport, 498–510. Lanham, MD: Rowman & Littlefield, 2020.

———. "Jerusalem in Modern Christian Thought." In *Jerusalem: Religious, National and International Dimensions*, edited by Mitri Raheb, 35–50. Bethlehem: Diyar, 2019.

———, ed. *Jerusalem: Religious, National and International Dimensions*. Diyar, 2019.

———. *The Politics of Persecution: Middle Eastern Christians in an Age of Empire*. Waco, TX: Baylor University Press, 2021.

———. "The Revolution in the Arab World. Liberation: The Promise and the Illusion; A Palestinian Christian Perspective." In *The Reemergence of Liberation Theologies: Models for the Twenty-First Century*, edited by Thia Cooper, New Approaches to Religion and Power, 101–10. New York: Palgrave Macmillan, 2013.

Raheb, Mitri, and Mark A. Lamport, eds. *The Rowman & Littlefield Handbook of Christianity in the Middle East*. Lanham, MD: Rowman & Littlefield, 2020.

———. *Surviving Jewel: The Enduring Story of Christianity in the Middle East*. Eugene, OR: Cascade, 2022.

Ross, Kenneth R., et al., eds. *Christianity in North Africa and West Asia*. Edinburgh: Edinburgh University Press, 2018.

TOI Staff. "Meeting Biden, J'lem Christian Leader Describes 'Attacks by Israeli Radical Groups.'" *Times of Israel*, July 16, 2022. https://www.timesofisrael.com/meeting-biden-christian-leader-described-attacks-by-israeli-radical-groups/.

Welby, Justin, and Hosam Naoum. "Let Us Pray for the Christians Being Driven from the Holy Land." *Times*, Dec. 19, 2021. https://www.thetimes.co.uk/article/let-us-pray-for-the-christians-being-driven-from-the-holy-land-f27wwksdh.

Appendices

I

Number and percentage of Palestinian Christians in the 1948 Territories over time

Year	Number of Christians (in thousands)	Percentage of Christians out of the entire Palestinian population in Israel
1949	34	21%
1965	51.3	19.1%
1975	c. 67	15%
1990	c. 92	13.1%
2001	c. 110	11.3%
2020	124.6	7.9%

II

Average household size[1]

Christian households	3.39
Muslim households	4.53
Druze	3.68
Jewish	3.07

III

Household differences by religion

	Couples without children	With children, youngest up to seventeen years old	With children, youngest older than seventeen years old	Couple, with children up to seventeen years old	Couple, with children eighteen years old and older
Christian	23%	43%	17%	6%	18%
Jewish	29%	45%	12%	6%	6%
Muslim	10%	64%	15%	6%	5%

1. Christian households with six persons and over made up just 7 percent, compared to 31 percent of Muslim households and 9 percent of Jewish households.

IV

Students in higher education

	Completed education at a university	Completed education at a college	Completed education at the Open University	Completed education at an educational college
Arab Christians	50.1%	32.3%	8.9%	8.7%
Broader Arab community	35.4%	28.3%	18.3%	18%
Hebrew education	35.8%	40.3%	11.7%	12.1%

V

Patterns of education

Discipline	Percentage of all students	Arab Christians	Arab Muslims
Humanities	3%	2%	2.2%
Literature and languages	1.4%	1.9%	2.3%
Arts	3.9%	4.5%	2.3%
Social sciences	17%	14.8%	14.7%
Business administration and management science	10.7%	9.1%	12.2%
Law	6.3%	8.5%	5.3%
Medicine	1%	1.6%	0.5%
Allied health professions	6.8%	9.9%	10.6%
Mathematics, statistics, and computer science	9.2%	10%	6.5%
Exact sciences	1.4%	0.7%	1%
Biology and agriculture	3.1%	3.6%	3.1%
Engineering and planning	18.9%	22.%	12%

www.ingramcontent.com/pod-product-compliance
Lightning Source LLC
Chambersburg PA
CBHW060338100426
42812CB00003B/1040